The Economic Impact of Digital Technologies

The Economic Impact of Digital Technologies

Measuring Inclusion and Diffusion in Europe

Edited by

Paolo Guerrieri

Professor of Economics, College of Europe, Bruges, Belgium and University of Rome 'La Sapienza', Italy

Sara Bentivegna

Professor of New Media, University of Rome 'La Sapienza', Italy

IN ASSOCIATION WITH THE COLLEGE OF EUROPE

Edward Elgar

Cheltenham, UK • Northampton, MA, USA

Published by
Edward Elgar Publishing Limited
The Lypiatts
15 Lansdown Road
Cheltenham
Glos GL50 2JA
UK

Edward Elgar Publishing, Inc.
William Pratt House
9 Dewey Court
Northampton
Massachusetts 01060
USA

A catalogue record for this book
is available from the British Library

Library of Congress Control Number: 2011924312

ISBN 978 0 85793 188 7

Typeset by Servis Filmsetting Ltd, Stockport, Cheshire
Printed and bound by MPG Books Group, UK

Contents

Contributors

Marco Bee, Assistant Professor, Department of Economics, University of Trento, Italy.

Sara Bentivegna, Professor of New Media at the Faculty of Political Sciences, Sociology and Communication, University of Rome 'La Sapienza', Italy.

Giovanni Di Franco, Associate Professor of Methodology of Social Research at the Department of Sociology, University of Salerno, Italy.

Giuseppe Espa, Professor of Statistics, Department of Economics, University of Trento, Italy.

Rinaldo Evangelista, Associate Professor of Economics, University of Camerino, Italy.

Roberto Gabriele, Assistant Professor, Department of Computer and Management Sciences, University of Trento, Italy.

Paolo Guerrieri, Professor of Economics at University of Rome 'La Sapienza', Italy and College of Europe, Bruges.

Valentina Meliciani, Professor of Economics, University of Teramo, Italy.

Jacques Pelkmans, Jan Tinbergen Chair for European Economics, Director, European Economic Studies, College of Europe, Bruges.

Preface

This Final Report originates from a study, 'Analysis of e-Inclusion impact resulting from advanced R&D based on economic modelling in relation to innovation capacity, capital formation, productivity, and empowerment', conducted for the European Commission (Contract no 30-CE-0220618/00-21) by the College of Europe, Bruges. An Intermediate Report has been prepared. This volume presents the main findings of the study and provides an in-depth overview of the methodology, policy simulations, the underlying theoretical framework, and literature references.

The study was conducted between December 2008 and September 2010 by a project team including Paolo Guerrieri (Director), Sara Bentivegna (Chapters 1–4), Giovanni Di Franco (Appendix), Rinaldo Evangelista (Chapter 5), Valentina Meliciani (Chapter 6), Marco Bee, Roberto Gabriele and Giuseppe Espa (Chapter 7), and Jacques Pelkmans (Chapter 8).

We would like to thank the steering committee of experts which guided the project, including Professor Peter Golding (Northumbria University) and Dr.ssa Barbara Ubaldi (OECD) for their precious contributions.

During the course of the study the project team also received very valuable and helpful comments and suggestions on work in progress at three workshops held in Brussels. We would like to thank all participants at these meetings.

As editors of this volume we would also like to thank all the people who contributed to the process that led to its publication. Special thanks to Nikolas Bader, Jesús Ballesteros, Elisa Molino, Bernadette Kerckhove, Cordula Singer and Barbara Cassani from the College of Europe, and Roberta Bracciale and Isabella Mingo from the University of Pisa and University of Rome 'La Sapienza', for their support for the initiative. The College of Europe provided valuable support throughout the course of the study.

Additionally, the authors would like to acknowledge the contribution of the European Commission team: Loris Di Pietrantonio who designed the study specifications, Elena Neculaescu and Jan Komarek who reviewed and commented on the intermediate and final reports.

However, any errors or omissions are solely the responsibility of the authors.

Legal notice

Introduction

Differences in economic performance between industrialized countries are largely explained by the level of investment and research in, and use of, information and communication technologies (ICT), and by the competitiveness of the information society and media industries. ICT services, skills, media and content are a growing part of the economy and society. Indeed, the implementation of the Europe 2020 strategy, intended to modernize the European economy and to build a knowledge-based economy, is strictly linked to an 'information society for all', in other words a widespread use of ICT in public services, SMEs and households.

Progress in e-inclusion, however, is still slow. Social differences in ICT use persist and in some cases are even widening. Most of the Riga targets will be difficult to achieve if current trends continue. Therefore much more should be done to achieve e-inclusion, and EU intervention is justified to guarantee equal access and effective participation in the information society, internal market coherence and e-inclusion co-ordination actions.

At the end of the 1990s, when the European Council began to deliberate upon and formulate plans of action with regard to the role of ICT within the European economy, the theme of ICT diffusion slowly began to attract the attention of policy makers and researchers. To achieve this main goal, over the years many intervention plans have been prepared and implemented. In this perspective a path articulated on two tracks has been followed: the first devoted to finding and describing the modalities and the pace of ICT diffusion – early defined in the much quoted and well known expression 'digital divide' – the other one focusing on policies and interventions able to reduce the digital gap and favour a more balanced technological diffusion. In the initial phase, attention and efforts were all concentrated towards reinforcement and expansion of networks and electronic services; that is, on the enlargement of the size of the user population. Faced with such needs – preliminary and essential to the construction of an 'information society for all' – the issue of social impact of digital inclusion/exclusion inevitably remained in the background.

It came to the fore in the subsequent plan, 'eEurope 2005: An information society for all' (CEC, 2002), presented at the European Council in Seville in June 2002. In the light of the progress made within the ambit of *e*Europe 2002, the new plan concentrated on two categories of action: 'on the one hand, it was intended to stimulate services, applications and content both for public online services and e-business; on the other, it refers to the basic broadband infrastructure and issues linked to security' (p. 3). The new attention given to the spread and availability of broadband and multi-platform access implies a different approach to the services offered and the role of the user. Two years after the formulation of the *e*Europe 2005 plan, the Commission set forth the '*e*Europe 2005 Action Plan: an update' (CEC, 2004), which dedicated greater attention to the issue of e-inclusion and the need 'to understand in more detail the various facets of this complex issue' (p. 3).

The new strategic plan 'i2010 – A European information society for growth and employment' (CEC, 2005), presented in 2005, follows this route even more clearly. The issue of the inclusion of citizens in the information society thus becomes one of the Commission's priorities. The aim of a European society based upon the inclusion of its members is linked to the spread of broadband access and, more generally, to the achievement of digital convergence, the improvement of the services on offer in terms of both accessibility and costs, the spread of basic digital awareness and the improvement of citizens' health made possible by the new e-health services. Attention is extremely clearly directed towards the social impact of ICT and the need to guarantee the advantages of their use to an ever-greater number of citizens. Reference to various dimensions of access (both material and skill access), as well as the implementation of public services, indicates a distinctly richer and more structured interpretation of the themes of e-inclusion than in the past.

In 2006 this approach and the objectives for an EU e-inclusion policy were agreed in the Riga 'Ministerial Declaration on an Inclusive Information Society' (June 2006) which set concrete targets for Internet usage and availability, digital literacy, and accessibility of ICT by 2010. It also identified a number of priority areas for action: namely ICT and ageing, geographical digital divides, e-accessibility (that is, the usability of ICT for people with disabilities), digital literacy and competences, ICT for cultural diversity, and inclusive e-government. As a follow-up, in November 2007 the Commission adopted a 'Communication on a European e-inclusion initiative' (CEC, 2007a) which considers failure to access or use ICT to be a major form of social and economic exclusion, affecting cohesion and prosperity in Europe.

Furthermore in the final part of the 'e-Inclusion' Ministerial Conference held in Wien (2 December 2008), the Presidency of the European Union emphasizes that: (i) measures to improve digital inclusion constitute an investment in the future and have to be at the centre of public policies addressing the information society; (ii) a strong political commitment, targeted at vulnerable social groups, is necessary in order to improve digital inclusion; and (iii) broadband is becoming an 'essential commodity' like water and electricity. it is today an indispensable service for the effective participation in global trade, economy, education, culture, politics and society.

Therefore, the key issue becomes the 'difference' made by ICT in the everyday life of people and in the whole society. This contribution is not restricted to the economic dimension alone. It involves the social dimension as well. Thus the issue of e-inclusion becomes something that is worth achieving (CEC, 2007b) if we want to build 'a growing and sustainable well being for all society' (p. 8). In order to build one Europe, including digitally, it is necessary to create an 'Internet ecosystem' which has its foundations in a social system that promotes the economic development and social welfare of its citizens by reducing inequality in all its various aspects. This appears to be the objective of 'Europe 2020' (CEC, 2010a), the new strategy for Europe, as it poses as its priority the 'development of an economy based on knowledge and innovation' and places among the seven flagship initiatives 'a digital agenda for Europe'.

Despite all these valuable initiatives, as the CEC's 'impact assessment' (2007b) recognizes, much more must be done to achieve e-inclusion and EU intervention is justified to guarantee equal access to and effective participation in the information society, internal market coherence and e-inclusion co-ordination actions. In this regard, the 'European e-inclusion initiative' (CEC, 2007a) clearly recognized that e-inclusion should not be seen as a problem only but also as an economic opportunity. On economic grounds an inclusive information society brings large market opportunities for the ICT sector, contributes to productivity growth and reduces the cost of social and economic exclusion. In other words, bridging broadband and accessibility gaps, or improving digital competences, translates into new jobs and services.

These economic benefits, however, are difficult to estimate. On the macroeconomic quantification of the inclusive potentials of ICT and its impact on economic performance (productivity, consumer welfare, employability and economic growth) there are very few contributions in the current socioeconomic literature.

The purpose of this study is to start to fill this gap and strengthen the evidence on the economic benefits (and costs) deriving from investment in inclusive information society technology and services. The study will gather data, propose indicators and composite indexes of digital development and e-inclusion (and its flip-side, e-exclusion), and use econometric models to assess the relationship between inclusive ICT and wider economic and social performance.

Despite a growing literature on digital inequality and e-inclusion, the quantitative and qualitative understanding of ICT and e-services usage remains extremely poor and uncoordinated: it is not yet possible to find fully consolidated and reliable datasets and indicators to provide a broad quantitative perspective and facilitate benchmarking for monitoring the process of e-inclusion. Facing these difficulties, and in order to define and measure e-inclusion, we moved beyond the distinction between 'haves' and 'have-nots' in terms of access only, and instead propose a multi-focal approach to this complex concept in continual evolution (see Chapter 1).

More specifically, in Chapters 2–4 we adopt a multi-perspective and multi-dimensional approach (infrastructure, usage, impact on quality of life) so as to to provide a quantitative evaluation, indicators and a dataset to monitor e-inclusion for all 27 EU Member States and explain their main determinants.

On the operational front our goal is to produce the European Digital Development Index (EDDI), in order to monitor and capture the level of advancement of digital inclusion in the EU27 and in all member countries and compare progress made between 2004 and 2009. The composite and longitudinal nature of the EDDI – based on the indexes measuring the subdimensions of infrastructure, usage and impact from 2004 to 2009 – will contribute to individuate the main obstacles to ending the digital exclusion and to monitor progress that has been made in terms of the Riga targets. Its main objective is to provide policy makers with a useful tool to benchmark and assess the e-inclusion processes.

Another key goal of this research is to strengthen the quantitative evidence on e-inclusion and the understanding of the relationship between indicators of e-inclusion and wider economic and social performance. In this perspective, in Chapter 5 we review and compare the existing analyses and models, focusing on the relationship between inclusive ICT and European performance in terms of growth, job creation, and social inclusion.

To select the most suitable model and econometric tools we focus on a set of reference parameters related to: (a) methodological approach; (b) structural specification; and (c) performance variables (Chapters 6 and 7). The selected econometric tools and International Futures (IFs) model meet the following requirements: (i) they are internationally used; and (ii) they are able to assess e-inclusion policy initiatives in multiple dimensions (economic and social) and geographically within Europe, across Europe and in a global context. More specifically they incorporate the properties of ICT in a satisfactory way. ICT is general purpose technology (GPT), whose impact on the economy cannot be understood in the framework of the simple production function and must be assessed taking into account, among other aspects, its interaction with the regulatory framework, the structure of the economy, and the evolution of skills and organization (Guerrieri and Padoan, 2007).

We use and improve the selected IFs model and assess the impact of ICT on inclusion and economic growth generated by digital inclusion in the EU27. We focus also on the most relevant and measurable factors emerging from the literature and the statistical data at micro level. We provide quantified estimates of impacts of various credible forward-looking policy scenarios and run policy simulations using different assumptions with regard to digital inclusion policies.

These policy simulations help us to provide conclusions and identify policy recommendations that are relevant for the post-i2010 strategic framework, keeping in mind the peculiar characteristics of ICT as general purpose technology (which requires that ICT be activated together with other enabling strategies) (Chapter 8). This final part develops an encompassing EU policy framework for pursuing e-inclusion. It attempts to come to grips with what e-inclusion can be understood to comprise (following the EDDI approach) in an EU perspective, and how it relates to traditional and new ICT policies at EU and national levels.

1. Digital development in Europe: a theoretical framework

1.1 DEFINITIONS OF DIGITAL INCLUSION: BEYOND THE DISTINCTION BETWEEN 'HAVES' AND 'HAVE-NOTS'

In the early phase of study on the diffusion of ICT, the predominant approach was clearly based on the distinction between 'haves' and 'have-nots'. This distinction became widely known as the digital divide, defined as 'the gap between those who have access to the new technologies and those who do not' (US Department of Commerce, 1999, p. xiii). Embedded in a sort of technological determinism, the concept of the digital divide – even if connected to a range of economic, social, cultural and technological differences – maintains a predominant dichotomy in terms of access only, insofar as it utilizes the binary categories of *information haves* and *information have-nots*.

Having mightily entered the everyday vocabulary, the expression 'digital divide' has had a unique destiny: the more it spread, the more it was criticized and revised by scholars. The inflection point of the parabola describing this destiny can be identified soon after 2000, when articles and volumes declining the concept of digital divide in terms of criticism and analytical revision started to circulate. Examples include 'From the "digital divide" to "digital inequality"' (DiMaggio and Hargittai, 2001), 'Second thoughts: toward a critique of the digital divide' (Gunkel, 2003), *Virtual Inequality. Beyond the Digital Divide* (Mossberger et al., 2003), *Technology and Social Inclusion. Rethinking the Digital Divide* (Warschauer, 2003), and 'Reconsidering political and popular understandings of the digital divide' (Selwyn, 2004).

The perception of the presence of this cultural wave represents the first step towards a close critical examination of a central concept of the study of social and communicative transformation in present-day societies. The first cause of surprise when looking back into the 1990s in search of the author of the lucky expression 'digital divide' is the impossibility of establishing certain parentage. Scholars who have dedicated themselves with obstinacy to this task (Gunkel, 2003; van Dijk, 2006) agree on identifying its official entry into literature with the report 'Falling through the net: defining the digital divide' – the third report published by the Department of Commerce's National Telecommunication and Information Administration (US Department of Commerce, 1999). Although the expression was used in that report, Larry Irving – under whose direction the report was at the time – has always denied that he coined the term. During a public meeting organized by the Benton Foundation he claimed to have 'stolen' the expression, although he could not recollect the source.[1] The difficulty of ascribing the parentage of such a successful term indicates the climate of creative effervescence that accompanied the initial phase of Internet diffusion. Further indicators of such a climate can be found in the multifarious and diversified meanings attributed to it. Throughout much of the 1990s, this term was in fact used to indicate differences in educational opportunities, inequalities regarding Internet access in schools, differences in working opportunities or even technical incompatibilities (Gunkel, 2003).

The report drafted by the Department of Commerce marks the end of loose interpretation for the term and intentionally provides the definition as being 'the divide between those with access to new technologies and those without' (US Department of Commerce, 1999, p.xiii). Ever since, the sphere of application and interpretation has been well defined and limited to mean Internet access on behalf of the population, which translates into a clear binary classification between the 'information haves' and the 'information have-nots'. On the basis of this clear dichotomy, the following gaps have been identified: global (between countries), social (between different segments of the same society), and democratic (between those who have access to the new virtual space and those who do not) (Norris, 2001). Within any context, digital divide has constantly referred to the level of access, with the consequent classification of individuals into those who have access on the one hand and those who do not on the other.

According to DiMaggio et al. (2004), the adoption of this analytical category based on binary classification is the outcome of an interpretative distortion resulting from the extension of the principle of concession of universal service that has been attributed to the telephone in the United States. Indeed, in their opinion 'the view of the digital divide as a gap between people with and without Internet access was natural at the onset of diffusion, because the Internet was viewed through the lens of a decades-old policy commitment to the principle of universal telephone service' (p.363). In line with this formulation, the first reports published by the US Department of Commerce have paid particular attention to the differentiation between urban and rural areas, considering the family, rather than the individual, as a unit of analysis when monitoring Internet diffusion.

In addition to producing an incomplete picture of the phenomenon, the reference – implicit or explicit as it may have been – to such an approach has brought about false expectations regarding the time it will take to reduce the gap between the 'online' and the 'offline'. In fact, delays have been increased by the expectation of the progressive lowering of prices – of hardware, software and connection costs – to shorten the distance between the various groups, marginalizing the role played by other factors in the decision to get connected to the Internet. Some academics believe that such a clear characterization between those who have access and those who do not, known today as the 'early digital divide', has produced more problems than benefits (Gunkel, 2003; van Dijk, 2005, 2006). Others believe that 'the dichotomous view of the digital divide as a distinction between people who do and do not have Internet access was natural and appropriate at the beginning of the diffusion process' (DiMaggio and Hargittai, 2001, p. 2). On the other hand, research experience gained in recent years has produced a number of arguments in favour of a progressive marginalization of the access element, considered a main indicator for subdividing individuals into haves and have-nots. This division has been defined as both too reductive and highly problematic (Bertot, 2003), as well as unclear and confused (Warschauer, 2001). But what exactly are the reductive, problematic or confused elements connoting the concept of digital divide? Furthermore, once these elements have been analysed, will this term still stand or should it be replaced with a more adequate one?

Before proceeding, we should clarify that the evocative capacity of the expression digital divide to describe new forms of social exclusion deriving from the diffusion of new communication technologies is in no way coming under criticism here. From this perspective one can only agree with Selwyn (2004) when he states that, despite the weakness of the concept, it has had the undeniable merit of imposing the question of informative inequality at the centre of the debate in present-day societies. What is being criticized, however, are the limitations of a term that is essentially centred on the element of access, to the disadvantage of other equally important factors, thereby overlooking the fact that access is different from use and that there are a variety of ways in which this technology is actually employed. We are also liable to forget that the adoption of a similar interpretation could generate some serious misunderstandings with regard to the reduction of inequalities between individuals: data concerning the proliferation of the Internet among the population, as well as the reduction of certain inequalities, risks masking those inequalities that persist – or increase progressively – in the way that technology is used and the role it plays in expanding personal opportunities.

Getting to the heart of the concept analysis, the first important objection to be raised concerns the binary structure used to complicate the issue of the relationship between individuals and technologies. Whatever the aspect in question, 'it represents its problematic according to a binary logic, dividing things into one of two types, where the one option is nominally defined as the negative or antithesis of the other' (Gunkel, 2003, p. 505). The result is a classification between the 'information haves' and its opposite term the 'information have-nots'. This dichotomous structure automatically sweeps aside any intermediate positions, denying their existence and cognitive importance. Consequently, all individuals fall into one of two categories, in open contrast with the personal experience of each one of us and with the research data collected over the years. Rather than bringing to light and underlining the differences in behaviour of the individuals within the group of those who use the Internet and among those who do not, this classification gives us a black and white picture that lacks the subtle shading of reality. On the other hand, a consideration of the varied modes of access, use and competence that govern the way individuals interact with the Internet calls for a new definition of digital divide as 'a gradation based on different degrees of access to information technology' (Warschauer, 2001, p. 1).

Based on such a reference, van Dijk (2005) for instance develops a spectrum of six positions regarding Internet access (the 'truly un-connected', the 'net evaders', the 'net dropouts', the 'intermittent users', the 'continuous users', and the 'home broadband users'). Bentivegna (2009), on the other hand, develops a well-constructed typology with five positions (the 'unconnecteds', the 'monomorphes', the 'utilitarians', the 'polimorphes', the 'netizers'). The Pew Internet & American Life Project (2009), finally, identifies as many as ten profiles ('digital collaborators', 'ambivalent networkers', 'media movers', 'roving nodes', 'mobile newbies', 'desktop veterans', 'drifting surfers', 'information encumbered', 'tech indifferent', 'off the network'). Even if developed with reference to specific situations, these examples show the complexity of the positions included in the two greater groups of users and non-users. It is also important to stress how they contribute to cleaning up the apodicticity of the binary classification: it is much more frequent and common to pass from one condition to the other than is generally believed. Moreover, the differentiations do not only concern access dimensions but also extend to the digital competences of individuals and how these means are used. Therefore, rather than referring to a binary structure, the relationship between individuals and the Internet refers to a multiple structure that results from the combination of a multiplicity of variables. Metaphorically, this combination has been defined as a 'rainbow' (Clement and Shade, 2000) due to the presence of physical means, software, contents, services, infrastructure and so on.

Moreover, the very concept of digital divide is open to question in that it contains elements that refer to so-called 'technological determinism'. Ignoring the distinctions within the 'soft' or 'hard' approach that can be adopted by technological determinism (Gunkel, 2003), we find the common suggestion that 'access to the technology concerned is able to fix existing social problems, among them problems of social inequality, democracy, freedom, social relationships, and community building' (van Dijk, 2005, p. 5). The main problem is therefore reduced to that of access to digital technologies, marginalizing the importance of other factors that contribute to creating conditions of social inequality. Against this approach, focusing on technologies rather than on social transformations, Warschauer (2003) provides convincing examples of failed experiences aimed at improving the everyday life of citizens through the use of new technologies. From India to Egypt, the negative experiences bring the scholar to the conclusion that 'access to ICT is embedded in a complex array of factors encompassing physical, digital, human, and social resources and relationships' (p. 6). It is thus deceitful, if not counterproductive, to implement plans for technology diffusion without ensuring that individuals use it for activities that are believed to be important in everyday life.

Another criticism of the concept of digital divide refers to its characterization in static rather than dynamic terms. The difficulty of filling a gap in the presence of continuous and new technological updates is also pointed out. In short, those individuals who are already connected are believed to continue enlarging their range of technological opportunities through new applications, skills and uses, thus introducing further differentiations. The reduction of the difference between the 'connected' and the 'unconnected' does not necessarily mean the closure of a gap, with the possibility of even greater distances generated in other areas. With this in mind one can only agree with Compaine (2001) when he states that the digital divide is a 'moving target' that is constantly repositioning itself. With the clear intention of resizing the problem's social relevance, the same author stresses the mobility aspect, recalling that. . .

> in the original iteration of the NTIA surveys. . ., it [digital divide] meant primarily personal computer ownership. More recently it has come to incorporate Internet access. The latest noises is that it further delineates those with high speed (broadband) access from slower dial-up modem access. (p. xiii)

The criticisms and analytical reviews that have accompanied the digital divide in recent years have induced some scholars to make a clear choice for the replacement of the concept. DiMaggio and Hargittai (2001), for instance, have stated very clearly that the digital divide paradigm served researchers and policy makers during the opening years of Internet diffusion. But the ongoing expansion of Internet access, along with continuing institutional change, require that we move beyond that paradigm if we are to document and explain important dimensions of digital inequality as Internet penetration continues to increase. (DiMaggio and Hargittai, 2001, p. 18)

On the same wavelength we have Warschauer (2003) who, although acknowledging the historical value of the concept of digital divide, prefers to use alternative concepts that are deemed to be more useful for researchers when facing cognitive challenges. These include 'digital inclusion' and 'digital inequalities'. Unlike the digital divide, which is a one-dimensional concept built on access size, the concepts of digital inclusion and digital inequalities are characterized by their multidimensionality, based on more significant factors that combine to condition how individuals interact with the Internet. Along the same lines, Hargittai (2004) affirms that 'it is important to realize that the term digital divide is misleading because it suggests a one-dimensional divide. Rather, divides exist on multiple dimensions – technological access, autonomy, social support, skill, type of uses' (p. 141).

Although it is undeniable that the concept of digital divide played an essential role in describing the initial phase of Internet diffusion and bringing to the fore the need for governmental intervention to guarantee the development of communicative infrastructures, its cognitive function no longer applies. There is now a need to turn to new analytical categories and conceptual constructions. Consequently it is necessary to go beyond the digital divide and address the lack of sociological sophistication (Webster, 1995) that accompanied the term during its early years.

1.2   DIGITAL INEQUALITIES AS A MOVING TARGET

To go beyond the concept of digital divide and, above all, beyond a one-dimensional approach centred on access, it is vital to identify the other areas where the relation between the Internet and the individuals in present-day societies can be explored. This involves both piecing together the picture of how individuals relate to the Internet and identifying the 'moving' aspects of existing inequality. In order to do this, we need to go one step back to take another look at access size. Rather than rehabilitating positions that have already been amply objected to, it is necessary to acknowledge that inequality in access is important, in that it conditions and accentuates all other factors. Acknowledging such relevance necessarily implies that access size be placed within a wider theoretical context than that used for the classic approach to the expression digital divide (DiMaggio et al., 2004) – a context characterized by a strong concern for the impact of technologies on social inequalities. Written reports indicate that the degree of technology-related inequalities can be found in motivation, access, skill and use (van Dijk, 2005) – or rather in the accessibility of the offer, in informative mobilization (intended as the ability to use information resources), and in information awareness (the ability to use means to obtain resources) (Kim and Kim, 2001).

Apart from the different emphasis given to the motivations that are at the basis of access, it would appear that the two proposals have much in common. In truth, separating motivations from access appears a little forced and is still the result of an interpretation that, despite its intentions, establishes the central importance of the availability of physical means to establish a connection. From a point of view that goes beyond the classic approach of the digital divide, the overlap between the two areas seems clear: people connect when they are motivated to do so. In virtue of this consideration, the concept has been subdivided into three areas: access, skills and use.

With regards to access size, it is worth noting that unlike in the past, when the sole consideration was whether or not there was a connection to the Internet, today there is the question of the quality and autonomy of the connection. In practice, this means that we need to keep paying attention to the data on Internet connection diffusion on both a global and a national level whilst monitoring the achievements of fast connections that allow users to take advantage of all the facilities of an increasingly sophisticated offer requiring ad hoc skills. It is no coincidence that today access is classified as either 'formal' (physically available) and 'effective' (for people with skills that allow them to benefit from technology, Wilson, 2000), or 'technological' (technical means for connection) and 'social' (ability to use them). Whichever pair applies, both distinguish between the physical and technical availability of a connection and the skills required to make the best use of it.

Regarding the physical availability of a connection, it is important to first establish whether broadband is present or absent. A good many studies and research papers have amply documented how broadband provides those who use it with a greater degree of satisfaction, enabling them to take advantage of much of what the Internet has to offer. Empirical data from the US and Europe shows those with broadband as 'strong' users of a wide range of opportunities, often committed to the production of contents and practically always on (Davison and Cotton, 2003; Dutton et al., 2003; Horrigan and Rainie, 2002; Fox, 2005). Unsurprisingly, these individuals have been classified as belonging to the so-called 'broadband élite' (Horrigan and Rainie, 2002).

Just the availability of a connection, however, still does not tell us much: a useful informative integration comes from the place where the connection happens. The fact that we connect to the Internet from home, from work, from the place where we study, from a friend's or in a public place has great influence on the quality of our relationship with the Internet (Bimber, 2000). It is in fact the individual's autonomy of use that changes (DiMaggio et al., 2004). On the other hand it is not difficult to guess that a connection from work first of all is affected by the software available, the firewalls that may be working, the problems concerning privacy, as well as the rules of use to be observed. Access from the workplace is not, however, in itself the only limitation that produces inequalities regarding autonomy of use. This can also be conditioned by the hierarchical structure of the organization: managers may well enjoy benefits (in terms of hardware, software, connection speed, absence of filters and limitations of any kind) that have an important impact on the quality of use of the Internet. Ultimately it could be proffered that, when someone is accessing the Internet from work, their individual autonomy is closely related to the degree of seniority within the functional hierarchical structure. Autonomy is also subject to significant variation when a person is connecting from home, however. With regards to this, numerous studies referring to the 'domestication of the Internet' provide convincing data in support of an interpretation that takes into account – for Internet use within the family – the interlocking relationships and structures involving all members of the family (Bakardjieva, 2005; Berker et al., 2006; Haddon, 2004).

Another element that influences the degree of autonomy of use concerns the acquisition of major digital skills – those who have the freedom of using a 'good quality' connection are also in the position to improve their digital skills through what is known as learning by doing, one of the preferred ways in which individuals increase their technological literacy. While learning by doing is certainly a popular learning system, it is however closely related to the process of appropriation of technology that stands at the base of true ability to take advantage of the opportunities that the Internet, in particular, and the personal computer in general, have to offer.

The elements that allow optimal exploitation of the offer – those that regulate accessibility – must also be associated with the degree of access. Much progress has been made in this direction, particularly in Europe, although results are fairly limited and the problems remain far from solved. One should also bear in mind the problem of access to the contents themselves, which continue to be mainly in English and, according to Warschauer (2003), do not represent subject matter or culture beyond the confines of that pertaining to the American middle class: 'the massive amount of digital content being created on the Internet does not necessarily meet the needs of diverse communities around the world, and this has important consequences for issues of social inclusion' (p. 81). When focusing our attention on the element of access we must also therefore consider the nature of the offer available as well as its capacity to satisfy individual needs. In view of this particular detail it becomes easier to understand why some people prefer not to use the Internet, increasing the numbers of the so-called 'want nots' group (van Dijk, 2006).

A general interest in the field and, ideally, a fast connection, are the two main elements that lead to satisfactory Internet use. When associated with experience of the Internet, these elements can even be multiplied and emphasized, provided the individual has the skills necessary to help improve his or her performance. In order to fully understand the relevance of such skills, it should suffice to consider the huge quantity of information available online via continuous research and selection activities. Not only do individuals have to master huge quantities of data (the so-called 'information overload'), they must also cope with a constantly changing universe where new communicative forms are being realized (for instance, the web 2.0 innovations). To take full advantage of the opportunities offered by the Internet, it is thus necessary to have certain skills, variously termed 'computer literacy', 'electronic literacy', 'digital literacy', or 'multimedia literacy'. According to Warschauer (2003), 'electronic literacy' is the term that best describes the totality of issues linked to the relationship between technology and literacy, being 'an umbrella term that encompasses several other generic literacies of the information era, including computer literacy, information literacy, multimedia literacy, and computer-mediated communication literacy' (p. 111).

Although these forms of literacy are based on the peculiarities of technology, they also reflect many aspects of the social environment in which they appear. It will not have escaped the reader's attention that the skills in question produce inequalities regarding both the ability of use and application. At the same time, they are the result of further inequalities of a social and cultural kind. For the moment it would be useful to focus our attention on the aspects that compose this totality of knowledge and skills, with 'digital skills' intended as being 'the collection of skills needed to operate computers and their networks, to search and select the information they contain and to use them for one's own purposes' (van Dijk, 2005, p. 73). But on what levels is the concept of digital skills articulated? In concrete terms, what activities does it refer to? According to the same scholar (2005, 2006), digital skills can be divided into three levels:

'operational skills', 'informational skills' and 'strategic skills'. Operational skills are those used to work the computer along with the network software and hardware. Informational skills are those used to search, select and process the information obtained from the computer and from the net. Finally, strategic skills are those that allow us to reach specific goals and, in more general terms, to improve our position in society. Proficiency therefore ranges from basic skills – that allow us to use a computer and to surf the Internet – to more articulate skills that enable us to obtain results of various kinds. An even more detailed attempt at subdividing digital skills was eventually offered by Hargittai (2007), who identifies as many as eleven levels: safe and effective ways of communication; knowledge of how to take part in conversation groups and share contents; knowledge and use of tools; knowledge of what is available online; ability to find contents; effectiveness in web navigation; ability to establish source and contents of a message; understanding of privacy-related topics; understanding of safety-related topics; knowledge of where to get assistance; and personalization ability. Predictably enough, those who can master a large number or all of the above levels 'will be in a considerably better position to derive benefits from digital media than those who lack expertise in these domains' (p. 135). It is just as easy to predict that an unequal distribution of skills among individuals will translate into a further source of inequality. Furthermore, as we shall see later, if one of the objectives of Internet diffusion is social inclusion, we cannot ignore the danger deriving from the consequences of verticalized differentiation of individual digital skills.

Quality of access, the availability of increasingly sophisticated technological equipment enabling a steady connection, along with the skills that allow us to reach objectives that are of a consistently improved quality, are elements that reflect on the sphere of Internet use. An initial useful indicator for evaluating possible differences in use can be obtained by classifying the Internet as a 'meta-medium: or rather a set of stratified services making it easy to build new media with nearly any characteristics' (Agree, 1998, p. 3). This means that the Internet can become what people want it to be: from entertainment involving teenagers in role-playing games to support for school activities when teachers assign online researches for homework, relocating on the labour market when specific skills are required for certain tasks or commercial transactions when, for instance, a woman buys a bag she was not able to find in the shops of her hometown.

To have an idea of the multiplicity of areas of activity in which people on the Internet are involved, let it suffice to recall that a recently published synthesis by Pew Internet & American Life Project (2007) listed as many as 72. The list naturally contains the current activities of the American population, spread into percentages. So, for instance, 91 per cent consult emails and use search engines, 38 per cent pay bills online, 27 per cent download music and 11 per cent engage in social relations on dating websites. The great number of activities that it is possible to carry out on the Internet have been gathered and classified by this research institute into seven groups: communication, information research, information production, downloading, media streaming, commercial and economic transactions, entertainment. Although these groups help reduce the wealth of initial data, they are not mutually exclusive – entertainment, for instance, can be pursued through both downloading and media streaming.

The availability of such a range of opportunities and whether an individual is able to make the most of them depends on the availability of economic, social, cultural and technological resources that are not equally distributed – and which become progressively less so in relation to differences in consumption of what the web has to offer. According to van Dijk (2005) this inequality becomes structural once 'some segments of the population systematically and permanently use and benefit from advanced computer and Internet applications for information, communication, work, business and education, and others only use the basic or simple applications for information, communication and shopping, and enjoy more application for entertainment' (p. 129). If this was simply a case of individual trends and interests with no effects on significant areas of activity in present-day society, these differences could well be dismissed as just a diversified use of the media that has always existed, much like a difference in ability to take advantage of available information (Tichenor et al., 1970).[2] This 'minimalist' interpretation is, however, confuted by the transformation of present-day society towards an 'information society', 'knowledge society' or 'network society' – where the ability to acquire and process information has become a prerequisite for full individual citizenship: from work to education, healthcare and even social life. Those who are excluded from communication and information structures are also effectively excluded from political and cultural citizenship (Lash, 1994).

The complexity and size of the issue covered by the concept of digital inequality, along with its cumulative nature, clearly underline how this is indeed a moving target, undergoing constant redefinition and renegotiation, in virtue of the fact that it is a central element in the process of social inclusion in contemporary society. If in the recent past technologies were considered 'enabling' due to their ability to enable individuals to use new tools, today they have become 'empowering' because they broaden and improve the individual's sphere of intervention and application. The mobile trait that we have assigned to the objective of overcoming digital inequalities finds its *raison d'être* in the acknowledgement of the deep and rooted existence of inequality in society. With present-day societies increasingly structured around the web, ICT is conceived not just as another medium 'but as an infrastructure in many ways connected to inequalities. It even assists in deepening the disparities' (Sassi, 2005, p. 694).

1.3   NEW FORMS OF EXCLUSION IN THE NETWORK SOCIETY

In order to fully understand the range of the effects caused by a diversified use of new technology, it is necessary to reconstruct the social and economic changes that have deeply transformed present-day societies. In the eyes of their citizens, these societies display clear elements of discontinuity with the past. Among other things, the present is characterized by phenomena such as globalization, significant differentiations in social stratification, a widespread lack of clear identification (such as class, religion or politics). Other elements also play a part in building up this picture of contemporary society – a progressive individualization (Beck, 2000), a renewed need to feel part of a community (Bauman, 2001) and the establishment of a new form of modernity, defined alternately as 'second' (Beck, 2000), 'liquid' (Bauman, 2002) or 'reflexive' (Giddens, 1990). All these aspects and their diffusion can be placed within the broader framework of the transformation of society and its organizational models. A common element of the various approaches can be found in the acknowledgement of 'a radical change in the organization of human coexistence and of the social conditions of today's living policies' (Bauman, 2002, p. xvii). To avoid embarking on what would inevitably be a lengthy and articulated debate, the changes currently underway can be summed up as marking the end of an era: the modern era – 'the age of technological industrialism, class divisions, mass societies and markets, conflicting ideologies, and political authority organized at the level of territorial, sovereign nation-states' (Barney, 2004, p. 4).

But if this is indeed the era we have left behind, how can we define the one we have just entered? What distinguishes and identifies the present day? A careful observer of reflections on contemporary society has pinpointed information as being an often-quoted innovative element: 'we are told that we are entering an information age, that a new "mode of information" predominates, that ours is now an "e-society", that we must come to terms with a "weightless economy" driven by information, that we have moved into a "global information economy"' (Webster, 2002, p. 2). The concept of information that is usually intended when talking about information society is characterized by its quality of being both 'means' and 'product' of a multitude of processes. This initial, elementary definition of information society already seems to underline the role played by new technologies, in particular the Internet, in the distribution of power in advanced societies. It must however be said that the very term information society has been criticized by a number of sources. Webster, for instance, after a systematic reflection on the use of the term information, states that although there is certainly an increase in the quantity of circulating information (in the form of products, occupation, means and so on), this is not so for quality. Giddens (1987) expresses similar perplexities when he states 'even if it is assumed that we are now entering the information age, modern societies have been "information societies" from their beginning' (p. 27). Similar feelings also appear in Castells (1996), who denies the novelty of the term, arguing that past societies were also based on information.

In order to interpret the changes that are taking place, Castells suggests the use of the terms 'informational', which indicates 'the attribute of a specific form of social organization in which information generation, processing and transmission become the fundamental sources of productivity and power' (1996, p. 21). This new form of social organization leads to the establishment of 'informational capitalism' which replaces the industrial one. At the same time, a new organizational model is established, that is, that related to the network. The attributes that characterize present-day society in the light of the network society theory developed by Castells (ibid.) are the following: the shift of capitalistic economies from an industrial to an information base; the organization of the capitalistic economy which is globally active on the network model; the repositioning of human activities in terms of spatial and temporal organization in response to technologies which permit real time long-distance communication; and the distribution of power based on network access and flows control (Barney, 2004). The identification traits of a society that can be compared to a network society consist, in brief, in the presence of an infrastructure of sophisticated communication and information technologies capable of permitting the implementation of numerous activities in the social, political and economic sphere, and in the reproduction and institutionalization of the network organization as a widespread form of human and social relationship model.

The network model becomes the predominant model, organized on the basis of the node, link, and flow. The node is a separate point connected to at least one other point; the link allows one node to communicate with another; the flow is what is communicated from one node to another through the link. In a given network, whether this concerns micro-social relationships or economic relationships, the dynamics develop at the single node level: a number of links are established between them permitting the transition of flows. The aim is to extend the relationship network as a consequence of the inclusion within the organization. This inclusion, however, is not definitive; in fact, it is the result of a competitive dynamic which continuously redefines the relationships between the various nodes. If any relationships are judged as no longer convenient, the related nodes are removed. In brief we can say that, the relationships within the network survive only as long as they generate benefits for the subjects involved; when this is no longer the case, the relationships are suspended and new ones are established.

This model fits in perfectly with the disembedding and reembedding process referred to by Giddens (1990) to illustrate his concept of reflexive modernity. In present-day societies, the individual's life is increasingly less connected with and dependent on the intermediate bodies of society. In the past, the individual behaviours were the result of the respect of values and rules proper to the context in which the same individuals belonged. Nowadays, individuals enjoy greater freedom of choice, and they are free from any restrictions and obligations imposed by the community. From this point of view, Giddens sustains that we live in a 'post-traditional society', where everything can be negotiated and questioned. For this to occur, however, individuals must be constantly aware of their surroundings, or they must exercise a continuous reflexivity. In the exercise of such surveillance, the constant gathering of information in order to evaluate the various situations and make choices is crucial. It appears evident that social relationships become increasingly more unstable and similar to those characterizing the network organization model: links survive only if they are convenient and functional for the nodes/individuals involved. In this dynamic competition, individuals find themselves in a condition of solitude, which urges them to search for biographical solutions to systemic contradictions (Beck, 2000), that is, to try to implement a solitary self-realization project. Relationship networks between similar nodes/subjects are built in what has also been defined as a situation of networked individualism, with the inevitable consequence of producing new and numerous forms of exclusion. This, moreover, is no surprise if we only consider that the trait identifying the dynamic of network relationships is that of competition.

To sum up the above, we may proceed with the reconstruction of the fine net of relations that makes the digital divide issue dependent on the social changes underway. In a society where the individual's condition of solitude has become a constant which accompanies the latter in all his or her activities, the opportunities to establish contact with other individuals takes on the form of a network within which relationships are established between the various nodes, in a perspective of reciprocal advantage. Such relationships, which cease to exist when they no longer provide fewer benefits or provide fewer benefits than others, allow individuals to acquire the information necessary to carry out a sort of surveillance over the world that surrounds them, and thus create a sense of proximity and belonging to a community, although of a temporary nature (for example, the 'peg communities' referred to by Bauman).

The possibility to obtain useful information is fundamentally important to individuals who find themselves in an increasingly disembedded condition. The reader will certainly have noted that the opportunity to obtain information and the propensity to associate nodes having similar characteristics may lead to new forms of exclusion, which are typical of a society in which reflexive modernity and a network organization prevail. Such new forms of exclusion concern, in particular, all those subjects who are excluded from the communication and information structures, making up a category which is even more disadvantaged than the proletarian one in the age of modernity, and who live at the bottom of what is frequently defined as the society 'of two thirds'. In other words, a growing trend toward polarization takes place, that is, the simultaneous growth of the summit and of the bottom of the social ladder (Sassi, 2005): 'global' citizens are in a position to make choices starting from the access to a wide range of information; the 'excluded' citizens are unable to implement the surveillance process on an ever-changing society and swell the ranks of that 'fourth world' referred to by Castells (1996) to indicate all those who are excluded from the network society. The risk posed by these new forms of social differentiation leads Lash (2002) to sustain that, today, exclusion has become more serious and meaningful than exploitation. In his opinion, in fact, in those societies where information has become the trait characterizing both individual and social relationships, inequality is increasingly less dependent on production relationships between workers and employers and more dependent on the opportunity to gain access to the communication structures, to the extent of possibly transforming itself into an exclusion from the political and cultural citizenship (Lash, 1994).

The social changes that have swept and continue to sweep across the present-day societies described above reflect a scenario which helps us to gain a better understanding of the risks involved in a radicalization of the digital divide. We are not faced with a 'Mercedes Divide', as Michael K. Powell[3] has cynically sustained. On the contrary, we are faced with a risk for the economic, political, social and cultural development of the world we live in. In this respect, it is worth mentioning a passage from the position taken by the G8 countries during the meeting held in Okinawa (2000):

Our vision of an information society is one that better enables people to fulfil their potential and realise their aspirations. To this end we must ensure that IT serves the mutually supportive goals of creating sustainable economic growth, enhancing the public welfare, and fostering social cohesion, and work to fully realize its potential to strengthen democracy, increase transparency and accountability in governance, promote human rights, enhance cultural diversity, and to foster international peace and stability.[4]

On the same wavelength, there are several interventions on the part of the European Community that are intended to increase investments in communication and information technologies so as to build an inclusive society capable of promoting development, employment and a better quality of life for its citizens. The awareness that the new technologies play a significant role in determining situations of social inclusion or exclusion forces the issue of digital divide on the agenda of policy makers and researchers (Mossberger et al., 2008). Such a position is fuelled and strengthened by the awareness that a new network society model has now been established, that the new technologies play a fundamental role in numerous fields of present-day life, and that the ability to use such technologies determines the difference between marginality and social inclusion.

The belief that the digital divide constitutes a problem for the fair and balanced development of present-day societies inevitably implies the need for a careful examination of the evolution of the phenomenon and of the future scenarios. Depending on the interpretation context, in fact, the problem can be presented as 'naturally' solvable (consistently with the approach adopted in studies on the diffusion of technology) over a more or less extended period of time, or such as to require the implementation of ad hoc interventions (consistently with the approach adopted in studies on social exclusion). As regards the importance of the interpretation given, it is hard to disagree with Hacker and Mason (2003): 'the ways in which the digital divide is framed are related not only to statistics but also to politics and ethics' (p. 114).

In the early phase of the advent of the new technologies, the approach inspired by Rogers' theory of systematic diffusion of innovations (2003) has clearly prevailed. In his broad and accurate study, the American researcher theorized and analysed the innovation diffusion patterns starting from their nature, the existing communication channels, the different implementation times and the present social structure. Among the numerous examples provided, that of the diffusion of wheat seeds among Iowa farmers (Ryan and Gross, 1943) forms the basis for constructing a user type still applied today in marketing: the early adopters, the early majority, the late majority, the laggards. Using the temporal and diffusion rhythm

Normalization model

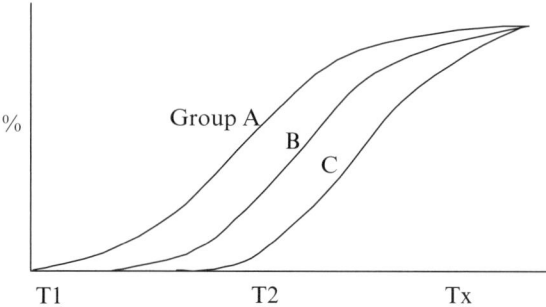

Stratification model

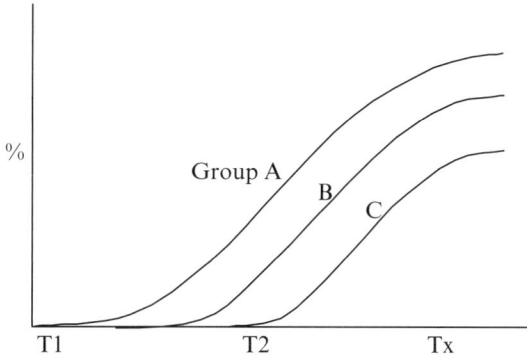

Figure 1.1   The cumulative S-shaped curve of technological diffusion

variables, the groups of subjects were projected on two axes forming an S-shaped curve, which is the result of the contribution of various types of users, positioned in line with the time required to appropriate innovation. The underlying assumption of the model is that, in the course of time, innovation will reach a point of saturation and will eventually involve all the individuals, with only one hardly definable unknown (the temporal variable) (Figure 1.1).

The S-shaped diffusion curve forms the basis of the interpretation, defined as 'optimistic', which considers the digital divide issue almost exclusively in terms of access. This application of the curve to the study on new technologies has led to the so-called normalization model (Norris, 2001), that is, a model in which the gaps between the various subjects are bridged in the course of time, creating a sort of curve overlap. It is important to underline that this interpretation is based on a one-dimensional view of inequalities; and it is only by virtue of such a limitation, that those who adopt it may assume that the reduction of computer and connectivity prices (the result of the mechanisms used by the competition and of the functioning of the economic market) will automatically cause the catchment areas to expand. According to a number of scholars, the automatism underlying the normalization model is based on the fact that the differences between the groups in the pace at which they acquire the Internet affect their positioning on the diffusion curve; this curve seems inevitably to culminate in full access to all (Leigh and Atkinson, 2001).

This extremely linear interpretation can be challenged by the following question:

> But *can* we assume that different groups are merely at different points on the same curve? Perhaps the most important question facing policy makers is whether disadvantaged groups are simply a few paces behind or, by contrast, are becoming marooned as the rest of the world moves ahead. If the former is true, we can count on time to bridge the divide; if the *trajectories* are different, public policy must play a larger role to reduce inequality. (DiMaggio et al., 2004, p. 363; italics original)

As easily intuitable, the normalization hypothesis is optimistic, as it is based on the belief that all the groups move towards the same level, although at a different pace. There are essentially two elements which support this interpretation: (1) indeed, Internet diffusion times have been very short (in a 10-year period, according to the data from ITU[5] sources, Internet users in the world increased from 0.46 to 13.8 out of 100 individuals), and at a faster pace than those of radio and television; and (2) some differences in the nature, generation and residence (understood as urban or rural) have narrowed over the last few years. In brief, the tendency of the data to reduce the gaps confirms the interpretation based on the acknowledgement that 'any new communication technology that has important impacts will, at least temporarily, advantage some individuals and disadvantage others' (Rogers, 2001, p. 107); time, however, works towards bridging that gap between individuals.

Those who challenge this optimistic interpretation have developed numerous arguments: (1) despite the increasingly wider diffusion of the Internet, the rate of adoption in developing countries is far below that registered in developed countries (James, 2007); (2) although some differences have narrowed, the economic, cultural and social resources continue to have a strong impact on the appropriation opportunities of the individuals; (3) the S curve may perhaps represent the access dimension but certainly not that of usage; and (4) the characteristics of the new technologies lead to the creation of new differences: the intensity, expertise and quality of Internet usage are in themselves a source of new gaps, as the adoption phase must be followed by the appropriation phase, which is certainly slower than that of the development of the technology market. Whichever context is preferred, the common denominator of the perplexities expressed above can be traced in the flat rejection of an interpretation inspired by a mechanistic theory on the diffusion of technological innovation. Even if we were to accept Rogers' argument (2001) as to what qualifies the Internet as an innovation – or 'characterised by a very high degree of *relative advantage* (defined as the degree to which an innovation is perceived as providing greater benefits than the previous idea that it replaces)' (p. 97) – the comparison with other innovations, whether the radio, television or the telephone, for example, is not altogether relevant and satisfactory. By making such a comparison, in fact, we forget that the Internet is different from the television media, for example, because it requires the skills necessary for mobilization and information awareness (Kim and Kim, 2001), or ability and willingness in the choices made. In short, we tend to forget 'the inherent complexities of the processes of diffusion, adoption and integration of the Internet as a new medium in society' (Bonfadelli, 2002, p. 81).

In addition to creating different areas of study, these two approaches form the basis of several political interpretations (Yu, 2006). In fact, it is evident that to consider the diffusion and appropriation of the Internet as a problem that can be solved 'naturally' by the market mechanisms, implies a non-intervention policy; conversely, the belief that the problem is of a structural nature, and that it reproduces old mechanisms of social exclusion by amplifying them, implies an intervention policy. Positioned along the traditional right–left axis, the existing ideological views take on clearly defined features and provide just as clear solutions:

> For those on the left, it may be desirable to associate digital inequalities with all other social inequalities and to see little possibility for progress short of revolutionary political changes in the entire economic and political system. For those on the right, it may also be desirable to see digital inequalities as part of other inequities, but with a different ethical bent – the assumption that the inequities are simply natural and inevitable consequences of human competition and unequal abilities and therefore undeserving of intensive concern. (Hacker, and Mason, 2003, p. 100)

By taking into account this interpretational axis, it is possible to identify distinct areas of analysis with the consequent intervention or non-intervention proposals.

The interpretation that considers digital inequalities as inevitable (Compaine, 2001; Foster, 2000; Mueller, 2001) is clearly in favour of non-intervention. According to this interpretation, the inequalities in the relationship between certain groups of the population and the Internet are normal and inevitable, as are those existing in the field of health, education and employment opportunities. If inequalities have always existed and still exist today, it follows that there is not one specific feature that characterizes technology. Ad hoc interventions are not only rejected in the light of the normal functioning mechanism of the economic market (in a market economy, the producers of technological goods try to increase the size of their clientele by making their prices accessible to an increasingly larger number of individuals) but, also, with reference to considerations of social justice, which would be upset in the case where public investments are used in favour of given interventions rather than others. In conclusion, those who favour this approach support a limited government role in facilitating the functioning of the market and its competitiveness, including by accelerating the process for deregulating the telecommunications sector.

Another interpretation recognizes the existence of the digital inequalities issue, although mainly in an economic context. According to this interpretation, digital inequalities have contributed to arresting the development of the ICT market, preventing the expansion of the technological production sector and of electronic trade (Antonelli, 2003; Sehrt, 2004; Wong, 2002). According to this point of view, the reduction of digital inequalities plays a key role in removing the obstacles which hamper market development and in creating economic growth and development opportunities. Once it is acknowledged that the market functioning mechanisms alone are not capable of solving the problem, the need for government intervention to reduce the gap is supported. The problem, however, for those who adopt this interpretation, is and remains strictly of an economic nature.

In political terms, on the other hand, there is an interpretation developed by researchers who consider the question of digital inequalities of fundamental importance to present-day societies (Golding, 2000; Golding and Murdock, 2001; Hacker and Mason, 2003). In their opinion, the problem does not concern economic development but, rather, social inclusion. The real issue lies in the disparity of opportunities enjoyed by certain sectors of society – in terms of education, employment and political participation – whilst others are excluded. Precisely because of the significant social consequences deriving from the conditions of exclusion, an interpretation that conceptualizes the digital divide as a technological gap that could be bridged with technological solutions is flatly rejected. With great intellectual clarity and rigour, Golding and Murdock (2001) argue that the conceptualization of the issue in similar terms inevitably leads to a discussion centred on commercial interests. The social and political relevance of the problem forms the basis of an explicit request for government intervention in guaranteeing Internet access to the citizens by investing in infrastructures, digital literacy of the population, and in providing meaningful content to users. As regards the developing countries, reference is made to the need to implement a mechanism of exchange with the more developed countries and to pay attention and respect to the traditions and culture of the populations involved.

Last but not least is the interpretation which clearly denies that the issue may be posed strictly in economic or technological terms. The issue is rather of a social nature (Alden, 2003; Burkett, 2000) but, precisely because it is a social issue, it can be treated on an equal footing with many other issues concerning present-day societies. It is in fact submitted that there is a potential risk that the attention paid to digital inequalities may reduce the importance of other issues such as world hunger, environmental pollution and so on. In conclusion, therefore, it would not be desirable to have any intervention which would reduce inequalities, which are not only technological, but also reflect those which clearly mark off the distance between developed and developing countries.

1.4 MODELLING DIGITALIZATION PROCESSES

The acknowledgement of the central role of digital inclusion in present-day societies represents the first step along the road leading to the creation of a new form of social cohesion based on the use of ICT. In order to achieve this objective, however, there is a need not only for ad hoc policy-making interventions, but also to identify the knowledge and measurement instruments. The reference to the digital inequalities paradigm facilitates this task thanks to the social roots of technology, which is theorized on its construction side as much as on its usage side. In brief, what is shown of technology is its involvement in an ongoing reinvention process, as much on the part of those who design it as on the part of those who actually use it; this ongoing reinvention process generates their constant adaptation to the social practices and needs, resulting in an internal rather than external impact on society (DiMaggio et al., 2004). The same paradigm also provides a focus on the strong connection linking digital inequalities with social inequalities, in a perspective based on the realization that technology is ever more socially embedded. On the other hand, empirical studies on the use of ICT in England and Italy reach similar conclusions that there is strong evidence that many of those who are digitally excluded are also socially excluded (Bentivegna, 2009; Digital Inclusion Team, 2007). The emphasis on the existence of this link is of fundamental importance for the making of policies which may be useful in reducing the differentiation and social exclusion processes that mark present-day societies.[6] From this point of view, therefore, 'e-inclusion is both the symmetric counter part of e-exclusion and also a policy objective and programme aiming at reducing digital inequalities thus directly or indirectly contributing to the process of social inclusion as a whole' (CEC, 2007b, p.116). In order to achieve this objective, we need to correctly identify the dimensions of the concept of e-inclusion.

The definition of digital inclusion provided by the Riga Ministerial Declaration (2006), understood as a focus 'on participation of all individuals and communities in all aspects of the information society', such as to produce an improvement in economic performance, in employment opportunities, and in social participation and cohesion, indicates the general coordinates required to identify the dimensions which make up the concept. On the one hand, in fact, reference is made to the breadth of the range of subjects who should be involved (all individuals and communities); on the other hand, explicit reference is made to the consequences of the digital inclusion processes. This attempt to provide a definition is the first step in a process which, at a later time, identifies the indicators and, finally, condenses them into empirical indices. In fact, the construction of an e-inclusion summary index is the final result that needs to be achieved in order to monitor the digital inclusion processes, whether across countries at a given point in time or within countries over time. For this Lazarsfeldian process to occur, however, the dimensions and subdimensions of e-inclusion need to be carefully contemplated and identified.

Before proceeding in this direction, however, it is important to introduce certain elements which interact significantly with the dimension-based representation of the concept. Among these, there is certainly that which defines digital inclusion as a 'moving target': that is, a phenomenon which is closely connected with the changes in the technological innovation process. As technological applications change, the digital inclusion process connected to them inevitably changes. By way of example, it will suffice to refer to the digital inclusion process in 2009 – based on broadband availability – and to note the considerable differences between 2009 and the same process in 2004 – characterized by slower connections. In brief, in order to understand the real nature of the digital inclusion process – inevitably interconnected with technological change – its 'in progress' nature must be constantly taken into consideration.

Another factor which needs to be taken into consideration, moreover, is that the digital inclusion process aims not only to expand the number of individuals who are able to improve their quality of life as a result of ICT-related developments, but also to impact the overall level of a country's economic and social development. This means that digital inclusion has an impact at the individual level as much as at the social level, and at the micro level as much as at the meso and macro levels.

The simultaneous presence of these levels generates significant problems about the individuation of the indicators that can be useful to describe the phenomenon: the passage from the subjective perception to the impersonal registration of the overall effect of the digitalization processes in the banking sector, for instance, constitutes an evident exemplification of the existing tension between the different levels.

Before describing the conceptualization of digital inclusion and its dimensions, it is important to offer a brief review of the previous indexes used to measure the concept. Measuring digital inclusion, in fact, has been a longstanding goal shared by all those who monitor the evolution of ICT in contemporary societies. As evidence of this, there have been a number of very interesting attempts to construct summary measures of this issue, such as SIBIS (SIBIS, 2003) DiDiX 'Digital Divide Index' (Husing and Selhofer, 2004), DAI 'Digital Access Index' (ITU, 2003), Infostate Index (Sciadas, 2005), DOI 'Digital Opportunity Index' (ITU, 2005), and IDI 'ICT Development Index' (ITU, 2009, 2010).

All these indexes, even though they vary in terms of number of countries sampled and indicators used, share a common structure based on the degree of development of technological infrastructures and on Internet diffusion in the various settings. According to Barzilai-Nahon (2006), author of an interesting review of the literature on the topic, there are two general types of indexes commonly used: 'focused monoptical indices and comprehensive indices. Monoptical indices are more widely available, while comprehensive ones are rare' (p. 269). The obvious reason for the prevalence of the former over the latter is that they facilitate the retrieval of information on individual, mainly technological, dimensions. This imbalance in the existing index vis-à-vis the technological aspect generates that monoptical feature which Barzilai-Nahon speaks about, as well as a continuous revision due to the technological transformation that is taking place in ICT. It should be stressed, moreover, that, with rare exceptions, the majority of existing indexes are used to measure the degree of technological development in any country, whether Sweden, Senegal, South Korea, or Bangladesh, which clearly and inevitably entails the need to set aside specific frameworks.

A notable exception to this approach is the recent Broadband Performance Index (BPI), which was developed in Europe 'to measure the relative performance of countries in the wide broadband economy' (CEC, 2009, p. 14). Unfortunately, the index was calculated for a one-year period only (2008) and, therefore, it cannot be used in a diachronic logic. Nevertheless, this index has the merit of having introduced a multidimensional approach (six dimensions are used), which is much more useful in understanding complex issues such as, for example, broadband development in Europe.

This brief overview of the various indexes designed to monitor ICT evolution constitutes the framework within which the 'comprehensive' index proposed herein is integrated and structured into a temporal dimension, so as to enable benchmarking of the various values obtained overall, and into the different dimensions making up the index. In fact, the index proposed here does not merely take account of the purely technological dimension, but also adopts a broader concept of digital inclusion.

After having introduced and briefly presented these elements which together define the framework in which is posed the concept of digital inclusion nowadays, we can move on to define its dimensions and subdimensions. Going back to the definition of digital inclusion formulated for the Riga Ministerial Declaration (2006), understood as a focus on participation of all individuals in all aspects of the information society so as to benefit the economy, labour, and social participation and cohesion, it is possible to define the dimensions of the concept.

Before reaching this specification, however, it is necessary to clear some matters of conceptual and methodological order. For example, which strategy has to be elaborated to reach the accurate registration of the individuals involved in the many areas of the information society? And, furthermore, how does one catch the signals of improvement in the different areas touched by the digitalization processes, for example economic, working, social, cultural and so on? If we exclude the eventuality of turning to subjective evaluations offered by the same individuals involved in the process of construction of the information society, the only workable alternative remains the accurate registration of the many activities realized online, with consequent advantages at both the individual and social level. In fact, be it the search for employment or the purchase of goods and services, the reading of newspapers or the fulfilment of paperwork, the benefits lie both in the everyday life of the individual and in collective advantage, above all in cost reduction and wealth production.

The registration of the activities carried out online as well as the extent of the number of individuals that carry them out configure themselves as a proxy for the ongoing digitalization processes. Through this research strategy, the focus of attention is on the progressive digitalization of fundamental areas in individual and collective life, so as to build a picture of the wide digital inclusion of individuals, communities and societies. The reading that allows this approach characterizes itself by the emphasis put on the final result of the process under consideration – digitalization – rather than on the single elements that contribute to generate it. In other

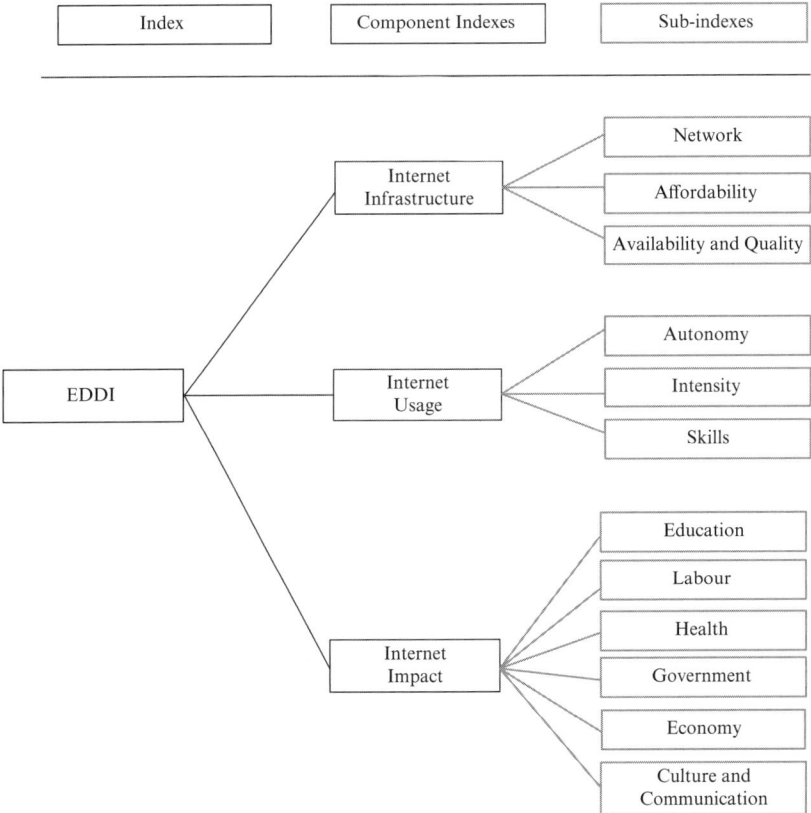

Figure 1.2   European digital development index (EDDI)

words, rather than giving answers about the digital inclusion of single individuals, answers are given about the overall degree of development of the digitalization processes in a single state or in the whole of Europe.

The description of the state of digitalization of a society can take place only through the description of its constitutive dimensions. In the light of the observations formulated in the previous pages, one of the dimensions which makes up the concept is that of infrastructure. The provision of access points and forms of connection is the first step in the process of domestication of technology and its use in improving quality of life and participation in an information society. This is particularly relevant for broadband connection, which enables a dramatic change in the use of multimedia products and enables individuals to assume the role of content producers.

It is in any case true that the infrastructure dimension does not fully define the concept of digitalization – as has been widely discussed – but certainly no digital inclusion process can be implemented without it. Unlike digital inclusion in the past, when it was interpreted in dichotomic terms and constituted the pillar of the digital divide paradigm, the dimension of infrastructure of modern-day e-inclusion can only be structured into subdimensions capable of representing the large number of existing nuances. It is thought that the subdimensions of e-inclusion can be identified first in the availability (of a home computer, Internet connection at home) and in the quality of connection (broadband connection), that is, in the full control of access and in the possibility to access all available services. In order to establish the conditions of autonomy and a good quality of access, however, there are a number of prerequisites which must be fulfilled or which make these two subdimensions actually significant.

First, it is essential that a technological network be available to the subjects (whether individuals, households or enterprises) to stimulate the context in which they are set, creating the necessary conditions for making Internet access actually attainable. Although its meaning may vary, the presence of any subdimensions in the network (or infrastructure) is traced in the various indexes created to register the diffusion of ICT: from the ICT Opportunity Index – which is the result of the synthesis of two different indexes proposed by the ITU (2003) and Orbicom (Sciadas, 2005) to the ICT Development Index (ITU, 2009). Even though the created indexes are used for different purposes, the attention to the technological infrastructure – defined as network in the case at issue – is an inevitable step in the correct interpretation of the subjects' choices concerning ICT access.

Another essential element for a correct interpretation is accessibility in economic terms. In addition to the availability of a technological network, in fact, it appears self-evident that there is a need for accessibility in terms of reduced and affordable rates and low equipment costs. This, in brief, is a form of access in economic terms which is useful in describing the effective availability of the technological supply. In the light of these considerations, the dimension of infrastructure can be structured into three subdimensions, considered fit to represent and reproduce its full meaning: 'network; affordability; and availability and quality'.

The evidence from the literature established at international level identifies usage as a further dimension of the concept of digital inclusion: indeed, it is widely acknowledged that, for digital inclusion processes to be successful and to produce positive outcomes at the overall level, it is essential to possess the necessary skills to guarantee a satisfactory technological appropriation. Autonomy in Internet usage is a fundamental element in determining the success of the technological appropriation process: only when the possibility to navigate in full autonomy exists – understood as access availability and choice of content – is it possible to establish the conditions for fully realizing the digital experience, and for individuals to search for new applications and uses. The conditions of autonomy go hand in hand with those of intensity: also in the latter case, a frequent use of the Internet facilitates the acquisition of greater skills necessary to carry out more complex activities.

Access autonomy and intensity of use prepare the ground on which the subdimensions of informational skills and Internet skills are applied. As regards the first type of skills, which consist in a basic knowledge of the personal computer and how it works, they are required to carry out certain operations of an increasing level of complexity: from copy and paste to the installation of programmes. These basic features of technological literacy, although they are related to a specific connection device such as the personal computer, constitute the common basis for the use of the Internet. Compared with the Internet skills, finally, they certify the individual's ability to use the technology and, hence, indicate the size of the sphere of 'movement'. It is clear that autonomy and intensity of use, combined with advanced and composite informational and Internet skills, facilitate the digital inclusion process: the ability to carry out complex operations facilitates and affects the size of the scope as well as the daily quality of life. Thus it is proposed that the dimension of usage be structured into three subdimensions: autonomy, intensity, and skills.

As said before, the last dimension of the e-inclusion concept presumably lies in the spheres in which the most significant outcomes, at both individual and social level, occur. Unfortunately, as is known, the 'impact of digital inclusion is often very difficult to isolate or to quantify' (FreshMinds, 2008). Nevertheless, during the structuring of the concept, it is possible to assume a number of subdimensions on the basis of the definition of e-inclusion formulated during the Riga Conference. Within the 'impact' dimension, the following subdimensions can be identified: economy, education, employment and labour, health, government interaction, and culture, communication and recreation. Such subdimensions, although they certainly do not address the full complexity of the concept, render part of its meaning clear and, at the same time, are the most easily translatable (into indicators) in empirical terms. The impact of e-inclusion at the various levels, for example, can be brought together in the illustrated representation of the economy subdimension: from the use of e-banking to that of e-commerce. The numerous activities pertaining to individual training both for personal cultural growth and for professional improvement with a view to entry in employment can be brought together in the education subdimension.

Employment-seeking activities as well as other spheres of employment

in which ICT constitutes a specialization or delocalization feature can
be brought together in the employment and labour subdimension. The
activities related to the search for health information and medical assistance provided through online consultation and prescriptions are grouped
together in the health subdimension. And the various activities pertaining
to relations between citizens and the public administrations, in a range of
possibilities from a simple information request to the full management of
procedures online can be brought together in the government interaction
subdimension. Lastly, the chaotic and lively sphere of communication and
entertainment developed in terms of media product consumption (TV and
newspapers), downloading games and music, communication production
and cultural products can be brought together in the culture, communication and recreation subdimension. Indeed, the subdimensions identified
above do not render the full meaning of the concept of e-inclusion with
respect to its impact on individuals. The choice of transforming the dimensions into indicators inevitably entails a selection which is inspired by the
availability of data rather than by their evocative ability. Despite such
limits, however, the subdimensions of *economy, education, employment
and labour, health, government interaction,* and *culture, communication
and recreation* have the ability, in our opinion, to accurately represent the
consequences of the digital inclusion process at both individual and social
level.

1.5   THE SELECTION OF INDICATORS

Despite the growing literature on digital inequalities and digitalization,
it is not yet possible to find fully consolidated and reliable quantitative
datasets and indicators to provide a broad quantitative perspective and
facilitate benchmarking for monitoring the process of digitalization. In
order to find indicators able to represent dimensions and subdimensions of
the digitalization concept, a number of databases containing information
on ICT have been consulted.

The database with the largest quantity of information related to the
diffusion and use of ICT is undoubtedly that of Eurostat,[7] as a result
of its institutional task of providing material useful for benchmarking
the process of e-inclusion as requested in numerous interventions by the
European Commission. Other databases which contain interesting information, although emphasizing more the economic side, are those provided
by the OECD[8] and by the World Development Indicators (WDI).[9] Finally,
the ITU[10] database pays careful attention to recording the changes in the
technological infrastructure and costs. The selection of the indicators used

to construct the index of digitalization is based on examination of those included in different databases and on checking their completeness for the time span selected (from 2004 to 2009).

Starting from the analysis of the indicators used to describe the infrastructure dimension, it is worth remembering that the availability of a good technological infrastructure and of a qualitative connection is the *sine qua non* for a positive outcome of the technological appropriation process. The provision of access points and forms of connections is the first step in the process of domestication of technology and its use in improving quality of life and participation in an information society.

On the basis of this consideration, the infrastructure dimension has been broken down into three subdimensions, which can help to shed light on various aspects of the real access opportunities offered to individuals. More specifically, the following subdimensions were examined: network; affordability; and availability and quality. These subdimensions, which represent three aspects of the infrastructure dimension, can provide information on the greater or lesser user-friendliness of the Internet. Starting with an initial dataset containing 35 indicators, on which a number of 'quality' inspections and analyses in principal components were conducted to identify the most significant factors (see Appendix), we obtained a final dataset containing eight indicators divided between the three infrastructure subdimensions.

Within the network subdimension are the indicators (broadband penetration rate; international Internet bandwidth per inhabitant (bit/s); secure Internet servers per 1 million people) that describe the degree of development of the infrastructure that makes it possible to use the Internet and makes the difference in terms of quality. This subdimension is very similar to that of 'infodensity', which was developed as part of the construction of the ICT Opportunity Index,[11] although it is essentially different in terms of the specific attention given to indicators related to the diffusion of the Internet.[12]

From a reading of the indicators used, it is quite apparent that the role played by this subdimension within the more general access dimension consists in registering the degree of development of the infrastructure available in a given country – or in the whole of Europe – for disseminating and developing the use of the Internet. It appears evident, in fact, that people will be less likely to buy online or complete administrative procedures through the Internet if the protection of their online transactions is not guaranteed. Likewise, difficulties in transmitting information or the lack of broadband coverage will affect the type of activities that users will choose to carry out on the Internet.

The role played by the affordability subdimension is, in terms of explanatory power, just as intuitive. In this case, the economic cost of using the Internet represents a major and direct obstacle to its diffusion.[13] Unfortunately, it must be stated that there are no indicators available which make the presence of such an obstacle immediately clear (like those, for example, designed to register the cost of tariffs). There is only one indicator available (the fixed broadband Internet access tariffs per month) which helps to determine the value of the 'price basket'[14] recently developed by ITU and WDI. Unfortunately, this indicator is available only for the years 2008–09 and, consequently, it cannot be applied to this study, which is of a dynamic rather than a static nature. In order to register the role played by the cost variable it was deemed appropriate to use the information and communication technology expenditure per capita indicator, developed by WDI, which is available for a sufficient number of years.[15] This indicator, even though it has less evocative and explanatory power than the data on monthly tariffs, was deemed satisfactory and hence used to describe the degree of affordability of the Internet in the various countries.

Finally, the third dimension comprises indicators describing the availability and quality of Internet connections. That is the last element of a picture which aims to describe the conditions of user access. In the latter case, emphasis is placed on the availability of a network[16] and on its quality. The indicators which refer to the diffusion of subscriptions to the Internet (Internet subscribers fixed broadband per 100 inhabitants, Internet subscribers fixed per 100 inhabitants) constitute a sort of 'framework' on which the indicators connected to the actual access to the Internet on the part of households and individuals are based (level of Internet access of households, percentage of households using a broadband connection).

The approach selected in this research differs from one focusing strictly on broadband diffusion and quality: this dimension was explored, for example, by the interesting Indexing Broadband Performance (CEC, 2009) experience, as well as by the American contributions aimed at finding a satisfactory explanation for the international broadband leadership (Atkinson et al., 2008). The results produced by both of these studies are extremely useful in providing an explanation of the different performances registered in the broadband connection dimension, but reveal little or no information on its evolution over the course of time. Such poor attention to the diachronic dimension was the consequence of the use of only recently acquired indicators (broadband speed, broadband prices), which cannot be used to reconstruct the evolution that occurred in Europe in recent years. Furthermore, adopting an approach which focuses strictly on broadband connection necessarily entails the neglect not only of the diachronic dimension, but also of important differences in the European situation. For example, if we only consider the number of households that had access to the Internet and those that had a broadband connection, a clear discrepancy immediately emerges: in 2009, 63 per cent had the former and 55 per cent had the latter. This showed that 8 per cent of households had Internet access through a low-quality connection only. The risk of taking account strictly of broadband connections is that the share of users who have already entered the world of Internet, albeit through medium or low-quality connections, is entirely neglected. In our opinion, these subjects should be included in the global picture, especially in light of the historical comparative nature of this study. On the other hand, it is obvious that in the coming years connection will be measured and assessed in terms of broadband speed (and the related costs), and any differences between individuals and countries will be constructed on that variable.

The fact that mere Internet access does not necessarily mean effective usage is widely accepted by all those who study the phenomenon of digital inclusion. According to the most widely accepted approach among researchers, actual appropriation of the Internet occurs in a context of autonomy (Bimber, 2000; DiMaggio et al., 2004; van Dijk, 2005, 2009; Warschauer, 2003); that is, only through frequent use of the Internet is it possible to acquire the skills necessary to master it. On the other hand, it can be easily divined that establishing a connection in a place where the degree of autonomy is limited – such as the workplace, for example – is subject to a variety of conditions: the software available, the firewalls installed, if any, the privacy-related issues and the Internet use regulations in place.[17] Many of the factors considered in relation to the limitation of autonomy of use at the workplace can also be applied to the place of education, where young people are given the possibility to use the Internet. In this case too, there are numerous variables that affect and limit the degree of autonomy in Internet usage: the availability of workstations, the software made available to students, the quality of connection and the time allocated by the overall school curriculum for using the computer lab. Last but not least in order of importance, is the objective limit of the regulated access to the school or university facilities as provided for in the related training modules.

Proceeding with the analysis of the dimension of autonomy, it is necessary to take a closer look at what is occurring in the household context. In this respect, the numerous studies conducted on the 'domestication of the Internet' have provided evidence which strongly supports the view that Internet use in the household entails an interrelationship between relational and structural dynamics which involve all family members (Bakardjieva, 2005; Berker et al., 2006; Haddon, 2004) in an ongoing negotiation on the use of the Internet. Regulations and 'taking turns' are often applied in the household to guarantee access to all family members or to transform navigation on the Internet from an individual activity to a group activity involving the entire family (Bakardjieva, 2005).

Alongside the 'traditional' connecting methods established at the workplace, in the household or at the place of education, there is another new method that needs to be considered here, and which will bring significant changes in the near future to the very structure of the concept of autonomy. Reference is made here to Internet navigation by means of devices such as palm-tops or netbooks, or via wireless connections guaranteed by Wi-Fi access points. It is evident that true autonomy in Internet use can be achieved under these circumstances, whereby the dimension of 'connectivity' that comes with the development of digitalization of contemporary societies is materialized. At the time of writing, however, such materialization of autonomy has yet to become widespread due to a number of reasons – costs, coverage and so on – and, as a result, it was not taken into account in this research.[18]

In the light of the observations made above and of the evidence provided by the application of the Principal Components Analysis (PCA), connection from home was deemed to best represent autonomy of use. In fact, the possibility to connect to the Internet from home is a fundamental requisite in facilitating the technology appropriation process. Furthermore, it is self-evident that having a connection available for hours on end enables one to carry out numerous activities and, at the same time, acquire the necessary skills, which are indispensable in taking up the so-called web 2.0.

A similar reasoning was applied in relation to the intensity of Internet usage, that is, to the frequency with which the Internet is used. In this case, the indicator selected was that which measures access on a daily basis, whereas those which measure access on a weekly or monthly basis were eliminated. This decision was determined by the interpretation of digitalization process adopted in this research: that is, a transformation of the daily life of individuals (from work to study, from entertainment to e-commerce) as a result of the use of the Internet. It appears evident, in fact, that access to the Internet on a weekly or even less frequent basis cannot be interpreted as an indicator of a digitalization process within a given country.

To conclude the analysis of the spheres which, in our opinion, are fundamental in structuring the dimension of Internet usage, it is necessary to analyse the skills that permit individuals to improve, or even to master, the use of the Internet. In order to fully understand the importance of such skills, it will suffice to consider the enormous quantity of information that is available on the web. Individuals need not only master an enormous quantity of data, but also navigate in an ever-changing universe in which new forms of communication emerge (consider, for example, the innovations brought about by web 2.0). In order to fully benefit from the opportunities that the Internet has to offer, therefore, it is necessary to acquire skills, defined variously as 'computer literacy', 'electronic literacy', 'digital literacy', or 'multimedia literacy'. Focusing, for a moment, on the elements that make up this set of skills and knowledge, it may be useful to adopt the definition 'digital skills' coined by van Dijk (2005), understood as 'the entire set of skills necessary to operate a computer and navigate on the web, search and select information contained therein, and use such information to achieve one's objectives' (p. 73). More precisely, digital skills can be structured into three levels: 'operational skills', 'informational skills' and 'strategic skills'. Operational skills are those used by individuals to operate a computer and to work with the web software and hardware. Informational skills are used to search, select and process information obtained from the computer and from the web. Lastly, strategic skills are those which permit one to achieve specific objectives and, more generally, improve one's position in society. An attempt to further disaggregate digital skills was made by Hargittai (2007) who thus identified as many as eleven dimensions.

Obviously, such disaggregation of data can hardly be supported at empirical level, especially as part of a comparative approach which is based on 27 countries. It is therefore necessary to reduce the level of complexity of the dimensions examined and transform the concept of skills into a representative set of indicators. An effective way to simplify this is offered by Eurostat, which makes a distinction between 'personal computer skills'[19] and 'Internet skills',[20] which are very similar to the operational skills and informational skills identified by van Dijk (2005). 'Internet skills' were first used to monitor the level of diffusion of skills among the population. The results of the analysis (see Appendix) supported this choice, showing a significant overlapping between the two clusters of skills: in other words, the subjects who were in possession of Internet skills were also in possession of personal computer skills. Furthermore, such superposition is not surprising at all, if we consider the number of computer skills that each one of us uses during navigation. In summary, it may be stated that those who possess skills in the use of the Internet also possess skills in the use of the personal computer.

Further reflection, however, led to a sharp upturn, that is, to the use of personal computer skills instead of Internet skills. The latter, in fact, were often found throughout the activities carried out over the web. For example, it certainly requires skills to use Skype but, at the same time, it appears to be an activity that may or may not interest individuals belonging to a circle which finds it more convenient to communicate over the

Internet than to use the traditional telephone. Similarly, 'creating a web page' certainly requires specific 'technical' skills but, before that, there needs to be interest on the part of the individual in creating a personal web page, whether for personal or work reasons. If there is no such interest, it is very unlikely that the individual will acquire the skills necessary to create a web page. This superposition between 'skills' and 'activities' in connection with personal interest undermines the validity of the indicator, and makes it difficult to use it in a survey such as this one, aimed at measuring digitalization of European citizens. As regards 'computer personal skills', the application of PCA made it possible to identify three indicators which can best represent the entire area: 'copying or moving a file or folder', 'using basic arithmetic formulas in a spreadsheet'; 'connecting and installing new devices'. As we can see, these three indicators summarize the main applications that can be performed on a personal computer and which are considered the 'basics' in a process of domestication of technology.

To sum up, the usage dimension was structured into three subdimensions (autonomy, intensity and skills) and, from an operational viewpoint, this led to a selection of five indicators for the three subdimensions: (1) percentage of individuals who accessed the Internet at home, (2) percentage of individuals who accessed the Internet every day or almost every day, (3) percentage of individuals who have copied or moved a file or folder, (4) percentage of individuals who have used basic arithmetic formulae in a spreadsheet, (5) percentage of individuals who have connected and installed new devices.

In the definition of e-inclusion adopted as a reference in this paper, an important role is played, along with the Internet access and usage dimensions, by the impact dimension: that is, the whole area in which the positive effects of individual and social empowerment resulting from the technology appropriation process are felt. This is the most consistent dimension of all, lending itself to easy and immediate interpretation and application in people's daily lives. Unfortunately, from an empirical research perspective, quantifying 'the impact of digital inclusion is often very difficult' (FreshMinds, 2008).

The impact dimension has been subdivided into six subdimensions, which can help to shed light on the different areas in which empowerment effects can be felt at both individual and social level. More specifically, the subdimensions that were examined are the following: economy; employment and labour; education; health; government; and culture, communication and entertainment. Based on an initial dataset comprising 31 indicators, which were subjected to quality tests and principal component analyses to identify the most significant factors (see Appendix), we have come up with a final dataset containing 14 indicators.

For the economic subdimension, we have used indicators which effectively measure changes in people's lifestyles, thus widely expanding the spectrum of opportunities available. For that reason, we have eliminated indicators which measure 'one-time' behaviours, or rather, a simple search of information on goods and services. The indicators we have selected, in contrast, are capable of measuring real change in people's daily lives. Internet banking, for example, is an opportunity which, on the one hand, may offer better and cheaper services, and on the other hand, cuts the costs of visiting bank counters. Hence, there is an economic improvement – by virtue of competition – but also an improvement in terms of simpler relations with one's bank – which increasingly becomes a pull rather than push mode – as well as the freedom to choose any operator without territorial strings attached. Other changes in people's lifestyles may derive from the spread of business transactions carried out through the net. The micro market that has formed around the Internet is populated by millions and millions of buyers and sellers who put up their goods for sale and/or buy others on a daily basis. In this case, the size of the market – which takes on the characteristics of a global market – helps to create the best conditions for keeping costs down to a minimum, whilst the mechanisms supported by the same navigators for assessing the reliability of vendors regulate each specific transaction. If we put this in the context of daily life, the familiarity with e-commerce activity can translate into an opportunity, for a young girl living in the English provinces, to purchase a pair of sunglasses manufactured in the United States at a lower price than that offered by the local town shop. Another example of economic savings is provided by the sophisticated world of services related to travel and accommodation. The constantly developing e-travelling market is one of the more popular Internet applications among navigators, and certainly one of the most liked. In synergy with the low cost airlines, the use of the Internet has helped to extend the boundaries of the army of travellers, to the extent of making them almost coincide with those of the population living in the wealthy contemporary societies.

The second subdimension that we have selected comprises indicators which are connected to the complex world of labour, with respect to both those who already have a place in it and those who seek employment. For the latter subjects, especially the young, the Internet is an opportunity for research and applications. Rather than limiting their job search to a limited geographical area, Internet users can take as reference point an independently selected universe, in which to offer their services or evaluate what it has to offer. For those who, on the other hand, already have a place in the labour market, the Internet represents an instrument which becomes part of the work routine; that is, it enables one to carry on a business activity away from the office or company premises. In both cases – even with all the obvious differences – the quality of the work performed changes significantly.

The education subdimension comprises all the indicators which contribute to determining 'human capital', that is, that valuable asset which is becoming increasingly significant for the development of the information society. Human capital, understood as the whole of knowledge, skills and information (Becker, 1964), is closely connected to the education dimension, which extends throughout the lifespan of individuals. In this context, the opportunities offered by the Internet acquire significant relevance: from online university to courses on specific subjects of interest, from professional courses to post educational programs.

As regards the health subdimension, the only indicator that we have been able to find limits itself to measuring online information searches on injury, disease or nutrition. This indicator clearly reveals an interest in certain subjects as well as the opportunity to satisfy that interest through the Internet, but it provides no information on the use of the Internet in the health sector: for example, the possibility to provide online prescriptions, or link up with family doctors and pharmacies or analysis laboratories. Eurostat's periodical surveys, which constitute the main source of data for all those who are interested in studying the impact of the Internet on individuals, do not provide any information on this aspect. It is hoped that, in the near future, an ad hoc section will be added to the standard field survey relating to the use of ICT in the health sector, on the part of the patients and of all the other subjects, for whatever reason.

The government dimension, on the other hand, is rich and highly structured. The section on Internet use in the sphere of relations between citizens and public administrations, which has been for years at the centre of initiatives by individual countries and the European Commission, draws a lot of interest and provides various field data. However, the initial set of four indicators – percentage of individuals who used the Internet for obtaining information from public authorities' websites, percentage of individuals who used the Internet for downloading official forms, percentage of individuals who used the Internet for sending completed forms, percentage of individuals who used the Internet for interaction with public authorities – was reduced in the light of the correlation coefficient values. Over the course of all the years examined in this study, the calculation of the correlation coefficient between the four variables has produced results exceeding the .900 mark, testifying to the fact that they are superposable.

Finally, a good number of indicators was obtained to describe the cultural, communication and recreational subdimension. Certainly the richest and most structured section – as well as the most frequented – it comprises the most common communication opportunities, such as electronic mail and chat rooms, the consumption of radio and television on alternative platforms, downloading of games, music, magazines and software, and the reading of newspapers free of charge or on payment. In summary, these are some of the many activities that Internet users carry out over the web, and which constitute the contemporary forms of communication and cultural consumption. There is no doubt that, with respect to this subdimension, there is a direct impact in terms of individual empowerment. Many of the activities included in this field, in fact, typically tend to establish the citizenship of those who practice them in the contemporary world.

As a result of the observations set out above and of the application of the analysis in main components conducted on a set of variables, the following indicators were selected for the six subdimensions identified: (1) percentage of individuals who used the Internet for training and education; (2) percentage of individuals who used the Internet for looking for a job or sending a job application; (3) percentage of persons employed using computers connected to the Internet in their normal routine; (4) percentage of individuals who used the Internet for seeking health information on injury, disease or nutrition; (5) percentage of individuals who used the Internet for interaction with public authorities; (6) percentage of individuals who used Internet banking; (7) percentage of individuals who ordered goods or services for private use over the Internet; (8) percentage of individuals who used the Internet for services related to travel and accommodation; (9) percentage of individuals who used the Internet for sending/receiving emails; (10) percentage of individuals who used the Internet for playing/downloading games and music; (11) percentage of individuals who used the Internet for reading/downloading online newspapers/news magazines; (12) percentage of individuals who used the Internet for listening to web radios/for watching web television; (13) percentage of individuals who used the Internet for downloading software; (14) percentage of individuals who used the Internet for other communication uses (chat sites, and so on).

The indicators' selection presented in the previous pages and summarized in Table 1.1, has been the result of an approach that aims to describe and to measure the state of the digitalization process in Europe in a diachronic perspective and multidimensionally. The European Digitalization Development Index (EDDI), in fact, can be used to detect the state of the digitalization process in Europe, in a single member state, in a specific year of our timespan and in the course of the whole arc of time considered. Even as a proxy of the digitalization process, the EDDI can be a measure of great utility in the processes of benchmarking ICT in Europe.

Table 1.1   The European Digitalization Development Index (EDDI), dimensions, subdimensions, and indicators[a]

Infrastructure	Usage	Impact
Network 1. Broadband penetration rate (2004–09 Eurostat) 2. International Internet bandwidth per inhabitant (bit/s) (2004–09 WDI) 3. Secure Internet servers (1 million people) (2004–09 WDI) **Affordability** 1. Information and communication technology expenditure per capita (2004–09 WDI) **Availability and quality** 1. Internet subscribers fixed broadband per 100 inhabitants (2004–09 ITU) 2. Internet subscribers fixed per 100 inhabitants (2004–09 ITU)	**Autonomy** 1. Percentage of individuals who accessed Internet at home (2004–09 Eurostat) **Intensity** 1. Percentage of individuals who accessed Internet every day or almost every day (2004–09 Eurostat) **Skills** 1. Percentage of individuals who have copied or moved a file or folder (2004–09 Eurostat) 2. Percentage of individuals who have used basic arithmetic formulae in a spreadsheet (2004–09 Eurostat) 3. Percentage of individuals who have connected and installed new devices (2004–09 Eurostat)	**Education** 1. Percentage of individuals who used Internet for training and education (2004–09 Eurostat) **Labour** 1. Percentage of individuals who used Internet for looking for a job or sending a job application (2004–09 Eurostat) 2. Percentage of persons employed using computers connected to the Internet in their normal routine (2004–09 Eurostat) **Health** 1. Percentage of individuals who used Internet for seeking health information on injury, disease or nutrition (2004–09 Eurostat) **Government** 1. Percentage of individuals who used Internet for interaction with public authorities (2004–09 Eurostat) **Economy** 1. Percentage of individuals who used Internet for Internet banking (2004–09 Eurostat) 2. Percentage of individuals who ordered goods or services for private use over the Internet (2004–09 Eurostat) 3. Percentage of individuals who used Internet for using services related to travel and accommodation (2004–09 Eurostat)

3. Level of Internet access of households (Eurostat 2004–09)

4. Percentage of households using a broadband connection (Eurostat 2004–09)

Culture, communication and recreation

1. Percentage of individuals who used Internet for sending/receiving emails (2004–09 Eurostat)

2. Percentage of individuals who used Internet for playing/downloading games and music (2004–09 Eurostat)

3. Percentage of individuals who used Internet for reading/downloading newspapers/news magazines (2004–09 Eurostat)

4. Percentage of individuals who used Internet for listening to web radios/for watching web television (2004–09 Eurostat)

5. Percentage of individuals who used Internet for downloading software (2004–09 Eurostat)

6. Percentage of individuals who used Internet for other communication uses (chat sites, etc.) (2004–09 Eurostat)

Note: [a] 'Dimensions' are Infrastructure, Usage and Impact. 'Subdimensions' are in bold. Indicators are numbered items.

NOTES

1. 'I am certain I stole the term, but I am not certain who I stole it from. Jonathan Webber of the *Industry Standard* makes a compelling case that somewhere back around 1995 he and Amy Harmon (when both were with the *LA Times*) invented the term to describe the social division between those who were very involved in technology and those who were not. I believe I first heard the term in the late '95/early '96 time frame at a conference in a western state, Montana, North Dakota or South Dakota. We did not formally use the term at NTIA until months later, and the term did not gain the ubiquity it enjoys today until the release of the third "falling through the net" report in July '99. I hope that helps. The fairest thing to say is that no one at NTIA invented the term, digital divide. NTIA's reports were, however, the catalysts for the popularity, ubiquity and redefinition (from the *LA Times* original usage) of the term' (quoted in Gunkel, 2003, p. 501).
2. A structured discussion on the theory of knowledge divide can be found in Bentivegna (2003). Tichenor et al. (1970) articulated their work hypothesis thus: 'As the infusion of mass media information into a social system increases, segments of the population with higher socioeconomic status tend to acquire this information at a faster rate than the lower status segments, so that the gap in knowledge between these segments tends to increase rather than decrease' (pp. 159–60).
3. According to the *New York Times*, Michael K. Powell, the chairman of the Federal Communication Commission, 'said he thought digital divide was a dangerous phrase because it could be used to justify governmental entitlement programs that guaranteed poor people cheaper access to new technology. "I think there is a Mercedes divide" he said. "I'd like to have one; I can't afford one"' (quoted in Warschauer, 2003, p. 217).
4. The document is available at www.g8.utoronto.ca/summit/2000okinawa/gis.htm.
5. The data refer to the year 2006 and are contained in the Annual Report of the International Telecommunication Union, 2006.
6. As regards the link between digital inequalities and social inequalities in other countries, see Fuchs, 2009; Witte and Mannon, 2010.
7. The collection of Community statistics on the information society is based on the framework Regulation (EC) no. 808/2004 adopted by the European Parliament and the Council. It ensures harmonized data for all EU Member States and other participating EEA countries until 2010 and contains two modules: one on enterprises and one on households and individuals. As a framework regulation it allows adjustment to newly evolving needs by users and decision makers by annual implementing measures (Commission regulations, see links in Legislation).
8. The OECD Telecommunication Database contains data concerning the telecommunications industry. Data include variables covering revenue, investment, infrastructure, employment, equipment imports and exports, etc.
9. The World Development Indicators (WDI) is the statistical benchmark that helps measure the progress of development. The WDI provides a comprehensive overview of development drawing on data from the World Bank and more than 30 partners. The *World Development Indicators* publication is the World Bank's premier annual compilation of data about development. The 2009 WDI includes more than 800 indicators in over 90 tables organized in six sections: world view, people, environment, economy, states and markets, and global links.
10. The World Telecommunication/ICT Indicators (2009) database contains time series data for the years 1960, 1965, 1970 and annually from 1975–2008 for around 100 sets of telecommunication/ICT statistics covering telephone network, size and dimension, mobile services, Internet, quality of service, traffic, staff, tariffs, revenue and investments.
11. Sciadas, 2005.
12. The index developed by ORBICOM–ITU dedicated ample space to indicators related to the telecommunications structure (that is, main telephone lines per 100 inhabitants, digital lines/main lines, cable subscriptions per 100 households, and so on), in the aim of registering the state of diffusion of the information society in the world. This approach,

however, specifically due to its 'global' vocation, is not very suitable for providing information within a context such as that of Europe.

13. At the beginning, within the affordability subdimension were the following indicators: (1) percentage of households without broadband connection because it is too expensive; (2) percentage of households without broadband connection because the access costs are too expensive; (3) percentage of households without broadband because the equipment costs are too high. These indicators were selected because they measure the relevance of affordability barriers to the diffusion of broadband and could be very useful in order to elaborate an adequate policy to remove them. Unfortunately, after the check on the data's quality, many problems appeared, so the decision was made not to use them.

14. The price basket contains three indicators: (1) fixed broadband Internet access tariffs per month (in US$ or PPP), (2) mobile cellular prepaid tariff per month (in US$ or PPP), (3) residential fixed line telephone tariff per month (in US$ or PPP).

15. This indicator is available from the database of WDI from 2003 to 2007. In order to obtain the data related to 2008 and 2009, an estimate was made (see Appendix).

16. Within the initial set of indicators, there was the 'percentage of households without broadband connection because it is not available in the area'. This indicator was chosen because it measures the impact of lack of availability of one of the most important technologies for e-inclusion. Unfortunately, data were available just for one year (2007) and their quality was not good.

17. Such regulations may apply to the use of personal email, of social network sites like Facebook or to the downloading of material.

18. Besides, the available data provided by Eurostat (on the connecting device used, such as the mobile or handheld computer) are fragmented and, for many countries, they are incomplete and show very low performances.

19. 'Which of the following computer related activities have you already carried out?' (a) copying or moving a file or folder; (b) using copy and paste tools to duplicate or move information within a document; (c) using basic arithmetic formulas in a spreadsheet; (d) compressing (or zipping) files; (e) connecting and installing new devices (for example, a printer or a modem); (f) writing a computer program using a specialized programming language.

20. 'Which of the following Internet related activities have you already carried out?' (a) using a search engine to find information; (b) sending emails with attached files (documents, pictures, and so on); (c) posting messages to chatrooms, newsgroups or an online discussion forum; (d) using the Internet to make telephone calls; (e) using peer-to-peer file sharing for exchanging movies, music; (f) creating a web page.

2. The Internet in everyday life

2.1 DEVELOPMENT OF THE INTERNET INFRASTRUCTURE

As stated in Chapter 1, the availability of a good technological infrastructure is the *sine qua non* for a positive outcome of the Internet appropriation process. In fact, without access points and differentiated forms of connection, the individual process of domestication of technology is doomed to failure. To describe the state and quality of the Internet infrastructure in Europe and in the European Member States, three subdimensions (network; affordability; and availability and quality) have been identified to cast light on the various aspects of the real access opportunities offered to individuals.

In the disaggregation of the infrastructure dimension performed in this research, the network subdimension plays a fundamental role: it comprises indicators which monitor the conditions of the technological infrastructure existing in a given country. In other words, the network subdimension constitutes a sort of precondition for Internet diffusion and usage: there can be no development and improvement without a technological infrastructure. In recent years, increasingly greater attention has been attached to broadband penetration rate; that is, to the type of connection that permits one to carry out numerous activities (downloading of images, music, and so on), which would be impossible with the old connections.

This indicator shows how widely broadband access to the Internet has spread in the countries on the general level. In fact, the broadband penetration rate describes the number of dedicated high-speed connections per 100 inhabitants. Although at times criticized for using individuals and not households as the basis for calculating broadband penetration, this indicator has the undeniable advantage of providing a detailed description of the development and implementation of the technological infrastructure in a given country. Thus, for example, a quick glance at the analysis of this indicator reveals not only the large gaps separating the Netherlands (0.38) from Italy (0.20) or Denmark (0.37) from Spain (0.21), but also the growth trend that is taking place in single countries. If we analyse this detail by comparing 2004 and 2009, we can immediately see the sharp increase that was registered in Europe: from 0.06 to 0.23. This 17-point growth,

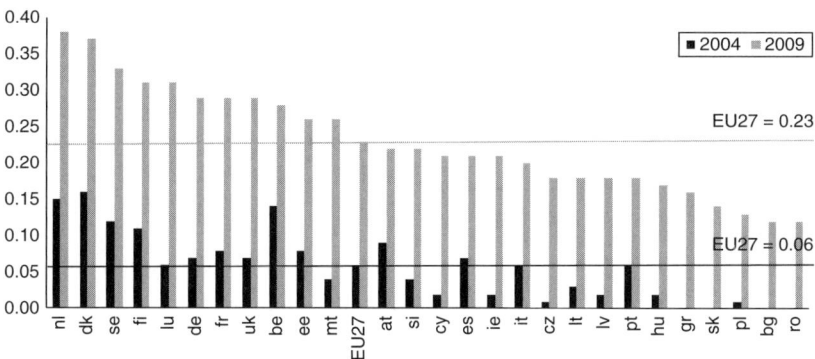

Note: Country abbreviations are from Eurostat.

Figure 2.1   Broadband penetration rate (2004–09)

however, is not evenly distributed across the various European countries: some of these even outperformed the average value (Luxembourg, the Netherlands, Sweden, UK, Germany, Denmark and France), while others registered lower values (Bulgaria, Czech Republic, Greece, Hungary, Italy) (Figure 2.1). This first analysis provides a picture of the European situation in which, next to the countries outperforming the European average (as many as 11 of them in 2009) are others lagging behind.

It is worth noting that in those cases where broadband diffusion was extensive, this result can be partly ascribed to national government policies devoted to encouraging broadband supply and to promoting broadband demand. Generally speaking, all EU Member States have put an emphasis on policies to increase the coverage of broadband. A significant number of countries have now set targets for broadband coverage of the population (often at 100 per cent). Strictly from a technological aspect, a number of Member States are making efforts to increase the coverage of wireless networks, to extend the coverage of mobile services, to invest in fibre-optic networks for very high speed access, and to expand the number of public access points in rural and socially disadvantaged areas (CEC, 2009).

From a political viewpoint, some governments in European countries have used an

explicit or implicit government mandate to pressure government-owned telecom providers to deploy broadband networks. Others have provided tax incentives, grants and low cost loans to make it cheaper for broadband providers to build infrastructure. Additionally, some governments have subsidized deployment of broadband by competitors by requiring incumbent providers to lease their networks to competitors at very low rates. (Atkinson et al., 2008, p. 22)

Government policies devoted to promote broadband are focused on promoting digital literacy and access to computers, encouraging the use of broadband in education and promoting the development of broadband applications with e-government initiatives. To sum up, there have been numerous initiatives supporting the development and establishment of broadband in Europe. If we take a closer look at the cluster of countries leading the broadband penetration field, it appears evident that the following paid particular attention to the policies described above: in the Netherlands, Denmark, Sweden, Finland, Luxembourg, United Kingdom, Belgium and Malta, broadband coverage is approaching 100 per cent. In 2007 Estonia set the 'Estonian Information Society Strategy 2013' with the aim that each member of society should lead a full life using the opportunities of the information society. In the meantime, Estonia has upgraded ICT infrastructure in schools. In brief, all the best-performing countries in the field of broadband penetration have been particularly active in developing policies targeted toward broadband deployment.

In order to provide a detailed description of the technological backbone in Europe, we used the broadband connection indicator together with other indicators measuring transmission capacity and connection security. These aspects were considered to be very important in diffusing and sustaining ICT usage among citizens: opportunities and security can indeed encourage the take-up of new technologies. Showing a mixed performance, standing around the 0.30 mark, the network subdimension summarizes the technological infrastructure situation and confirms the presence of large gaps between the various European countries. In 2009, for example, countries such as the Netherlands and Denmark came close to the 0.50 mark – followed closely by Sweden, Finland, Luxembourg, UK, Germany, Ireland, and Malta – and countries such as Romania and Bulgaria scored below the 0.10 mark. Within the two extremes of the continuum, we find – with values of approximately 0.20 – Italy, Hungary, Lithuania, Latvia, and Portugal. These data reveal a different 'speed' at which the various Member States of Europe are progressing in the field of technological development: we can see a cluster of countries that support and attempt to lead the development of ICT, with a clear impact on the technological infrastructure situation; on the other hand, another cluster of countries can be seen lagging behind in terms of infrastructure development, with inevitable repercussions on ICT; lastly, there is another cluster of countries which appears to be sceptical as to the central role of ICT in contemporary society and, as a consequence, refrains from implementing direct support measures.

The second subdimension taken into consideration for the purpose of monitoring infrastructure is that of affordability: as stated above, it was not possible to use indicators measuring connection costs in this research

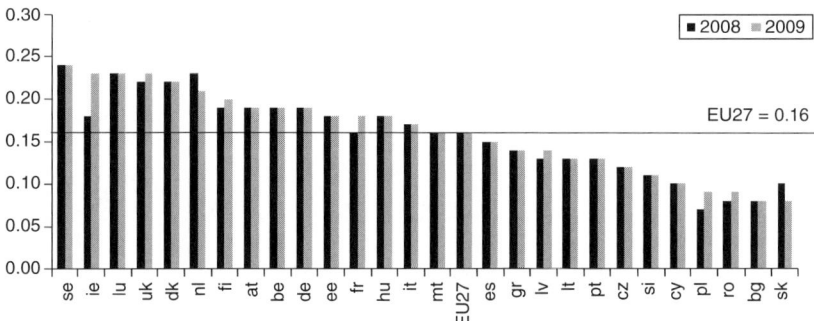

Figure 2.2   The affordability indicator: ICT expenditure per capita (2008–09)

due to the lack of relevant data for the time horizon examined. Those data, however, show a constant decline which brings the various countries' tariffs increasingly close,[1] making the variable increasingly less determinative. The indicator used in this study – the information and communication technology expenditure per capita – also shows a downward trend, as well as the presence of small gaps between the various countries and an average value standing stably at around 0.16. Figure 2.2 clearly reveals the presence of gaps and proximities separating the Member States, as well as the gap distancing the latter from the average value. If we take the most recent years – that is, from 2008 to 2009 – which are marked by a rapid establishment of technology, but also by the serious crisis that has affected the major world economies, we can see that the various countries are gradually moving closer in terms of ICT expenditure per capita. This progressive closing of the gaps may be attributed, on the one hand, to tariff reductions, and on the other hand, to the decreasing expenditure in this field as a consequence of the economic crisis.

Lastly, the subdimension of availability and quality of connection enables one to closely monitor the changes that occurred in the Internet catchment area (users and subscribers), as well as the type of connection, whether broadband or non-broadband. The most significant increases in the period examined were registered in this subdimension (+0.24), with an annual average growth of five points.

From an analysis of the data related to the individual subdimensions emerges a limited, albeit constant, growth in Europe's technological infrastructure, along with a more dynamic development in the sphere of availability and quality of connections. This trend, however, as we will see below, varies greatly between the various countries, which inevitably leads to the conclusion that Europe is progressing at multiple speeds.

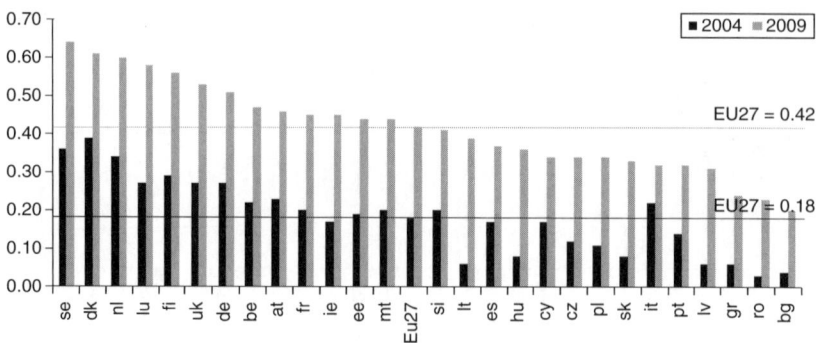

*Figure 2.3   The availability indicator: broadband and non-broadband
              connections by individuals and households (2004–09, %)*

2.2   THE INFRASTRUCTURE INDEX: DIFFERENT COUNTRIES, DIFFERENT SPEEDS

The picture that emerges from a joint reading of the indicators selected depicts a rather complex Internet infrastructure situation in Europe.

First, it indicates a slight increase of what may be defined as the Internet infrastructure. The overall data also point in this direction: in 2004, the European countries had a 0.24 access to the Internet; in 2009, this value was equal to 0.27. Despite the 3-point increase, its limited extent of growth cannot be denied. We will try further on to identify the reasons for such a limited growth trend as well as the barriers that were responsible for it; at this juncture it is however possible to make conjectures as to the crucial role that investments played in the development and consolidation of the Internet infrastructure (for example, broadband coverage).

Secondly, it confirms a different speed for each of the various groups of European countries: the EU15 increased from 0.30 in 2004 to 0.32 in 2009, the EU27 from 0.24 to 0.27. If we then take a close look at the perform-ance of each single country, the picture that emerges is even more varied: taking the EU27 figure as a reference, there are some countries which show, consistently over time, higher than average values (Denmark, the Netherlands, Sweden and Finland), whilst others constantly register below average values (Romania, Bulgaria, Greece, and Poland). This permanent discrepancy is confirmed despite the good recovery obtained by a number of countries belonging to the trailing group: for example, compared to an average growth of 3 points (EU27) in the period 2004–09, there are countries that registered an increment of 13 points (Lithuania), 6 (Poland) and 7 (Romania). Conversely, the frontrunner countries show much more limited increases (4 for Finland, 4 for the Netherlands, 3 for Denmark), although these were sufficient to confirm their good positions.

A historical comparative analysis of the data clearly shows that the year 2006 witnessed significant technological developments both in the single countries and in Europe as a whole. These developments were made possible thanks to the approval of the i2010 project and of the national projects that were subsequently implemented by individual countries. As the data in Table 2.1 clearly indicate, the year 2007 shows an inflection point representing a halt, and in some countries even a regression, subject to recovering lost ground in subsequent years.

To obtain an overview of the main trends and of the most significant discrepancies, we can put countries into four groups on the basis of the index values registered in the period 2004–09 (Table 2.2).[2] A comparison of the average values registered by each group provides further elements for discussion. Group 1 constantly registers values which are equal to more than double – and often even triple – those registered by group 4. This substantial differentiation can also be found if we compare group 2 with group 4 and, to a lesser degree – that is, stabilized at double the values – if we compare group 3 with group 4. Furthermore, it is worth noting that this differentiation of values in the infrastructure dimension in European countries remains constant throughout the years examined, thus empirically confirming the existence of multiple speeds in Europe. The trajectories of the four groups of countries continue to maintain substantial differences between them, to such an extent that it is difficult to imagine a possible convergence in the near future. This is because the increases registered in group 4 are counterbalanced by those occurring in group 1, and thus contribute to maintain the existing distance.

Finally, when one considers the countries that appear in the various groups, one notices interesting trajectories. The frontrunner group includes a platoon of countries – Denmark, Netherlands, Sweden, and Finland – which is relatively stable (except for sporadic shifts registered in the past). Next to these, on the other hand, are Luxembourg and the UK, both of which occupy a slightly fluctuating position. Such a variable position is due, in the case of Luxembourg, to a delay registered in the past regarding broadband penetration, as well as to a relatively slow connection speed in the past. In the case of the UK, its fluctuating position is attributed to the more limited value (compared with Denmark, the Netherlands, Sweden and Finland) of the ICT expenditure per capita. In the light of the importance attached to the development of the information society in the UK – reiterated and emphasized in the 'Digital Britain' plans – it can be expected that the country will once again permanently join group 1 and register the same values as those of the other countries.

Table 2.1   Infrastructure index values

	2004	2005	2006	2007	2008	2009
Austria	0.30	0.28	0.33	0.30	0.32	0.31
Belgium	0.30	0.30	0.33	0.31	0.31	0.31
Bulgaria	0.03	0.04	0.09	0.07	0.08	0.10
Cyprus	0.22	0.18	0.16	0.17	0.22	0.21
Czech Republic	0.18	0.16	0.20	0.18	0.21	0.22
Denmark	0.40	0.39	0.44	0.40	0.43	0.43
Estonia	0.26	0.24	0.31	0.27	0.30	0.29
Finland	0.32	0.31	0.39	0.35	0.37	0.36
France	0.27	0.27	0.29	0.28	0.30	0.30
Germany	0.31	0.29	0.35	0.32	0.34	0.34
Greece	0.16	0.13	0.14	0.13	0.16	0.18
Hungary	0.16	0.14	0.19	0.16	0.23	0.19
Ireland	0.29	0.27	0.31	0.29	0.30	0.32
Italy	0.25	0.22	0.24	0.21	0.18	0.23
Latvia	0.14	0.13	0.21	0.17	0.20	0.20
Lithuania	0.12	0.13	0.19	0.18	0.23	0.25
Luxembourg	0.33	0.34	0.38	0.37	0.37	0.39
Malta	0.27	0.26	0.29	0.26	0.28	0.29
Netherlands	0.37	0.39	0.43	0.41	0.40	0.41
Poland	0.13	0.11	0.15	0.13	0.21	0.18
Portugal	0.20	0.18	0.21	0.18	0.20	0.20
Romania	0.04	0.03	0.07	0.05	0.12	0.11
Slovakia	0.14	0.12	0.15	0.14	0.14	0.18
Slovenia	0.21	0.20	0.26	0.22	0.25	0.25
Spain	0.24	0.22	0.26	0.23	0.25	0.25
Sweden	0.37	0.37	0.40	0.39	0.36	0.40
United Kingdom	0.34	0.34	0.37	0.35	0.35	0.36
EU27	0.24	0.22	0.26	0.24	0.26	0.27
EU15	0.30	0.29	0.32	0.30	0.31	0.32

In the case of group 2 (Germany, Austria, Belgium, and France), a certain stability of composition was registered, with lower values compared to group 1 for all the indicators used. It should be noted, however, that this is a relatively positive performance, which enabled the group to rank above the EU15 average for several years. Frequent incursions have occurred within the group by countries such as Ireland, and, more rarely, Estonia.

Table 2.2   Infrastructure index in groups of countries

Year	Group 1	Group 2	Group 3	Group 4
2009 **EU27 = 0.27** **EU15 = 0.32**	Denmark, Sweden, Netherlands, Finland, Luxembourg, UK **x̄ = 0.39** **σ = 0.03**	Germany, Ireland, Austria, Belgium, France, Estonia, Malta **x̄ = 0.31** **σ = 0.02**	Spain, Lithuania, Slovenia, Italy, Cyprus, Czech Rep **x̄ = 0.24** **σ = 0.02**	Latvia, Portugal, Hungary, Greece, Poland, Slovakia, Romania, Bulgaria **x̄ = 0.17** **σ = 0.04**
2008 **EU27 = 0.26** **EU15 = 0.31**	Denmark, Sweden, Netherlands, Finland, Luxembourg, Germany **x̄ = 0.37** **σ = 0.02**	Malta, UK, Austria, Belgium, France, Estonia, Ireland **x̄ = 0.30** **σ = 0.02**	Spain, Portugal, Slovenia, Cyprus, Hungary, Lithuania Poland **x̄ = 0.22** **σ = 0.01**	Czech Rep, Latvia, Italy, G reece, Slovakia, Romania, Bulgaria **x̄ = 0.15** **σ = 0.05**
2007 **EU27 = 0.24** **EU15 = 0.30**	Denmark, Sweden Netherlands, Finland, Luxembourg, UK **x̄ = 0.37** **σ = 0.03**	Germany, Belgium, Austria, France, Ireland, Estonia, Malta **x̄ = 0.28** **σ = 0.02**	Spain, Portugal, Slovenia, Italy, Cyprus, Lithuania **x̄ = 0.19** **σ = 0.03**	Czech Rep, Latvia, Hungary, Greece, Slovakia, Poland, Bulgaria, Romania **x̄ = 0.12** **σ = 0.05**

Table 2.2 (continued)

Year	Group 1	Group 2	Group 3	Group 4
2006 **EU27= 0.26** **EU15= 0.32**	Denmark, Sweden, Netherlands, Finland, Luxembourg, UK **x̄ = 0.39** **σ = 0.02**	Germany, Belgium, Austria, Estonia, France, Ireland, Malta **x̄ = 0.30** **σ = 0.02**	Spain, Slovenia, Italy, Portugal, Latvia, Czech Rep **x̄ = 0.22** **σ = 0.03**	Hungary, Lithuania, Cyprus, Poland, Slovakia, Greece, Bulgaria, Romania **x̄ = 0.14** **σ = 0.04**
2005 **EU27 = 0.22** **EU15 = 0.29**	Denmark, Sweden, Netherlands Luxembourg, UK **x̄ = 0.35** **σ = 0.02**	Finland, Belgium, Germany, Austria, France, Ireland, Malta, Estonia **x̄ =0.27** **σ = 0.02**	Spain, Italy, Slovenia, Cyprus, Portugal, Czech Rep, Hungary **x̄ = 0.17** **σ = 0.03**	Greece, Lithuania, Latvia, Slovakia, Poland, Bulgaria, Romania **x̄ = 0.09** **σ = 0.04**
2004 **EU27 = 0.24** **EU15 = 0.30**	Denmark, Sweden, Netherlands, Finland Luxembourg, UK **x̄ = 0.34** **σ = 0.03**	Austria, Belgium, Germany, Ireland, France, Malta **x̄ = 0.28** **σ = 0.01**	Estonia, Italy, Spain, Cyprus, Slovenia, Portugal, Greece, Czech Rep **x̄ = 0.21** **σ = 0.03**	Hungary, Latvia, Slovakia, Poland, Lithuania, Bulgaria, Romania **x̄ = 0.10** **σ = 0.05**

As regards Ireland, its fluctuation between group 2 and group 3 can be attributed to a general low level of connectivity: in the year 2006, for example, 'broadband take-up was still below EU average and connectivity was still highly focused on narrowband' (CEC, 2007a, p. 27). To solve these problems, Ireland has been developing a 'National Knowledge Society Strategy'; nevertheless, 'in 2007, fixed broadband penetration reached 20.2% of the population, slightly below the EU27 average of 22.9%' (ibid.). In the case of Estonia, on the other hand, its fluctuating and unstable position is attributed not so much to the penetration of broadband – which, in fact, is above the average European value – as to the speed of connections: 'despite widespread connectivity, few of broadband subscriptions have speeds above 2MB/s (ibid.). The widespread use of the Internet and the political will to sustain the establishment of the information society in the country (by implementing projects such as the 'Estonian Information Society Strategy 2013', for example) point towards a good possibility of recovery from these problems in the years to come.

In group 3, a stable performance was registered on the part of countries such as Italy, Spain, Slovenia, Portugal, and Cyprus, combined with the fluctuating positions of Lithuania, the Czech Republic, and Hungary. These are countries which for years have been committed to sustaining and disseminating the Internet, although they cannot rely on an underlying solid technological infrastructure. Furthermore, despite the slight improvements in the diffusion of broadband, the overall situation concerning the development of the information society in these countries remains low, their values fluctuating between those of group 3 and of group 4. Finally, many countries of Eastern Europe appear in group 4 on a regular basis, and some of them have recently become members of the EU, with the addition of Greece. It is important to note that, in 2008, Italy slipped into the last group, confirming the difficulties it encountered in spurring the growth of the information society despite its contingency plans devised over the years.

At the end of this general presentation on data related to the Internet infrastructure dimension in Europe, which shows a strong differentiation in the consolidation of a basic infrastructure, it may be useful to pose the more specific question as to which areas show the longest delay phase or present the most significant problems. Looking beyond the performance of each individual country, it may be interesting to identify the points of strength and weakness at European level, and to analyse in detail the specific contribution made by the three subdimensions to the overall value of the infrastructure index.

In order to identify the contribution made by the various dimensions to the patterns and trends of infrastructure index data, it may be useful

Table 2.3   Contribution of each single dimension to the construction of the infrastructure index beta coefficient values

	Network	Affordability	Availability and quality	R-square	Standard error
2009	.254	.206	.572	.990	.009
2008	.271	.224	.453	.999	.002
2007	.364	.228	.441	1.000	.000
2006	.390	.233	.417	1.000	.000
2005	.374	.261	.402	1.000	.000
2004	.408	.289	.340	1.000	.000

to apply the regression analysis. Table 2.3 shows the values of the standardized beta coefficient calculated for all the years considered and for the three subdimensions. It can be noted immediately that there is a progressive decrease in the network subdimension and an equally strong and increasing contribution from the availability and quality subdimension. On the other hand, the same data show much lower and significantly decreasing values for the affordability dimension, confirming the progressive loss of relevance with respect to the other two subdimensions.

With reference to this decreasing trend, it is important to note that the affordability indicator measures the propensity to expenditure in the ICT sector rather than the costs of Internet access in the various countries. If we consider this piece of data, the progressive marginality of affordability in explaining the dynamic of access must be interpreted as the result of the increasingly reduced effect of ICT upon pro capita expenditure. In other words, it may be stated that the more economical becomes the use of ICT, and theoretically, therefore, the more accessible, the less the impact of expenditure. By way of example, it will suffice to provide data which testify to this progressive reduction of the value related to pro capita ICT expenditure in Europe (EU27): in 2003, that value was equal to 0.21, in 2004 it was 0.20, in 2005 0.19, in 2006 0.17, in 2007 and 2008 0.15. On the other hand, the studies that have been conducted on the cost of Internet connections – specifically the broadband connection – show that

> although retail broadband price comparison is a complex task because product characteristics, usage condition and quality of service greatly differ across offers, data indicate that the average price for a broadband standalone service with download speed between 2 and 4 MB/S has decreased from an average of around EURO/PPP 37 in April 2008 to EURO/PPP 29 in April 2009. (CEC, 2009, p. 13)

These results are in line with other data related to previous periods, albeit with the comparative difficulties arising from the specific characteristics of the services offered (Van Dijk Management Consultants, 2008).

Evidently, however, this does not mean that the economic dimension has become irrelevant in determining our infrastructure index. In fact, by breaking down the data in relation to each single country, it is possible to identify trends differentiated by groups of countries: in the period 2004–09, a significant reduction of the so-called 'rich' countries occurred (Belgium from 0.26 to 0.19; Netherlands from 0.28 to 0.21; Luxembourg from 0.28 to 0.23) whilst, conversely, the index values increased in the economically weaker countries (Hungary from 0.13 to 0.18; Lithuania from 0.12 to 0.13). However, beyond these persistent differences between countries, it may be noted that the diversified intervention strategies developed in the aim to create a single European area, as well as the measures adopted by each single country, have led to a reduction of the cost of ICT across much of the EU.

Going back to the contribution made by each subdimension to the overall value of the infrastructure index, it is apparent how the values registered by the network subdimension follow two separate trends in the period examined: from 2004 to 2007 the network subdimension, on a par with that of affordability, made a significant contribution to the construction of the index; from 2008 to 2009, on the other hand, that contribution decreased compared with that made by the availability subdimension. A possible explanation for the gradually decreasing importance of the network subdimension lies in the progressive reduction of the infrastructure to the benefit of the availability and quality of connections, when, on the one hand, the infrastructure became more stable and, on the other, quality services (such as broadband) became more widespread. In other words, the consolidation of the infrastructure – understood in this context simply as broadband penetration rate, international Internet bandwidth per inhabitant and secure Internet servers – becomes a prerequisite for the use of ICT, especially at a qualitative level such as that permitted by the use of broadband.

Again, these trends appear more evident in the case of the more technologically advanced countries (Denmark, Finland, Luxembourg, Netherlands, and Sweden) and have only recently appeared in countries with a lesser degree of ICT diffusion (Bulgaria, Romania, and Greece). This diversified growth pattern produces overall values which may at times appear contradictory, but which are in fact internally consistent and reflect the inevitable marginalization of the infrastructure dimension as a result of the establishment of ICT. Such establishment manifests itself in the consolidation of the Internet framework, on the one hand, and in the related household take-up, on the other. In other words, the purely technological dimension becomes less important when it is fully developed and may be considered fully taken up by the majority of the population.

2.3   THE DIMENSION OF THE USE OF THE INTERNET: THE USAGE INDEX

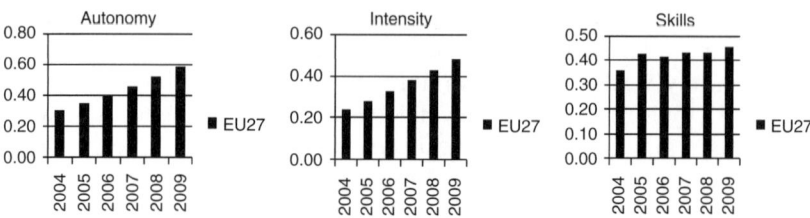

Figure 2.4   *Usage subdimensions: percentage of individuals who accessed the Internet at home (autonomy), every day or almost every day (intensity) and in digitally skilled form (skills) (2004–09)*

The usage index was structured into three subdimensions: autonomy, intensity and skills (Figure 2.4). Prior to delving deeper into the analysis of each subdimension, it is important to identify the general trends that can help to describe the evolution of Internet usage in the European context. Building on the analysis of the subdimension of autonomy, it can directly be seen that Internet usage among European citizens has become increasingly more autonomous: in fact, the value registered in 2004 was 0.31 (EU27), whilst the same value increased to 0.58 after only five years. This means that, over a five-year period, connection from home has become increasingly widespread and provides material evidence of the effectiveness of the national ICT policies adopted in recent years.

The availability of a connection from home, furthermore, constitutes a strong predictor of the intensity of Internet usage, thus confirming the validity of a theoretical approach that considers the dimension of autonomy as a fundamental factor in technology appropriation (DiMaggio et al., 2004). The regression analysis performed which takes daily intensity of Internet usage as the dependent variable, and availability of connection from home, from the workplace or from the place of education and broadband connection as independent variables clearly shows that, in the transition from 2004 to 2009, connection from home has become the most important variable in explaining intensity of use: an increase was registered from .284 in 2004 to .713 in 2009. As regards the values registered

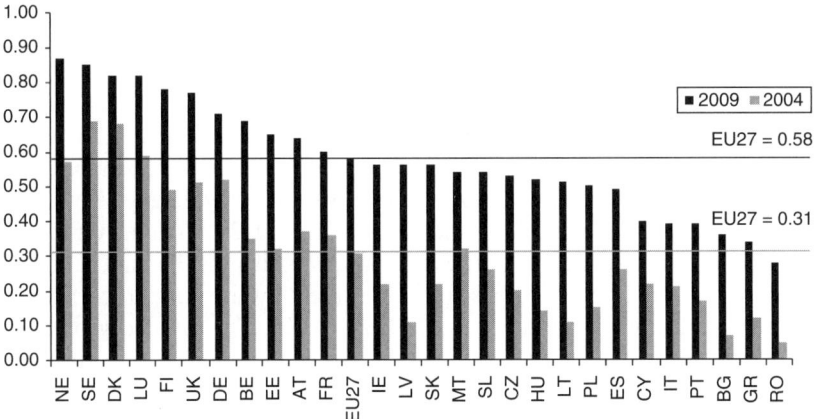

Figure 2.5   Autonomy: individuals who accessed the Internet at home

at European level, we can see a constant and progressive increase in this value, which doubled over the five-year period (from 0.24 in 2004 to 0.48 in 2009 in the EU27). This sharp increase in the subdimension's value, which, as we know, indicates daily connection frequency, determines – for a portion of the European population – the full entry of the Internet into people's daily lives.

The combination of autonomous Internet use and daily navigation is reflected – as is well known from the literature on the subject (Hargittai, 2004, 2007) – in the acquisition of skills, that is, of those skills necessary to improve the use of the Internet. Prior to delving further into the data related to their diffusion, it is important to consider the values of the correlation coefficients registered for the three variables (autonomy; intensity; skills). Over the time-horizon examined, the value associating the skills subdimension to that of autonomy and intensity never performed below 0.841, thus confirming the strong relationship that exists between these two areas.

Moving on now to an interpretation of the data, the indicators permit us to develop a fairly accurate overview of the 'styles' applied by European citizens in order to use the Internet. As regards the place of connection, in 2009 home has become the principal place. Over a six-year period, there was a significant increase of this value, rising from 0.31 in 2004 to 0.58 in 2009. If we look at the performance of each country, we are again confronted with significant differences (Figure 2.5): in 2004, a year in which the diffusion of the Internet was still limited, the value was 0.69 in Sweden, 0.68 in Denmark, 0.52 in the Netherlands, 0.51 in Germany

and 0.51 in the UK. Conversely, the 2004 data show a completely different situation in countries such as Romania (0.5), Bulgaria (0.7), Greece
(0.12), Poland (0.15) as well as Italy (0.21), Ireland (0.22) and Spain (0.26).
Six years later, the figure for Sweden reached 0.85, similar to that for the
Netherlands (0.87), Denmark (0.82), Finland (0.78) and the UK (0.77).
In the meanwhile, the countries which made up the trailing group registered some improvements although there was still a wide gap: Romania
reached 0.28, Bulgaria 0.36, Poland 0.50, Italy 0.39, Ireland 0.56 and
Spain 0.49. Among these countries, the case of Italy must be underlined as
it shows a fairly limited increase (+0.18), much lower than that registered
for the EU15 (+0.24) and for the EU27 (+0.27). This limited growth is
also lower than that registered for other countries included in the trailing
group (Ireland registered a 0.34 increase and Spain 0.23), which indicates
the many difficulties that Italy encountered in launching the use of the
Internet among its population. As regards the difficulties encountered in
Italy with respect to Internet diffusion, the failure to implement an up-to-
date national ICT strategy in the recent past (CEC, 2009, p. 78) is a strong
indication of the lack of attention paid by the government of that country
to the issue. An updated national ICT policy, on the other hand, can be
found in Spain (the 'Avanza' plan) and in Ireland ('A National Knowledge
Society Strategy'), thus supporting the validity of adopting specific policies. Evidence of the effect of addressing the issue, in the latter case, and of
a laissez-faire approach, in the former, was already indirectly provided by
simply comparing the data on the diffusion of broadband among households: in Spain, this value increased from 0.15 in 2004 to 0. 51 in 2009, in
Ireland from 0.3 to 0.54, in Italy from 0.15 to 0.39.

Looking now at the intensity of Internet access on the part of individuals, it is interesting to note the increasing importance of the Internet in
the daily life of individuals: in 2009, more than an half (0.56) of the EU15
community navigated the net on a daily basis. If we consider the EU27,
this figure is lower (0.51), but not dramatically so. If we take a closer
look at the data for each country, we again notice the different speeds at
which Europe embraces the world of the Internet (Figure 2.6). In 2004, in
Denmark the value reached 0.53, in Sweden 0.53, in the Netherlands 0.43,
in Finland 0.46 and in Luxembourg 0.36, registering values which were
constantly above the European average – both EU15 and EU27. At the
same time, there were countries which performed well below the average
European values: Romania 0.4, Bulgaria 0.7, Greece 0.9, Ireland 0.12,
Italy 0.24, and Spain (0.18).

The last indicator used for describing the spread of the use of the
Internet in Europe is that related to Internet skills. From 2004 to 2009
(that is, the period in which there were data available[3]), the average

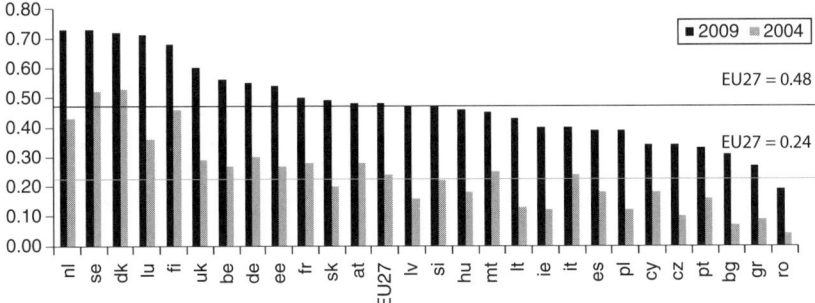

Figure 2.6   Intensity: individuals who accessed the Internet every day or almost every day

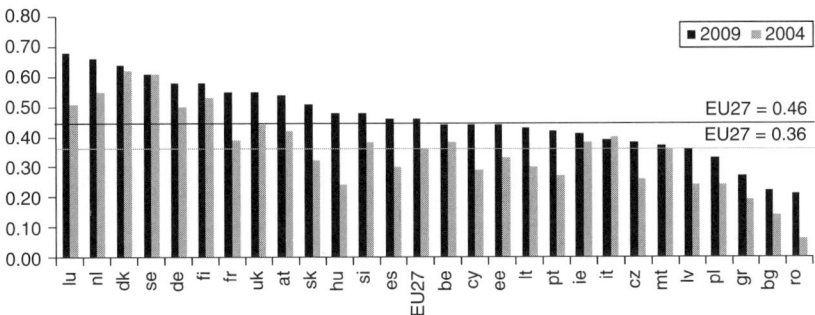

Figure 2.7   Intensity: individuals digitally skilled

value of the EU27 fluctuated from 0.36 to 0.46 whilst that of the EU15 fluctuated from 0.43 to 0.51. Compared to the other sub-indexes, that related to skills shows more limited increases and frequent fluctuations. Moving on now to a reading of the data, some surprising figures emerge: in 2009, next to the countries which traditionally showed a high performance in terms of technological applications such as Denmark (0.64), Luxembourg (0.68), the Netherlands (0.66), Finland (0.58), France (0.55) and the UK (0.55) now rank Estonia (0.44), Slovenia (0.48) and Spain (0.46) (Figure 2.7). Such high performances testify to the importance of daily use of the Internet – even in the presence of not always optimal infrastructures – as well as of the government policies which, over the years, encouraged and supported the development of the web. Making reference to the last few years only, it is important to note, in the case of Estonia, the 'Estonian Information Society Strategy 2013', which set as a main objective that each citizen should be able to benefit from the opportunities of the information society; in the case of Slovenia, 'Strategy for the Development of the Information Society in the Republic of Slovenia' which follows the European initiative i2010; and in the case of Spain, the 'Avanza plan' and 'Avanza Dos Plan', devoted to outlining new strategic lines for developing the information society for the period up to 2012.

Generally speaking, it is important to underline the existence of the so-called 'second digital divide' linked to the different ability to use the Internet. Even in countries like the Netherlands, traditionally frontrunners in Internet adoption, there are significant differences with respect to digital skills possessed. According to a survey conducted by the University of Twente, which indicated the presence of digital skills gaps within the Dutch population, the Dutch Government prepared the 'Digital skills and Digital Awareness Programme' (EC, eInclusion public policies, 2009). In addition to tackling the issue of unequal distribution of digital skills among the population, the programme also focused on the issue of cyber-security, an area closely connected to that of skills necessary to avoid fraud and to protect the privacy of citizens. In Hungary, an 'IT-mentor' programme was set up, in order to help people, and a 'Digital Literacy Action Plan' (2008–10) was formed, with the objective of reducing the country's proportion of people without digital skills. Finally, Lithuania and Denmark use their public libraries to offer Internet access and to improve fundamental skills. The purpose of this brief mention of the policies adopted by different countries is to underline the fact that the issue of 'digital skills' has raised increasing and more widespread concern, contextualized and problematized in relation to policies designed to increase the take-up and use of ICT by different sectors of society. It is important to stress that the digital skills issue

> should not be restricted to the school system only, as the 'lifelong learning' paradigm is now an established reality of the 21st century. ICT is essentially an empowering tool for the individual, for the enterprise, for the community, and the successfully inclusive Digital Competences public policy will be the one that will encompass all categories of citizens, whether they are at school, employed, unemployed or retired. (EC, eInclusion public policies, 2009, p. 67)

2.4 THE USAGE INDEX IN THE EUROPEAN COUNTRIES

If we now look at the usage index which was constructed on the basis of the subdimensions of autonomy, intensity and skills, it is possible to come up with an effective synthesis of the trends that have emerged up to now.

Table 2.4   Usage index values (2004–09)

Usage	2004	2005	2006	2007	2008	2009
Austria	0.36	0.41	0.46	0.52	0.52	0.55
Belgium	0.33	0.44	0.47	0.51	0.52	0.56
Bulgaria	0.09	0.14	0.15	0.20	0.24	0.30
Cyprus	0.23	0.23	0.26	0.28	0.32	0.39
Czech Republic	0.19	0.22	0.28	0.32	0.38	0.42
Denmark	0.61	0.67	0.70	0.69	0.71	0.73
Estonia	0.31	0.42	0.42	0.46	0.48	0.54
Finland	0.49	0.54	0.59	0.62	0.66	0.68
France	0.34	0.44	0.34	0.46	0.53	0.55
Germany	0.44	0.47	0.52	0.56	0.59	0.61
Greece	0.13	0.16	0.21	0.23	0.25	0.29
Hungary	0.19	0.25	0.34	0.40	0.45	0.49
Ireland	0.24	0.25	0.33	0.38	0.44	0.46
Italy	0.28	0.27	0.29	0.31	0.35	0.39
Latvia	0.17	0.26	0.31	0.38	0.42	0.46
Lithuania	0.18	0.22	0.28	0.35	0.41	0.46
Luxembourg	0.49	0.57	0.56	0.63	0.69	0.74
Malta	0.31	0.30	0.30	0.37	0.39	0.45
Netherlands	0.52	0.62	0.65	0.70	0.72	0.75
Poland	0.17	0.23	0.26	0.31	0.34	0.41
Portugal	0.20	0.25	0.26	0.30	0.34	0.38
Romania	0.05	0.11	0.11	0.14	0.18	0.23
Slovakia	0.25	0.31	0.32	0.38	0.47	0.52
Slovenia	0.29	0.36	0.41	0.44	0.45	0.50
Spain	0.25	0.30	0.33	0.37	0.40	0.45
Sweden	0.61	0.63	0.66	0.62	0.68	0.69
United Kingdom	0.41	0.48	0.48	0.55	0.58	0.64
EU27	0.30	0.35	0.38	0.43	0.46	0.51
EU15	0.38	0.43	0.46	0.50	0.53	0.56

At first sight, we can immediately see the limited but constant increase in index values for all the groups taken as a reference in the course of time: the EU15 increased from 0.38 to 0.56, the EU27 from 0.30 to 0.51 (Table 2.4).

When we consider the increase registered in the EU27 group in the period 2004–09 (+.21), we can see various trends which vary considerably from one country to another: (a) some countries, such as Denmark,

Finland, Luxembourg, the Netherlands, Sweden, and the UK, do not always show significant growth (that is, higher than average), but this does not prevent them from maintaining their position within the group with the highest values by virtue of their excellent initial conditions; (b) other countries, such as Austria, Czech Republic, France, Hungary, and Lithuania, show increases equal to or even higher than average, indicating rapid technological growth; (c) finally, countries such as Cyprus, Italy and Malta performed below the European average, and started with an unfavourable situation.

This initial overview enables us to identify a set of behavioural models which can be attributed to individual countries:

1. 'consolidating behaviours' – manifested by countries which have a solid technological tradition and continue to preserve it;
2. 'virtuous behaviours' – manifested by countries which are trying to quickly recover lost ground in the country's digitalization process;
3. 'resigned behaviours' – manifested by countries which are stuck in a situation of technological backwardness.

Regarding the results of each single country, the best performing ones for 2009 are the Netherlands (0.75), Luxembourg (0.74), Denmark (0.73), Sweden (0.69) and the worst ones are Romania (0.23), Greece (0.29), Bulgaria (0.30), Portugal (0.38), Cyprus (0.39) and Italy (0.39). Of the countries which are closely tailing the leading group, the following showed very significant increases: the Czech Republic (0.23), Estonia (0.23), Hungary (0.30), Ireland (0.22), Lithuania (0.28), Latvia (0.29), Poland (0.24), and Slovakia (0.27). Although the final index values are still not particularly high, these positive trends testify to a particularly rapid technological growth. Quite a different situation is observed, on the other hand, in countries such as Italy (+0.11) and Malta (+0.14), which appear to be stuck in the condition of straggler countries.

Table 2.5 shows countries grouped on the basis of the usage index,[4] so as to provide a clear overview of the various trends as well as confirmation of the existence of multiple speeds in Europe.

Group 1 comprises countries which constantly have the highest performances, in some cases three or more times higher than those of the lowest group (group 4), and which include a hard core of countries (the Netherlands, Denmark, Sweden, Finland and Luxembourg), with the addition in 2009 of the UK instead of Germany (shifted to group 2). It must be noted that these countries also obtained the highest score in the infrastructure index, which testifies to the importance of the availability of good technological provision. The high values registered in the case

Table 2.5 Usage index in groups of countries

Year	Group 1	Group 2	Group 3	Group 3
2009 EU27 = 0.51 EU15 = 0.52	Netherlands, Luxembourg, Denmark, Sweden, Finland, UK x̄ = 0.71 σ = 0.04	Germany, Belgium, Austria, France, Estonia, Slovakia, Slovenia x̄ = 0.55 σ = 0.03	Hungary, Ireland, Lithuania, Latvia, Spain, Malta, Czech Rep. x̄ = 0.46 σ = 0.02	Poland, Cyprus, Italy, Portugal, Bulgaria, Greece, Romania x̄ = 0.34 σ = 0.007
2008 EU27 = 0.47 EU15 = 0.47	Netherlands, Denmark, Luxembourg, Sweden, Finland, Germany x̄ = 0.68 σ = 0.05	UK, France, Austria, Belgium, Estonia, Slovakia x̄ = 0.52 σ = 0.04	Hungary, Slovenia, Ireland, Latvia, Lithuania, Spain, Malta, Czech Rep. x̄ = 0.42 σ = 0.03	Italy, Poland, Portugal, Cyprus, Greece, Bulgaria, Romania x̄ = 0.29 σ = 0.07
2007 EU27 = 0.43 EU15 = 0.44	Netherlands, Denmark, Luxembourg, Finland, Sweden, Germany x̄ = 0.64 σ = 0.05	UK, Austria, Belgium, Estonia, France, Slovenia, Hungary x̄ = 0.48 σ = 0.05	Ireland, Latvia, Slovakia, Spain, Malta, Lithuania, Czech Rep. x̄ = 0.36 σ = 0.02	Italy, Poland, Portugal, Cyprus, Greece, Bulgaria, Romania x̄ = 0.25 σ = 0.07

Table 2.5 (continued)

Year	Group 1	Group 2	Group 3	Group 3
2006 EU27 = 0.39 EU15 = 0.39	Denmark, Sweden, Netherlands, Finland, Luxembourg, Germany $\bar{x} = 0.61$ $\sigma = 0.06$	UK, Belgium, Austria, Estonia, Slovenia, France, Hungary $\bar{x} = 0.42$ $\sigma = 0.06$	Spain, Ireland, Slovakia, Latvia, Malta, Italy, Czech Rep., Lithuania $\bar{x} = 0.31$ $\sigma = 0.02$	Cyprus, Poland, Portugal, Greece, Bulgaria, Romania $\bar{x} = 0.21$ $\sigma = 0.06$
2005 EU27 = 0.36 EU15 = 0.37	Denmark, Sweden, Netherlands, UK, Luxembourg, Finland $\bar{x} = 0.59$ $\sigma = 0.07$	Germany, Belgium, France, Estonia, Austria, Slovenia, Slovakia $\bar{x} = 0.41$ $\sigma = 0.05$	Spain, Malta, Italy, Latvia, Hungary, Ireland, Portugal $\bar{x} = 0.27$ $\sigma = 0.02$	Cyprus, Poland, Czech Rep., Lithuania, Greece, Bulgaria, Romania $\bar{x} = 0.19$ $\sigma = 0.05$
2004 EU27 = 0.31 EU15 = 0.31	Denmark, Sweden, Netherlands, Finland, Luxembourg, Germany $\bar{x} = 0.53$ $\sigma = 0.07$	UK, Austria, France, Belgium, Estonia, Malta, Slovenia $\bar{x} = 0.34$ $\sigma = 0.04$	Italy, Spain, Slovakia, Ireland, Cyprus, Portugal $\bar{x} = 0.24$ $\sigma = 0.03$	Czech Rep., Hungary, Lithuania, Latvia, Poland, Greece, Bulgaria, Romania $\bar{x} = 0.15$ $\sigma = 0.05$

of the usage index lead one to believe in a sort of virtuous circle: a good infrastructure encourages and facilitates a widespread and structured use of the Internet, whilst an intense use of the Internet translates into the need to further develop the existing infrastructure. Further evidence of a sort of virtuous circle can be found if we analyse the integrated national ICT strategies developed by these countries in recent years (CEC, 2009): all of them have prepared specific policies aimed at reinforcing the infrastructure and broadband diffusion, the adoption of ICT in schools and the development of digital skills. In a nutshell, all of these countries have been engaged in formulating integrated national ICT strategies to maximize the benefits of ICT in their societies.

Along these lines, we find countries from group 2, although they registered different growth rates and results. This group of countries includes Germany (which only joined the cluster in 2009, after maintaining its position mostly in group 1), Belgium, France, Austria, Estonia, Slovakia and Slovenia. The average value achieved by the group was constantly above the European value (both EU27 and EU15), attesting to its good performance. This cluster of countries, which registered an annual average increase of approximately 5 points, best represents the ability of technological developments to recover lost ground and make up for past delays in a very short period of time, to the extent of enabling the cluster to position itself immediately below the frontrunners. Also in this case, evidently, the devising of strategies for the development and implementation of ICT has played a fundamental role in placing countries in a cluster that aims to live up to the European motto 'no one left behind'.

A completely different picture emerges, on the other hand, from the values registered in group 3, which performed constantly below the European average with gaps ranging from 5 to 10 points. A variety of patterns can be noted with respect to the performance of the countries included in this cluster: on the one hand, we see countries such as Hungary, Lithuania, Latvia, and the Czech Republic which are strongly committed to making up for structural delays and backwardness (and extremely dynamic at that), on the other hand, there are countries such as Ireland, Spain, and Malta, which are less active in terms of their progressive development of ICT. A reading of the data of the individual countries shows evidence of a vertical upward thrust bringing the former cluster closer to the forerunners and of a downward trend bringing the forerunners closer to the trailing group. In brief, this 'middle' group comprises different situations, moving in opposite directions.

The last group appears to be more homogeneous, with an often stagnant performance. The gap separating this group from the forerunners, reaching up to 40 points, does not show any signs of upgrading but, rather, of demotion. This is the case of Italy, which after holding a position in group 3 for three years, remained stably positioned in group 4 together with Poland, Cyprus, Portugal, Bulgaria, Greece and Romania. All these countries, with the exception of Italy, had deep structural gaps in technological infrastructure and in the diffusion of the Internet among the population. Although they are committed to revising and relaunching the i2010 initiative through national ICT strategies, they are still struggling to keep pace with the rest of Europe. As regards Italy, however, the i2010 initiative has not been updated and the country does not have a new national ICT strategy to close the gaps and to relaunch digitalization across the country.

2.5   PERSONAL AND SOCIAL EMPOWERMENT ON THE INTERNET: THE IMPACT INDEX

Over the course of the years examined in this study, the increase of Internet take-up in the various spheres of people's daily lives has been constant, though not evenly distributed. Generally speaking, high scores were registered in education (30-point increase in the EU27) followed by health (18-point increase), communication and culture (16-point increase) and government interaction (11-point increase). Trailing somewhat behind, although also showing a positive trend, are the labour subdimension (with a constant 8-point increase), and the economy subdimension (7 points) (Figure 2.8).

This first set of data suggests a slow but constant diffusion of Internet take-up, starting with certain areas which have shown a greater capacity of prompt reaction. Numerous factors connected with different areas have contributed to determining such a reaction: the increasingly central role of the social and communication dimension in contemporary society has made a strong contribution to the net increment that was registered in this area; similarly, the idea of 'lifelong learning' has contributed to firmly supporting a new use of the Internet in this sphere of daily life. With respect to the economic area, enterprises' interest in expanding their user base has certainly contributed to more attention being paid to the issue of online transaction security, and at the same time, it has accelerated the process for reshaping customer relations (as in the case of e-banking and e-travel transactions). In brief, the joint interest of enterprises and citizens alike has probably served as the driving force in the area's development. A similar virtuous mechanism can be found in the government area: the numerous initiatives and policies designed to simplify relations between public administrations and citizens have contributed to a rapid development of this mode of interaction.

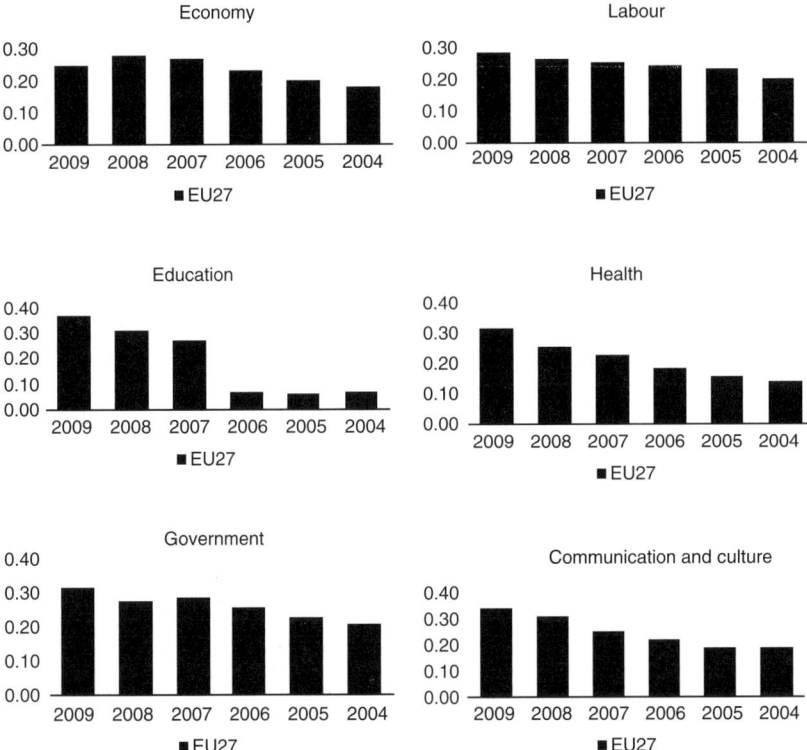

Figure 2.8   The subdimensions of Internet impact

Delving further into the analysis of the subdimensions, with regard to the economic area, it is important to note the gradual and constant growth (of approximately 2 points) that has occurred over the years, with the sole exception of a 4-point decrease registered in 2009. This detail is probably the result of the crisis that has hit the world economy in recent years and, by virtue of that, it cannot be interpreted as an indication of a halt in the sequence of development of the subdimension. If we analyse each country separately, we are reminded once again of the existence within Europe of multiple speeds: over the course of 2009, Denmark reached the 0.52 mark, the Netherlands 0.51 and Sweden 0.50, as opposed to Romania, Bulgaria, Cyprus, Portugal and Italy, which performed below the 0.12 mark. In between these two extremes, the other groups of countries fluctuate, inching closer to the top group and then slipping closer to the bottom one: immediately below the countries leading the economic area are Finland (0.46), Luxembourg (0.42), UK (0.42) and Germany (0.39); immediately above the trailing countries are Poland (0.17), Lithuania (0.14), Hungary (0.12), Czech Republic (0.15), and Malta (0.23). Spain (0.17), Austria (0.27), Ireland (0.24), Belgium (0.33), Estonia (0.28), and France (0.33) are positioned in the middle. Finally, it is worth noting that the countries with the best performance also registered the highest increases, confirming a growth trend that has yet to see its upper limit, and which will most likely widen further the gap with other 'straggler' countries.

The employment and labour area, on the other hand, is broadly stable. Before taking a closer look at the data for each country, we need to point out that the indicator 'percentage of persons employed working part of their time away from enterprise premises and accessing enterprise's IT system from there' has no longer been available from 2006 onwards. The disappearance of this indicator – which measured the presence of so-called teleworking – has contributed to reducing the overall rate of the sub-dimension index, thus producing a lull. Nevertheless, worthy of note is the good performance of Denmark and Sweden (0.42) and Finland (0.40). Other particularly positive situations can be observed in the countries of Northern Europe, while Romania, Bulgaria, Portugal, Czech Republic, and Poland continue to be the worst performers.

The educational area, on the other hand, showed a significantly positive trend over time (30-point increase). This strong increase clearly attests to the empowerment effect exerted by the Internet in people's lives, enabling them to acquire an education – be it formal or informal – in numerous fields and sectors. There is no doubt that the opportunity to follow online courses – whether formal or informal and on the most varied subjects – appears to be particularly welcomed by European citizens. If we analyse the rates achieved by each single country, we obtain a picture in which Finland (0.69) occupies the top position in 2009. As usual, however, among the straggler countries are Bulgaria (0.14), Romania (0.18), Slovakia (0.21) and Cyprus (0.25).

Another very popular activity among European citizens is the search for health information on the Internet. In reality, this subdimension, which has grown stably by 18 points, is one of the most dynamic over time. In this area, the countries of Northern Europe confirm the top position – Finland (0.56), the Netherlands (0.50), and Denmark (0.46) – with Luxembourg (0.54), Germany (0.48) and France (0.37) trailing close behind. The lowest rates were registered, as usual, in Romania (0.16), Bulgaria (0.10) and Greece (0.15).

Conversely, the use of the Internet for performing tasks involving public administrations is rather limited. The very low rates registered in many European countries seem at odds with the numerous initiatives undertaken over the years for promoting the use of the Internet for managing relations with public authorities: in fact, the data available show quite a different picture, from which great difficulties in spreading alternative forms of interaction clearly emerge. With the exception of a few countries, such as Denmark, Sweden, the Netherlands and Finland, which registered values above the 0.50 mark, the overall situation is clearly not a positive one: Austria stood at 0.39, Germany at 0.37, France at 0.39, the UK at 0.35, Spain at 0.30 and Italy at 0.17. It is important to stress these data in the light of the fact that all Member States are active in the implementation of policies in the area of e-government. An analysis conducted on this subject as part of the more recent Annual Information Society Report (CEC, 2009) on the policies of the various countries shows that 'within National governments, common policies include the expansion of office automation, the digitalisation of public administration, the networking of National governmental departments as well as between central and local authorities and the implementation of electronic public procurement' (pp. 84–85).

Lastly, the subdimension containing indicators relating to expression (email and other forms of communication), recreation (downloading music, games, movies), information (reading newspapers), remediation of media (listening to radio, watching TV) and technological upgrading (downloading software) is particularly dynamic, registering 16-point increases in the period from 2004 to 2009. The greatest capacity for prompt reaction in exploiting the new opportunities is once again attributed to Denmark (from 0.29 to 0.53), the Netherlands (from 0.30 to 0.52), Luxembourg (from 0.30 to 0.49), Sweden (from 0.29 to 0.44), Finland (from 0.33 to 0.44) and the UK (from 0.24 to 0.44). The greatest difficulties, on the other hand, continue to be experienced in Romania (from 0.05 to 0.18), Bulgaria (from 0.09 to 0.21), and Greece (from 0.09 to 0.19).

In order to measure the weight of each subdimension on the construction of the impact index – and consequently show the transformations that have occurred over time – we have conducted a regression analysis (Table 2.6).

Over the course of the years, the subdimensions of economy and government make the greatest contribution to the building of the impact index. The subdimension of education registered lower values but constant growth, as this area is highly requested by a large portion of the European population. Labour and health are on the progressive downturn, whilst the culture and communication area is quite stable. These data show the progressive take-up of Internet use in people's daily lives in a perspective of individual and collective empowerment: from economic benefits to those deriving from a significant broadening of the spectrum of communication, cultural and entertainment opportunities, and from the gradual transformation of relations with public administrations to the

Table 2.6   The weight of each subdimension on the construction of the impact index (beta coefficient)

	2004	2005	2006	2007	2008	2009
Economy	.250	.256	.291	.238	.254	.226
Labour	.159	.153	.151	.126	.116	.118
Education	.080	.066	.082	.172	.162	.193
Health	.205	.195	.188	.178	.171	.174
Government	.239	.247	.226	.219	.254	.223
Culture, communication	.140	.151	.158	.134	.154	.145

Note: Standard error = .000.

autonomous search for health information. The increase of beta values relating to the economic and government subdimensions clearly confirms their central role in the transformations that have involved the Internet in recent years.

The analysis of the subdimensions conducted thus far enables us to confirm, with full data documentation, the existence of multiple speeds in the take-up of the Internet among the 27 European countries. The impact that the Internet is capable of exerting on people's daily lives, constituting a real opportunity for individual and social empowerment, can be felt in certain areas whilst it is almost absent in others, thus confirming a new form of inequality between people.

2.6   THE IMPACT INDEX: INTERNET PRESENCE IN EVERYDAY LIFE

If we now look at the impact index, we can see that, over the course of the 2004–09 period, the performance of the index improved constantly, although at a slow pace, in the various European countries. In the EU27, the index rate moved from 0.16 in 2004 to 0.31 in 2009, with a limited maximum growth of two to three points (with the exception of 2006–07), and an overall increase of 15. In the EU15, the growth trend was similar, bringing the initial rate of 0.21 up to 0.36 (15 points).

If we now consider the performance of each country, we immediately note two different trends: on the one hand, there are countries which show a very rapid growth pattern, higher than the average increase; on the other hand, there are countries which are essentially static, showing very limited progress. In the leading position are Denmark (+22), Sweden (+19),

Table 2.7   The impact index values

	2004	2005	2006	2007	2008	2009
Austria	0.14	0.19	0.23	0.26	0.32	0.32
Belgium	0.20	0.19	0.22	0.25	0.25	0.31
Bulgaria	0.04	0.04	0.07	0.08	0.10	0.12
Cyprus	0.10	0.10	0.13	0.18	0.16	0.20
Czech Republic	0.08	0.07	0.14	0.17	0.20	0.23
Denmark	0.31	0.31	0.34	0.49	0.46	0.53
Estonia	0.18	0.22	0.22	0.27	0.31	0.35
Finland	0.33	0.36	0.39	0.47	0.50	0.51
France	0.19	0.23	0.17	0.33	0.38	0.37
Germany	0.25	0.28	0.30	0.38	0.36	0.39
Greece	0.07	0.06	0.08	0.12	0.15	0.16
Hungary	0.11	0.13	0.15	0.22	0.25	0.27
Ireland	0.11	0.13	0.18	0.24	0.27	0.28
Italy	0.19	0.11	0.12	0.17	0.19	0.21
Latvia	0.10	0.12	0.16	0.18	0.24	0.29
Lithuania	0.08	0.12	0.16	0.20	0.22	0.25
Luxembourg	0.32	0.33	0.31	0.44	0.45	0.50
Malta	0.17	0.15	0.16	0.22	0.24	0.29
Netherlands	0.30	0.34	0.38	0.45	0.45	0.47
Poland	0.09	0.10	0.12	0.17	0.20	0.22
Portugal	0.08	0.11	0.13	0.19	0.21	0.24
Romania	0.02	0.02	0.05	0.08	0.11	0.12
Slovakia	0.16	0.15	0.17	0.19	0.25	0.26
Slovenia	0.12	0.17	0.21	0.26	0.29	0.31
Spain	0.13	0.15	0.18	0.25	0.28	0.30
Sweden	0.27	0.33	0.33	0.40	0.44	0.46
United Kingdom	0.22	0.26	0.27	0.32	0.36	0.39
EU27	0.16	0.18	0.20	0.26	0.28	0.31
EU15	0.21	0.23	0.24	0.32	0.34	0.36

Slovenia (+19), Latvia (+19), Finland (+18), France (+18), Luxembourg (+18), the Netherlands (+17), and the UK (+17). In a different position, in what could really be defined as a standstill condition – albeit showing almost satisfactory rates – are Italy (+2), Bulgaria (+8), Greece (+9), Romania (+10), and Cyprus (+10). These countries show a fairly odd pattern, characterized by what may be defined as 'technological indifference' as opposed to the 'technological enthusiasm' characterizing the

first group. This piece of data may be the result of a modest technological infrastructure (see Section 2.2) combined with an equally modest
technology appropriation on the part of the population (see Section 2.3).

As above, the construction of groups of countries[5] in relation to the
impact index rates provides a clear overview (Table 2.8). Group 1, which
consists of traditionally 'strong' countries in terms of Internet take-up
such as those of Northern Europe, shows a positive trend, constantly
outperforming the EU27 and EU15 average. The 20–30 points gap separating this group from group 4 testifies to the different speeds at which
the two groups develop in the process of transformation in everyday life
as a result of Internet use. It is important to note that this gap remains
more or less unvaried over the course of time: 29 points separated the two
groups in 2009 and in 2008, 30 in 2007, and 24 in 2006, 25 in 2005 and 23
in 2004. Starting from 2008, Germany left group 1 whilst France held its
position there for only one year. The extreme cohesiveness of the cluster
and its stability over time are the clearest examples of the effectiveness of
the policies adopted over the years. Whether these were policies for the
autonomous implementation of the i2010 strategy or for specific measures
aimed at targeted areas, the results achieved were clearly satisfactory.
On the other hand, it should be borne in mind that in these countries,
a number of centres were established, for the dissemination of broadband knowledge (Broadband Expertise Centre, in Sweden), to improve
the climate of household and citizen trust toward the new technologies
(National Information Security Strategy in Finland), and to improve IT
skills among ethnic minorities (Digitale Trapvelden in the Netherlands).
These and many other measures that could be mentioned are all aimed at
encouraging the use of the Internet in the numerous activities that citizens
carry out on a day-to-day basis.

A similar commitment, albeit to a lesser extent, can be found in group
2. Although trailing behind the first group by between 11 and 16 points,
group 2 shows a constant and gradual improvement, achieving an
overall increase of 15 points. This group includes many countries which,
although they do not always enjoy a good technological infrastructure,
have always promoted the Internet culture: the clearest examples of this
are Estonia and Slovenia. It is important to stress that both of these
countries have finalized integrated national ICT strategies in order to
try to maximize the benefits of ICT in their societies. The 'Estonian
Information Society Strategy 2013' has the objective that each member of
society should lead a full life using the opportunities of the information
society in every possible way. The 'Strategy for the Development of the
Information Society in the Republic of Slovenia' seeks to promote further
the development of the information society, to promote competitiveness

and productivity, and to improve the quality of life of society as a whole and of each individual.

In addition to these countries, there are others which are always poised between an outstanding and a good position, namely Germany, the UK and France. These countries have also paid attention to the construction of ICT development strategies. The 2009 'Digital Britain' policy document sets out the next steps of the British government to maximize the economic and social opportunities of ICT with four action points: delivering an effective modern communication infrastructure, enabling Britain to be a global centre for the creative industries in the digital age, ensuring that people have the skills to flourish in the digital economy, and improving the digital delivery of public services. France, for its part, has developed a national strategy with the goal of making itself one of the best ICT countries by 2012, by providing 100 per cent coverage of fixed and mobile broadband and introducing digital television. The plan rests on four priorities: to provide access to the Internet for the whole population; to develop the production and supply of digital content; to increase and diversify usage and services within enterprises and households; to modernize the governance of the digital economy. Finally, Germany puts an emphasis on policies to increase the coverage of broadband (100 per cent broadband targets) and in implementing policies at regional level for raising the awareness of the positive impact of technology on the quality of life and employment. The positive results achieved over the six-year period examined, therefore, are the result of the intervention policies that proved to be effective in supporting Internet use among citizens in numerous spheres of daily life.

The same cannot be said, however, for group 3, which constantly performed below the European average. This cluster also has a 20 or so point gap from the top group. It is important to note that this gap increases slowly over the course of time: 18 points separated the two groups in 2004, 19 in 2005, 18 in 2006, 23 in 2007, 21 in 2008 and 22 in 2009. The 'core' of the group, in which other countries are sometimes included, comprises Ireland, Latvia, Slovakia, Hungary, Lithuania and Portugal. The cohesion of the cluster, from a geographical viewpoint as well, is weakened by Ireland and Portugal. These two countries are working hard to bridge the gap separating them from group 2 by implementing multi-faceted ICT strategies. Ireland is developing a 'National Knowledge Society Strategy', focused on development of its knowledge economy, and wants to accelerate the development of knowledge-intense areas (e-learning, digital traded services, and so on). More generally, 'the Strategy will bring together the various actions and supports which will result in Ireland having the ability to develop, produce, license and export products and services based on

Table 2.8 Impact index in group of countries

Year	Group 1	Group 2	Group 3	Group 4
2009 **EU27 = 0.31** **EU15 = 0.36**	Denmark, Finland, Luxembourg, Netherlands, Sweden $\bar{x} = 0.49$ $\sigma = 0.03$	Germany, UK, France, Estonia, Austria, Spain, Belgium, Slovenia $\bar{x} = 0.34$ $\sigma = 0.04$	Latvia, Malta, Ireland, Hungary, Slovakia, Lithuania, Portugal $\bar{x} = 0.27$ $\sigma = 0.02$	Czech Rep, Poland, Italy, Cyprus, Greece, Bulgaria, Romania $\bar{x} = 0.18$ $\sigma = 0.05$
2008 **EU27 = 0.28** **EU15 = 0.34**	Finland, Denmark, Luxembourg, Sweden, Netherlands, France $\bar{x} = 0.45$ $\sigma = 0.04$	Germany, UK, Austria, Estonia, Slovenia, Spain, Ireland $\bar{x} = 0.31$ $\sigma = 0.04$	Belgium, Hungary, Slovakia, Latvia, Malta, Lithuania, Portugal $\bar{x} = 0.24$ $\sigma = 0.02$	Czech Rep, Poland, Italy, Cyprus, Greece, Romania, Bulgaria $\bar{x} = 0.16$ $\sigma = 0.04$
2007 **EU27 = 0.26** **EU15 = 0.32**	Denmark, Finland, Netherlands, Sweden, Luxembourg, Germany $\bar{x} = 0.44$ $\sigma = 0.04$	France, UK, Estonia, Austria, Slovenia, Belgium, Spain $\bar{x} = 0.28$ $\sigma = 0.03$	Ireland, Hungary, Malta, Lithuania, Portugal, Slovakia $\bar{x} = 0.21$ $\sigma = 0.02$	Cyprus, Latvia, Italy, Czech Rep, Poland, Greece, Bulgaria, Romania $\bar{x} = 0.14$ $\sigma = 0.04$

Year	Group 1	Group 2	Group 3	Group 4
2006 EU27 = 0.20 EU15 = 0.24	Finland, Netherlands, Denmark, Sweden, Luxembourg, Germany $\bar{x} = 0.34$ $\sigma = 0.04$	UK, Austria, Belgium, Estonia, Slovenia, Spain, Ireland $\bar{x} = 0.22$ $\sigma = 0.03$	France, Slovakia, Lithuania, Latvia, Malta, Hungary, Czech Rep $\bar{x} = 0.16$ $\sigma = 0.01$	Cyprus, Portugal, Italy, Poland, Greece, Bulgaria, Romania $\bar{x} = 0.10$ $\sigma = 0.03$
2005 EU27 = 0.18 EU15 = 0.23	Finland, Netherlands, Luxembourg, Sweden, Denmark, Germany $\bar{x} = 0.33$ $\sigma = 0.03$	UK, France, Estonia, Austria, Belgium, Slovenia $\bar{x} = 0.21$ $\sigma = 0.03$	Spain, Malta, Slovakia, Hungary, Ireland, Lithuania, Latvia $\bar{x} = 0.14$ $\sigma = 0.01$	Italy, Portugal, Cyprus, Poland, Czech Rep, Greece, Bulgaria, Romania $\bar{x} = 0.08$ $\sigma = 0.03$
2004 EU27 = 0.16 EU15 = 0.21	Finland, Luxembourg, Denmark, Sweden, Netherlands, Germany $\bar{x} = 0.30$ $\sigma = 0.03$	UK, Belgium, France, Italy, Estonia, Malta, Slovakia $\bar{x} = 0.19$ $\sigma = 0.02$	Austria, Spain, Latvia, Slovenia, Hungary, Ireland, Cyprus $\bar{x} = 0.12$ $\sigma = 0.02$	Poland, Czech Rep, Lithuania, Portugal, Greece, Bulgaria, Romania $\bar{x} = 0.07$ $\sigma = 0.03$

knowledge-intense ideas' (CEC, 2009, p. 79). The 'Connecting Portugal' strategy 'focuses on optical fibre infrastructure, advanced broadband services and high-speed research network' (CEC, 2009, p. 8). The other countries in group 3 are engaged predominantly in making up for delays in technological infrastructure and in the diffusion of Internet use by the population.

Group 4, finally, confirms its marginal position in the take-up of the Internet, for example in the case of Poland, Greece, Romania and Bulgaria. The values separating this cluster from group 1 never dropped below the 23 point mark (2004), and reached up to 31 points in 2009. With the exception of Italy, which has maintained a stable position in the group since 2005, the other countries show a situation of general technological backwardness which prevents them from keeping pace with Europe as a whole. It is no coincidence that, in these countries, the national ICT strategies focus on guaranteeing connection and quality: in Greece, 'special emphasis is being put on the development of WiMax and satellite internet combined with WiFi, in order to cover as many areas as possible (and notably hard-to-access and remote areas)' (CEC, 2009, p. 82). In Bulgaria, on the other hand, the 'iCentres Network Projects' initiative was launched to expand the network of broadband Internet access points and promote citizens' access to the various electronic services. The anomalous presence of Italy in the cluster can be attributed to a sort of 'stagnation' that characterized this country's performance in the recent past, after the momentum it built up as a result of the adoption of i2010 in 2005. It is no coincidence that the greatest increase registered in this country occurred in the 2005–06 transition (+0.5). Since then, Italy has invested mainly in e-government (Piano e_GOV 2012) achieving satisfactory results although not good enough to quicken the pace of Internet take-up by individuals.

The countries' positions in the various groups confirm old allegiances and reveal new ones resulting from the use of the Internet on the part of individuals in their daily lives. In the following chapters we discuss a metrics for digital development and analyse the impact of the Internet on the daily life of people in traditionally disadvantaged groups.

NOTES

1. This is supported by the OECD (2007a) as well as by Van Dijk Management Consultants (2008).
2. For each year, four groups of countries have been aggregated on the basis of the score obtained in relation to the infrastructure index. After ranking the countries in decreasing order, three quartiles have been calculated to construct four groups. The first quartile divides the first 25% of the distribution from the remaining 75%; the second quartile

divides the distribution into two equal parts; the third quartile divides the 75% of the distribution from the last 25%. Therefore, in the first group there are 25% of the countries with the highest values of the infrastructure index; in the second there are the following 25% of the countries with middle-high values; in the third there are 25% of the countries with middle-low values; in the fourth group there are the countries with the lowest values of the distribution. Finally, the arithmetic mean and standard deviation have been calculated inside each group.

3. The data relating to skills are not available on a regular basis. Due to the missing data for the year 2008, we based our results on an estimate.

4. For each year, four groups of countries have been aggregated on the basis of the score obtained in relation to the usage index. After ranking the countries in decreasing order, three quartiles have been calculated to construct four groups. The first quartile divides the first 25% of the distribution from the remaining 75%; the second quartile divides the distribution into two equal parts; the third quartile divides the 75% of the distribution from the last 25%. Therefore, in the first group there are 25% of the countries with the highest values of the usage index; in the second there are the following 25% of the countries with middle-high values; in the third there are 25% of the countries with middle-low values; in the fourth group there are the countries with the lowest values of the distribution. Finally, the arithmetic mean and standard deviation have been calculated inside each group.

5. For each year, four groups of countries have been aggregated on the basis of the score obtained in relation to the impact index. After ranking the countries in decreasing order, three quartiles have been calculated to construct four groups. The first quartile divides the first 25% of the distribution from the remaining 75%; the second quartile divides the distribution into two equal parts; the third quartile divides the 75% of the distribution from the last 25%. Therefore, in the first group there are 25% of the countries with the highest values of the impact index; in the second there are the following 25% of the countries with middle-high values; in the third there are 25% of the countries with middle-low values; in the fourth group there are the countries with the lowest values of the distribution. Finally, the arithmetic mean and standard deviation have been calculated inside each group.

3. A metrics for digital development

3.1 THE EUROPEAN DIGITAL DEVELOPMENT INDEX

One of the earliest studies on factors affecting the variation in Internet connectivity highlighted that 'despite its overarching importance [of the Internet], little attention has been devoted to the study of its spread, especially on an international level. Given the potential wide-ranging effects of the technology, the level of diffusion in a country can influence the degree to which a country can hold its place in the global economy' (Hargittai, 1999a, p. 702).

Many things have changed since the days in which Hargittai denounced the lack of attention to these issues, one of them certainly being the renewed interest in the diffusion and adoption of the Internet. Today, in fact, there is even a need to introduce order into the rich and complex literature which embraces different scopes of analysis, types of data and variables used. With reference to this confusion resulting from the multitude and inequality of approaches, Howard et al. (2009) claim that there is a 'research divide on the digital divide'.

One of the richest strands is certainly that which analyses developed and developing countries. Among the numerous studies adopting the global approach, that conducted by Norris (2001) on 179 countries using cross-sectional data, is worthy of note. Taking as a dependent variable the proportion of the population online, Norris considers economic factors as the most relevant in predicting differences in access to the information society. According to Norris, 'economic development, measured by per capita GDP, was consistently important across all three models, indicating that more affluent societies have access to a richer range of information and communication technologies, among both traditional and digital media' (Norris, 2001, p. 63). A similar finding about the economic dimension, linked to education level of population, was made by Kiiski and Pohjola (2002), Robison and Crenshaw (2002) and Lucas and Sylla (2003) in presenting the empirical evidence of their studies. A more complex use of variables can be found in the work of Chinn and Fairlie (2004). In order to analyse 161 countries over the 1999–2001 period, the authors use economic variables, demographic variables, infrastructure indicators, telecommunications pricing measures and regulatory quality. The dependent variable, identified as computer and Internet penetration, is explained by the authors in relation to 'income per capita, communication infrastructure (as measured by telephone main lines density), access to electricity, institutional environment in the form of regulatory efficacy and the protection of property rights, and demographic characteristics' (p. 2).

Contributing to a further increase in the number of dimensions that can be used to explain the diffusion and adoption of the Internet are the works of Guillén and Suàrez (2005), Crenshaw and Robison (2006), and Milner (2006). From the analysis conducted by Guillén and Suàrez on 118 countries from 1997 through 2001, using as independent variables the world-system status, telecommunication policies and democracy, it emerged that '[the Internet] is a medium whose growth and diffusion are not only driven by technological and purely economic imperatives, but also by regulatory, political and sociological ones' (p. 700). In a study conducted on 80 developing countries by Crenshaw and Robison (2006), the authors agree on the need to expand the number of variables used to explain the diffusion of the Internet, arguing that 'while Internet development has been driven by the general affluence and high levels of education found in the developed world, this postindustrial template does not adequately capture Internet diffusion in developing countries' (p. 204). Recent studies adopting the global approach confirm the use of indicators related to the economic dimension, political dimension, telecommunication policies, and investments in business and technology (Azari and Pick, 2009; Howard and Mazaheri, 2009; Manrique and Manrique, 2009). Lastly, in his study conducted on 126 countries, Fuchs (2009) introduces the dimension of social inequality and, based on the data provided therein, sustains that 'the result was that for the year 2005 data, GDP per capita exerted the most important but not the only influence. Social inequality measured by the Gini coefficient, the level of democracy, and the degree of urbanization of a country were also found to be important influencing factors' (p. 55). To sum up, most researchers associate the diffusion of the Internet worldwide – understood strictly as access – with a country's economic development, level of education, the existing technological infrastructure, the regulations governing the telecommunications sector, and the political dimension.

At the end of this brief overview of the empirical literature on factors which explain the different levels of digitalization, the evocation of the term 'digital chasm' suggested by Howard et al. (2009) is by no means out of place. This is a chasm originating, *in primis*, from the unavailability of a measurement instrument able to realize the comparison between countries

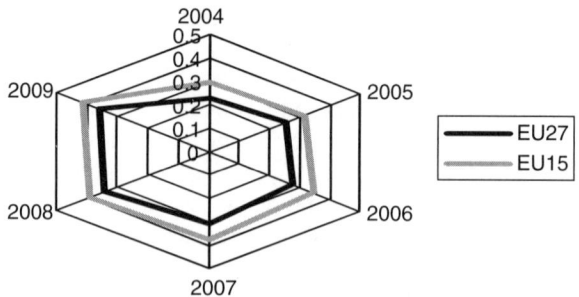

*Figure 3.1   EDDI: average performance of EU27 and EU15 countries
            (2004–09)*

and along the diachronical dimension. Very often, in fact, the data used
refer to different states of the digitalization process: from diffusion of main
telephone lines, for instance, to broadband coverage, or from availability of
personal computers to the presence of wi-fi connections. This accentuated
articulation comes directly from the approach of analysis selected, which
takes into account both developed and developing countries. In the case of
the European Digital Development Index (hereafter referred to as EDDI),
this problem doesn't exist: the countries analysed are all Member States of
the European Union. As already described (see Chapter 1), this index is a
measurement instrument capable of diagnosing all the relevant dimensions
of the digitalization development, namely infrastructure, usage and impact,
understood as opportunity for individual and social empowerment.

In a nutshell, EDDI makes it possible to diagnose the phase of digitalization in Europe, in individual states, and over the course of time.
Furthermore, it makes it possible to identify any points of strength or criti-
calities vis-à-vis individual dimensions. A selection of the various methods
adopted in the process is documented and discussed in the Appendix; in
this context, it is important to bear in mind that the index is the result of a
combination of the three indices (infrastructure, usage and impact) developed within the three dimensions – and all the subdimensions – over the
course of the period 2004–09. The three dimensions (infrastructure, usage
and impact), are structured into 12 subdimensions (network, affordability,
availability and quality, autonomy, intensity, skills, economy, labour,
education, health, government, and communication and culture).

Looking at the values obtained by the index in the period 2004–09,
for both the EU27 and EU15, we observe a clear trend line with values
increasing from 0.23 in 2004 to 0.36 in 2009 for the former, and from 0.29
to 0.41 for the latter (Figure 3.1).

Table 3.1   Growth and composition of EDDI

	Average value 2004	Average value 2009	Change in value 2004–2009
EDDI	0.23	0.36	+ 0.13
Infrastructure index	0.24	0.27	+ 0.03
Usage index	0.30	0.51	+ 0.21
Impact index	0.16	0.31	+ 0.15

Overall, within the relevant time horizon, the index shows a 13-point increase in the EU27 and a 12-point increase in the EU15. The figure shows a constant gap between the EU27 and the EU15, in the range of 5 to 6 points, which shows the different paces at which the various European countries progress. The fact that the gap remains constant is evidence of the structural nature of the divide separating the two clusters: in fact, it remains stable over time. The performance of the two clusters could even serve as the paradigm of the stratification model of ICT diffusion in contemporary societies theorized years ago (Norris, 2001).

On further perusal of the index, we can see the points of strength and weakness in EDDI's internal development. As already stated, this index not only monitors the development of digitalization in the 27 European Member States – thus measuring the overall and annual increase – but is also capable of identifying those areas which registered the greatest development and those which, in contrast, experienced the greatest difficulties in terms of expansion and establishment. Table 3.1 clearly shows that the two dimensions of usage and impact registered the largest growth, in confirmation of what was stated in Chapter 2 with regards to the diminishing effect of the infrastructure index on the index's overall values. In other words, this means that the technological infrastructure, which is fundamental in securing access to ICT, loses ground compared to the strengthened position of usage (understood as both intensity and autonomy) and of impact (understood as the progressive expansion and structuring of online activities or increased content supply).

In Figure 3.2, the display of the evolution of the three dimensions of EDDI over the period 2004–09 shows even more clearly the declining trend line of infrastructure, to the benefit of the other dimensions.

Additional information can be obtained by analysing a set of values relating to the three dimensions. It can be seen from the Table 3.2, showing the minimum, maximum and average values and the standard deviation, that the various dimensions behave differently over time: the infrastructure

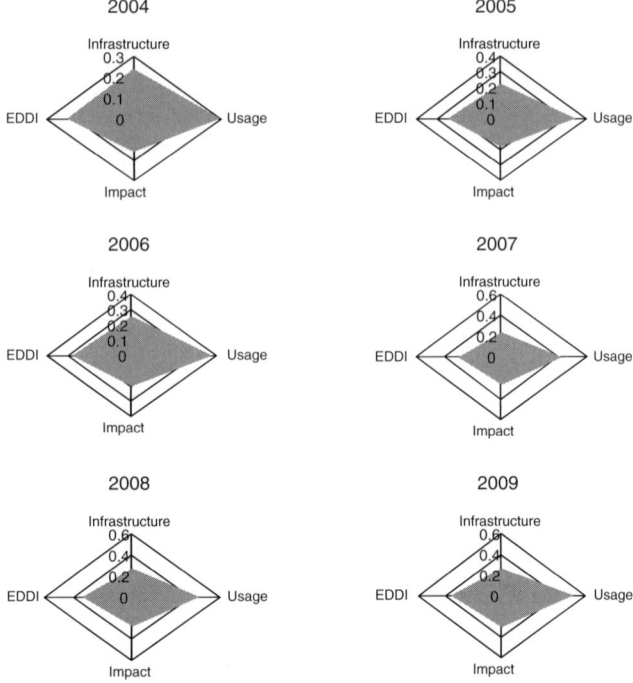

Figure 3.2   EDDI, infrastructure, usage and impact indexes: average performance of EU27 countries (2004–09)

dimension remains substantially stable compared to the average value, although it shows a decrease in standard deviation; the usage dimension registers a significant increase in average values and a slight decrease in standard deviation; finally, the impact dimension shows an increase in both average values and standard deviation. These values – including the related increases and decreases – provide still further evidence of the nature and direction of the shifts occurring in the index's three dimensions: the infrastructure dimension is confirmed as the backbone of technological development, with values within a range that narrows over time, whilst the usage and impact dimensions show values within a range that widens constantly over time.

3.2   THE PERFORMANCE OF EDDI IN EUROPE

As regards the Index values in Europe, both in relation to each Member State and to the various aggregations, major differences can be seen.

Table 3.2   Descriptive statistics of EDDI dimensions (2004–09)

	Minimum	Maximum	Mean	Standard deviation
2004				
Infrastructure	.03	.40	.2359	.09806
Usage	.05	.61	.2997	.14929
Impact	.02	.33	.1621	.08856
2005				
Infrastructure	.03	.39	.2233	.10103
Usage	.11	.67	.3533	.15778
Impact	.02	.36	.1759	.09820
2006				
Infrastructure	.07	.44	.2642	.10348
Usage	.11	.70	.3816	.15597
Impact	.05	.39	.1983	.09338
2007				
Infrastructure	.05	.41	.2425	.09987
Usage	.14	.70	.4263	.14817
Impact	.08	.49	.2579	.11513
2008				
Infrastructure	.08	.43	.2679	.08984
Usage	.18	.72	.4626	.14665
Impact	.10	.50	.2827	.11063
2009				
Infrastructure	.10	.41	.2670	.08822
Usage	.23	.75	.5053	.13946
Impact	.12	.53	.3097	.11405

Building on the analysis of the overall evolution of the index in the two European clusters, we saw in Figure 3.1 that a general upward trend occurred over the years: over the 2004–09 period, in fact, the EU27 values increased from 0.23 to 0.36 whilst those of the EU15 increased from 0.29 to 0.41. However, this initial data also indicates that there is a gap in the range of 5 to 6 points separating the EU27 from the EU15. If we then take a close look at the individual Member States, the situation appears to be uneven: there are states with high and constantly rising values, and other states that show lower values and are unable to gain ground over the former (Table 3.3). Thus in 2004, Denmark registered a value of 0.44, in sharp contrast to Romania (0.03), Bulgaria (0.06), Greece (0.12), Poland (0.13), Hungary and the Czech Republic (0.15).

If we analyse the data for 2006 – that is, the period around which broadband became widespread and various initiatives were launched in Europe

Table 3.3   EDDI values (2004–09)

Countries	2004	2005	2006	2007	2008	2009
Austria	0.27	0.29	0.34	0.36	0.39	0.39
Belgium	0.28	0.31	0.34	0.36	0.36	0.39
Bulgaria	0.06	0.08	0.10	0.12	0.14	0.17
Cyprus	0.19	0.17	0.18	0.21	0.23	0.27
Czech Republic	0.15	0.15	0.20	0.22	0.26	0.29
Denmark	0.44	0.46	0.49	0.53	0.53	0.55
Estonia	0.25	0.29	0.32	0.33	0.36	0.40
Finland	0.38	0.40	0.45	0.48	0.51	0.52
France	0.27	0.31	0.35	0.36	0.40	0.41
Germany	0.33	0.35	0.39	0.42	0.43	0.45
Greece	0.12	0.12	0.14	0.16	0.19	0.21
Hungary	0.15	0.17	0.23	0.26	0.31	0.31
Ireland	0.21	0.22	0.27	0.31	0.33	0.35
Italy	0.24	0.20	0.22	0.23	0.24	0.28
Latvia	0.14	0.17	0.23	0.25	0.29	0.32
Lithuania	0.13	0.15	0.21	0.24	0.28	0.32
Luxembourg	0.38	0.41	0.42	0.48	0.50	0.54
Malta	0.25	0.24	0.25	0.28	0.32	0.34
Netherlands	0.39	0.45	0.49	0.52	0.52	0.54
Poland	0.13	0.14	0.18	0.20	0.25	0.27
Portugal	0.16	0.18	0.20	0.22	0.27	0.27
Romania	0.03	0.05	0.08	0.09	0.14	0.15
Slovakia	0.18	0.19	0.21	0.24	0.29	0.32
Slovenia	0.21	0.24	0.29	0.31	0.33	0.35
Spain	0.21	0.23	0.26	0.28	0.31	0.33
Sweden	0.42	0.44	0.47	0.47	0.49	0.52
United Kingdom	0.32	0.36	0.38	0.41	0.42	0.46
EU27	0.23	0.25	0.28	0.31	0.34	0.36
EU15	0.29	0.32	0.35	0.37	0.39	0.41

to support the diffusion and use of the Internet – we can see a common upward trend which, however, does not affect relations between the various states. Thus Denmark, for example, reached the 0.49 mark, whilst Romania and Bulgaria still failed to pass above 0.10. Countries such as Hungary, Lithuania and Latvia, on the other hand, proved to be more dynamic, with values increasing by 8, 8 and 9 points, respectively. It is interesting to note that, again, there are states such as Italy and Malta which show a static performance and, in fact, even a slightly downward trend: the former decreased from 0.24 to 0.22, whilst the latter remained stable at 0.25.

In 2009, the year in which the EU27 registered a 13-point increase with respect to the starting year, many past trends remained constant: the northern European states, with Denmark in the lead, continue to show positive and constantly rising values; states close behind are Germany and the UK, attesting to the effectiveness of the structural investment and other policies; among the states lagging behind in the diffusion and support of digital inclusion are again those of eastern Europe, together with other countries from southern Europe (Greece, Portugal and Italy).

An effective summary of the main trends can be obtained by grouping countries[1] into clusters based on EDDI results achieved (Table 3.4). In the first instance, we can see a large gap between group 1 and group 4: in 2004, the gap stood at 28 points and, rather than decreasing, it even reached 29 points in 2009. This clearly suggests that there are various 'Europes' progressing toward the construction of the information society at differing, and hardly comparable, paces, which remain constant over time. Still more evidence of such a pace difference can be found in the gap separating the values registered in the groups under analysis from the average values: group 4 remains stable at 12–13 points below average, whilst group 1 maintains a 16-point lead over it. To sum up briefly, despite the gradually increasing EDDI values in Europe, there are countries which are still facing great difficulties in promoting digital inclusion.

By taking a closer look at the performance of individual clusters and states, we can see how each of these has progressed, regressed or strengthened its position in terms of ICT take-up and interpretation. Notably, the northern European states have strengthened their position and continue to represent the 'hard core' of group 1, that is, the cluster representing 'excellence' in European ICT usage. On the other hand, the fact that they have maintained their position in this group for so long hardly comes as a surprise, given the numerous integrated national ICT strategies that they have developed and implemented over the years. Their extended presence in group 1, therefore, is the natural consequence of the major financial and cultural investments that were made over the years.

Germany and the UK, on the other hand, show a fluctuating performance, constantly gravitating toward group 2. In 2004 Germany held a position in the excellence group, but in 2009 it was replaced by the UK and took the latter's position in group 2. This situation appears to be the result of a more aggressive policy on the Lisbon ambition for a dynamic, knowledge-based society, as stated by the Digital Britain strategy.

Group 2 comprises well-performing countries, although slightly underperforming those of group 1. The latter countries, in fact, constantly

Table 3.4 The EDDI in groups of countries

Year	Group 1	Group 2	Group 3	Group 4
2009 **EU27 = 0.36** **EU15 = 0.41**	Denmark, Sweden, Luxembourg, UK, Netherlands, Finland **x̄ = 0.52** **σ = 0.03**	Germany, France, Estonia, Austria, Belgium, Ireland, Slovenia **x̄ = 0.39** **σ = 0.03**	Malta, Spain, Lithuania, Latvia, Slovakia, Hungary, Czech Rep **x̄ = 0.32** **σ = 0.02**	Italy, Cyprus, Poland, Portugal, Greece, Bulgaria, Romania **x̄ = 0.23** **σ = 0.05**
2008 **EU27 = 0.34** **EU15 = 0.39**	Denmark, Sweden, Netherlands, Finland, Germany, Luxembourg **x̄ = 0.50** **σ = 0.04**	UK, France, Austria, Belgium, Estonia, Ireland, Slovenia **x̄ = 0.37** **σ = 0.03**	Malta, Spain, Latvia, Hungary, Slovakia, Lithuania, Portugal **x̄ = 0.30** **σ = 0.02**	Czech Rep, Poland, Italy, Cyprus, Greece, Bulgaria, Romania **x̄ = 0.21** **σ = 0.05**
2007 **EU27 = 0.31** **EU15 = 0.37**	Denmark, Sweden, Netherlands, Finland, Germany, Luxembourg **x̄ = 0.48** **σ = 0.04**	UK, Austria, Belgium, France, Estonia, Ireland, Slovenia **x̄ = 0.35** **σ = 0.04**	Spain, Malta, Latvia, Hungary, Lithuania, Slovakia **x̄ = 0.26** **σ = 0.02**	Italy, Portugal, Czech Rep, Cyprus, Poland, Greece, Bulgaria, Romania **x̄ = 0.18** **σ = 0.05**

2006 **EU27 = 0.28** **EU15 = 0.35**	Denmark, Sweden, Netherlands, Finland, Germany, Luxembourg $\bar{x}$ **= 0.45** **σ = 0.04**	UK, France, Austria Belgium, Estonia, Slovenia, Ireland $\bar{x}$ **= 0.33** **σ = 0.04**	Spain, Malta, Italy, Hungary, Latvia $\bar{x}$ **= 0.24** **σ = 0.02**	Lithuania, Slovakia, Czech Rep, Portugal, Cyprus, Poland, Greece, Bulgaria, Romania $\bar{x}$ **= 0.17** **σ = 0.05**
2005 **EU27 = 0.25** **EU15 = 0.32**	Denmark, Sweden, Netherlands, Luxembourg, Finland, UK $\bar{x}$ **= 0.42** **σ = 0.04**	Germany, Belgium, France, Austria, Estonia, Malta, Slovenia, Spain $\bar{x}$ **= 0.28** **σ = 0.04**	Ireland, Italy, Slovakia, Portugal $\bar{x}$ **= 0.20** **σ = 0.02**	Cyprus, Hungary, Latvia, Czech Rep, Lithuania, Poland, Greece, Bulgaria, Romania $\bar{x}$ **= 0.13** **σ = 0.04**
2004 **EU27=0.23** **EU15 = 0.29**	Denmark, Sweden, Netherlands, Finland, Germany, Luxembourg $\bar{x}$ **= 0.39** **σ = 0.04**	UK, Belgium, Austria, France, Estonia, Malta, Italy $\bar{x}$ **= 0.27** **σ =0.03**	Spain, Ireland, Slovenia, Cyprus, Slovakia, Portugal $\bar{x}$ **= 0.19** **σ = 0.02**	Czech Rep, Latvia, Hungary, Lithuania, Poland, Greece, Bulgaria, Romania $\bar{x}$ **= 0.11** **σ = 0.04**

performed above the European average, albeit narrowly, and maintained a 16-point lead over group 4. Group 2 comprises countries with a good technological infrastructure, a good level of ICT usage, a widespread awareness of the importance of digital skills as a result of focused policies and a good provision of e-public services. The position held by Estonia and Slovenia in the same group shows the relevance of the initiatives undertaken through national policy making, albeit with some structural delays vis-à-vis infrastructure. Also worthy of note is Italy's and Malta's demotion from the group 2, to stable positions in groups 4 and 3, respectively.

Spain, Slovakia, Hungary, Lithuania, the Czech Republic and Latvia, on the other hand, are positioned with Malta in group 3, constantly performing slightly below the EU27 benchmark (with a 4- to 5- point difference). With the exception of Malta, all these countries share a medium-low quality infrastructure, as well as a medium-low level of diffusion and ability to use the Internet. Overall, the situation in the group is characterized by a slowly strengthening Internet usage dimension owing to the lack of significant accelerating pressures.

Finally, group 4 comprises several countries with an 'historical' delay in promoting universal digital literacy: among these are Bulgaria, Romania, Poland, Greece, and Portugal. Constantly underperforming the EU27 average benchmark, with scores as low as half the average at times, these countries have to make up for a backward infrastructure and a slow Internet diffusion and usage, which is such as to hinder real empowerment of individuals. Their position in this group is by no means surprising, but the case of Italy is. This country, which once fluctuated between groups 2 and 3, dropped to group 4 where it has maintained a stable position since 2007. This trend appears all the more peculiar if we bear in mind that the years in which Italy's position 'stabilized' downwards are the same years in which greater attention and resources were extended to broadband connectivity. The past infrastructural delay (see Chapter 2), combined with the present delay in Internet take-up and usage by the population, create a situation of inertia extended over time.

An effective visual summary of the general picture in Europe is provided by Figures 3.3 and 3.4, showing the various positions assigned to Member States in the four different clusters. The maps show that digital inclusion was unevenly distributed in 2004 and that it continues to be so in 2009. We see, on the one hand, the rapidly increasing digital inclusion of the vast majority of the population of northern Europe and, on the other hand, southern Europe, with ramifications extending to eastern Europe, struggling to create an information society that should generate wealth and individual and collective development.

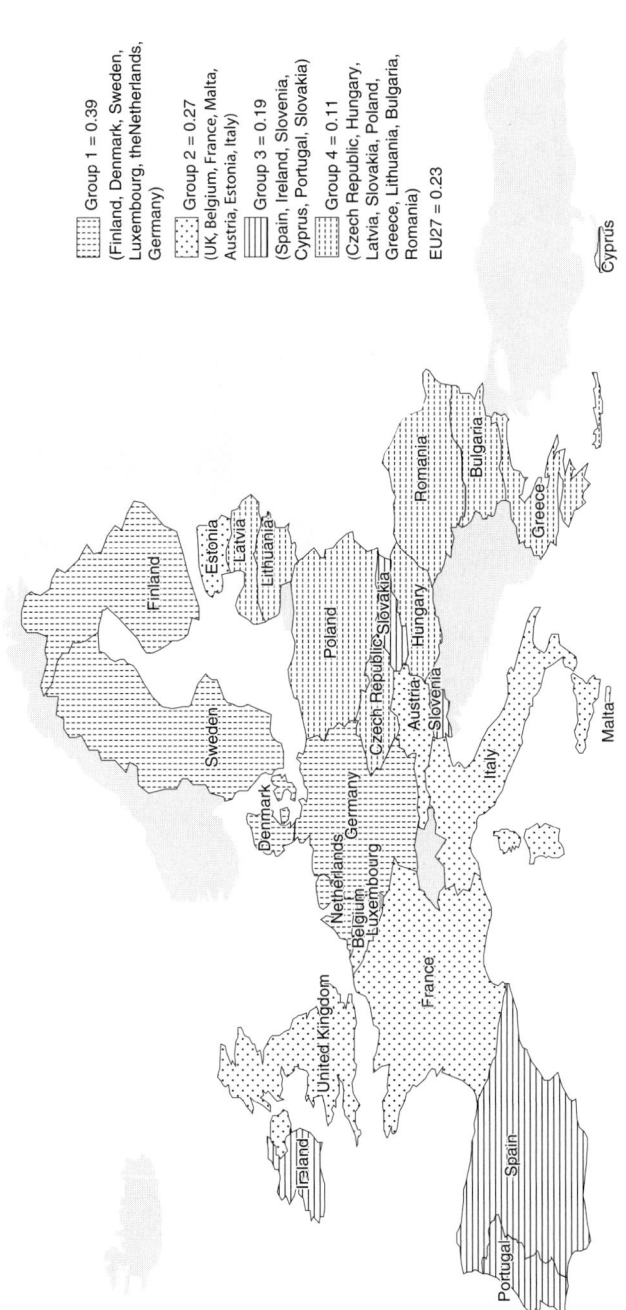

Group 1 = 0.39
(Finland, Denmark, Sweden, Luxembourg, theNetherlands, Germany)

Group 2 = 0.27
(UK, Belgium, France, Malta, Austria, Estonia, Italy)

Group 3 = 0.19
(Spain, Ireland, Slovenia, Cyprus, Portugal, Slovakia)

Group 4 = 0.11
(Czech Republic, Hungary, Latvia, Slovakia, Poland, Greece, Lithuania, Bulgaria, Romania)

EU27 = 0.23

Figure 3.3   EDDI in Europe (2004)

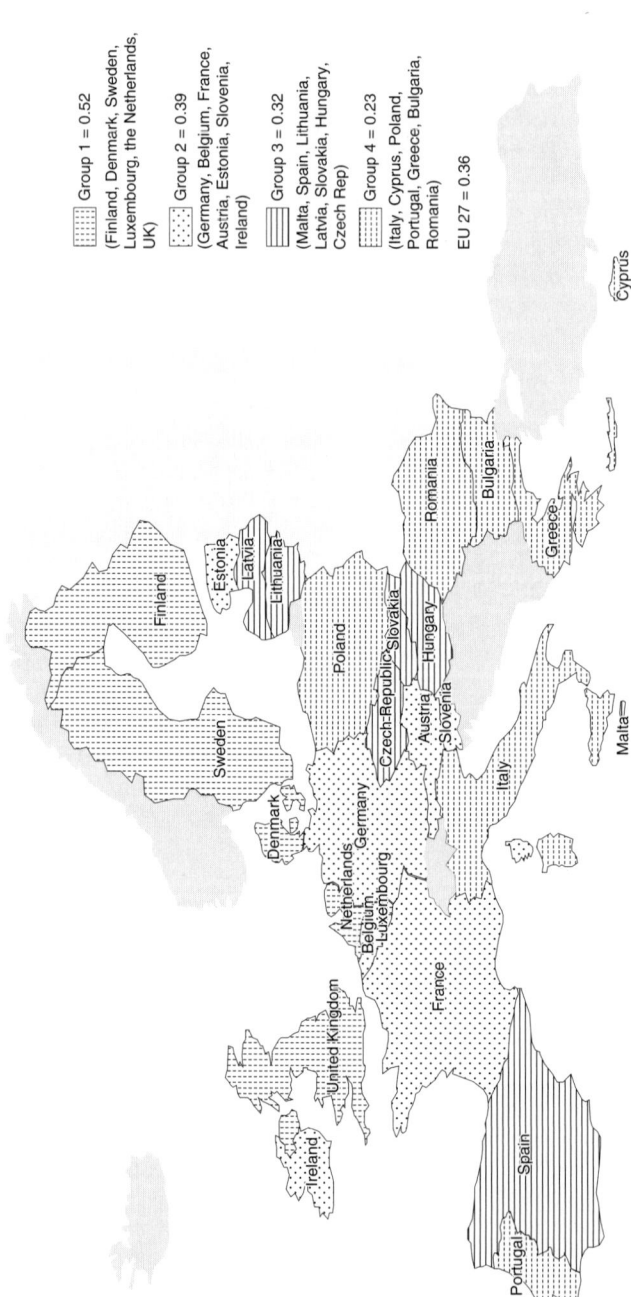

Group 1 = 0.52
(Finland, Denmark, Sweden, Luxembourg, the Netherlands, UK)

Group 2 = 0.39
(Germany, Belgium, France, Austria, Estonia, Slovenia, Ireland)

Group 3 = 0.32
(Malta, Spain, Lithuania, Latvia, Slovakia, Hungary, Czech Rep)

Group 4 = 0.23
(Italy, Cyprus, Poland, Portugal, Greece, Bulgaria, Romania)

EU 27 = 0.36

Figure 3.4   EDDI in Europe (2009)

3.3 THE COMPOSITION OF EDDI

The digital development index values shown above are the combined contribution of the three dimensions and numerous subdimensions used. In order to measure and evaluate the weight of each of them, and to highlight the changes that have occurred over time, we have conducted a regression analysis (Table 3.5).

Building on the analysis of the 2004 data, it can be seen that the usage dimension, again structured into autonomy, intensity and ability to use, had the greatest weight. The value with the second greatest weight in constructing the index was infrastructure. Finally, of much lesser weight was the impact dimension, that is, the area monitoring transformations in people's daily lives. This breakdown of the weight of each dimension indicates an enlargement of the catchment area of Internet take-up, combined with the technology appropriation process implemented in the presence of autonomy of use, intensity of use and skills development. In brief, the picture that emerges emphasizes diffusion and ability to use rather than a transformation in the management of a substantial package of activities. It is no coincidence that the dimension with the second greatest weight in determining the 2004 index value is that of infrastructure.

The subsequent year shows the contribution that was made by the dimensions with lesser weight. This is a year of transition, paving the way for 2006, when broadband connectivity was more widely distributed and the effects of EC Community and Member States' action plans were felt. It was in 2006 that the infrastructure dimension reached its peak, thus contributing to the construction of EDDI with a value of .412. Broadband penetration in the EU27 increased from 0.09 to 0.13, and, in the EU15, from 0.13 to 0.18. A similar trend was registered for broadband connectivity: from 0.21 to 0.29 in the EU27, and from 0.28 to 0.37 in the EU15. To sum up, all data support the view that 2006 was the year that witnessed the establishment of technological infrastructures in Europe.

Table 3.5   Regression results for EDDI (standardized beta coefficients)

	2004	2005	2006	2007	2008	2009
Infrastructure	.301	.290	.412	.280	.265	.268
Usage	.458	.452	.404	.416	.432	.436
Impact	.271	.281	.193	.323	.332	.317

Notes:
Dependent variable: EDDI.
Standard Error = 0.000.

Table 3.6   Regression analysis for EDDI (2009)

	Unstandardized coefficients		Standard coefficients		
	B	SE	Beta	t	Significance
(Constant)	.005	.008		.588	.563
Economic area	.151	.026	.206	5.743	.000
Skills	.152	.014	.166	10.515	.000
Availability	.223	.029	.240	7.812	.000
Cuture, communication	.146	.023	.130	6.386	.000
Affordability	.145	.023	.085	6.217	.000
Intensity	.132	.024	.173	5.605	.000

The year 2007, on the other hand, was an inflection point in the perform-ance of infrastructure: although still registering a high value, it fell signifi-cantly with respect to usage and impact. These two latter dimensions, in fact, assume a fundamental role, confirming the increasing relevance that they are to acquire over time. It is no coincidence that, in 2008 and 2009, the greatest contribution to the index and its construction came from the impact and usage dimensions. The new balance thus established between the various dimensions was the result of a strengthened infrastructure – accomplished over the previous years – and of the significant increase in the number of subjects using the Internet to carry out the activities that make up people's daily lives. The consequences of the individual and collective empowerment processes, that is, the identifying number of the information society, became increasingly evident and tangible.

A stepwise regression for 2009 certainly confirms this fundamental role (Table 3.6). Before identifying the contribution of the predictor variables, we should bear in mind that such a model accounts for 99.9 per cent of the variation in EDDI values. The picture that emerges from an analysis of the values relating to the contribution made by individual variables clearly shows the composite nature of digitalization processes in contemporary societies.

The first variable used to explain EDDI is that related to the economic area, that is, activities such as e-banking, e-commerce and e-travel (under-stood as the acquisition of travel services), which afford large savings in terms of both time and costs. In the light of the impact data analysed, it is no surprise that the first variable to be used in the model is the economic one: the economic subdimension registered the largest growth, attesting to its central role in people's daily lives. The second variable used to explain

EDDI is the ability to use the Internet and, hence, indirectly, the ability to carry out any activities on the web. In brief, this is further evidence of the new frontiers of the digital divide issue: whether the actual effective use of ICT – the second digital divide – or the performance of various activities – digital use divide. The third variable used in the model, on the other hand, is related to the availability and quality of connection, which is increasingly associated to broadband. This variable, relating to existing and available technological infrastructure, is in some ways a prerequisite for implementing the digital inclusion process. With respect to content, on the other hand, another applicable variable is that related to cultural, communication and recreational activities, a true cross-sectional area common to both young people and adults (albeit with the aid of various communication means), including individuals who make instrumental use of ICT (reading the newspaper) and those in search of new expressive spaces (managing a blog, creating video content, and so on). Lastly, other variables used in the model are those related to affordability and intensity of use – with varying weight – attesting to the entry of ICT into people's daily lives in terms of both costs and time dedicated to these.

The model thus obtained summarizes some of the major acquisitions developed with regards to the diffusion and new technology appropriation processes, highlighting that:

1. technological infrastructures have played an important role over the years, in a period that witnessed the gradual and increasing enlargement of the catchment area of Internet users; in particular, until the establishment of broadband connectivity, this dimension had a determining influence;
2. the establishment of broadband connectivity was accompanied by a significant improvement in the methods adopted to use the Internet: autonomy and intensity of connection combined with the acquisition of skills necessary to carry out a multitude of online activities;
3. starting from 2007, the dimension of impact – and, more specifically, that associated to the economic area – gained new ground and became a major contributor to the construction of the EDDI.

3.4   THE MULTIDIMENSIONAL NATURE OF EDDI

Having examined the contribution of individual dimensions in the construction of EDDI through the regression analysis, we now pay attention to the multidimensional nature of the same index in relation to individual countries, by taking a closer look at the performance of the three

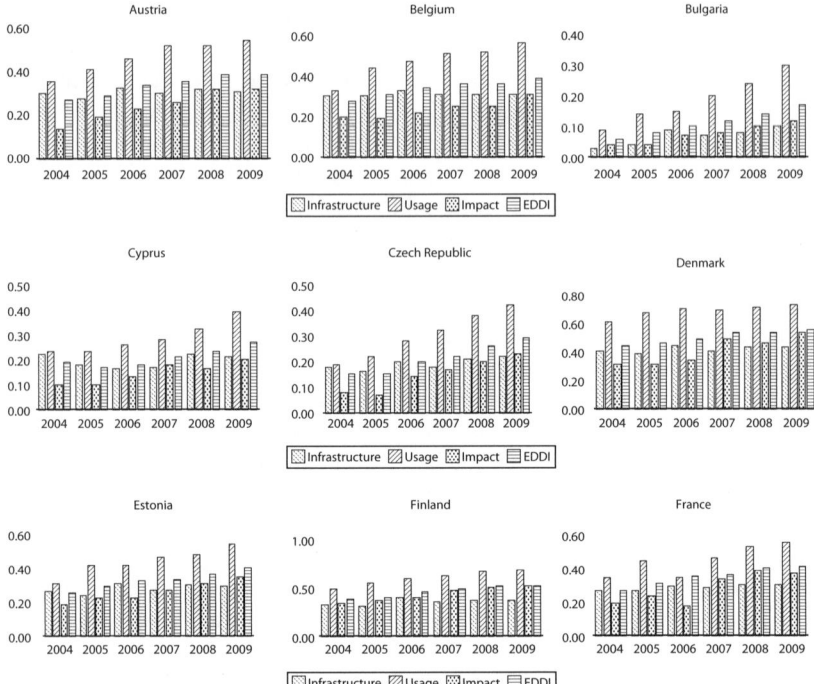

Figure 3.5   Average values of EDDI, infrastructure, usage and impact indexes for EU27 countries (2004–09)

dimensions over time and in the various countries. This diachronic and comparative analysis constitutes the very nature of the index proposed here. Such an interpretative approach makes it possible to identify not only the overall performance of a given country – an increase in the EDDI value, for instance – but also the dimension which most or least contributed to achieving its result.

Figure 3.5 shows the contribution of each dimension and the evolution of all the dimensions over the time. For each European Member State it is possible to find out the EDDI internal composition and its transformation. This index disaggregation is very useful for identifying the dimensions that need specific policies oriented to sustaining the country's digitalization.

Another interpretation of EDDI values is shown Table 3.7: in this case, we can see that 14 countries obtained an EDDI value above the European average (the Czech Republic, Estonia, Finland, France, Hungary, Ireland, Latvia, Lithuania, Luxembourg, the Netherlands, Poland, Slovakia, Slovenia and the UK). Within this group, the five countries that show the

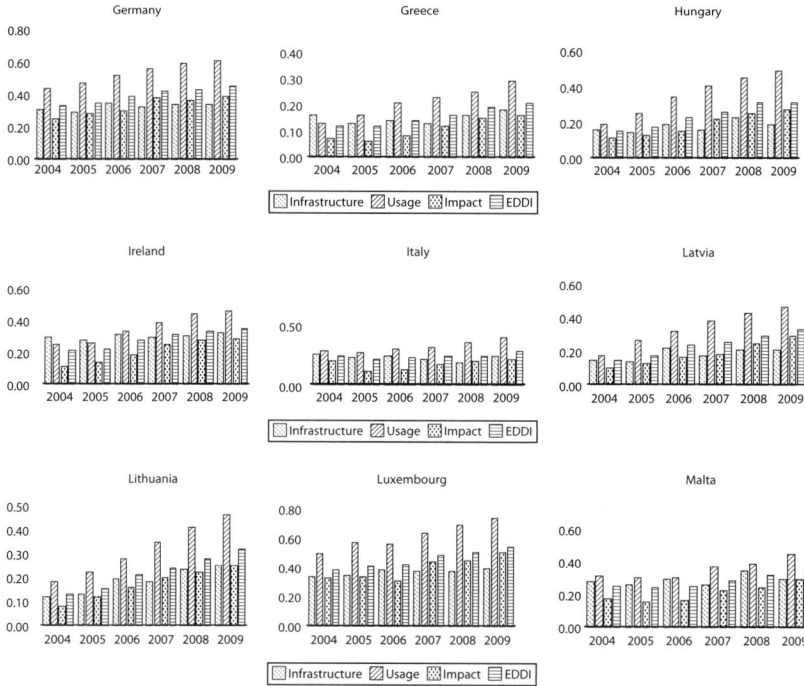

Figure 3.5 (continued)

highest changes in values are Lithuania, Latvia, Hungary, Estonia and the Netherlands. If we look more closely at the values for each country, we find that the changes are not uniform: Lithuania and Latvia show a 6-point increase in technological infrastructure, the Netherlands 4 points and Estonia and Hungary 3 points. As regards the usage values, the biggest changes are shown by Hungary (0.30), Latvia (0.29), and Lithuania (0.28). The Netherlands and Estonia both achieved a positive but more moderate result (0.23). Finally, regarding impact values, the five countries showed an increase in the range of 0.16 to 0.19.

In all these cases the achieved values were above the European average, and confirm a truly excellent performance. In particular, an infrastructure value that far exceeds the European average (6 points versus 3) shows that there has been a significant acceleration in this dimension, attesting to the development of focused policies in infrastructure provision to achieve complete coverage of the population (recently, especially, in relation to broadband). Investing in technological infrastructure is a must for all those countries that have yet to develop one, and which have registered

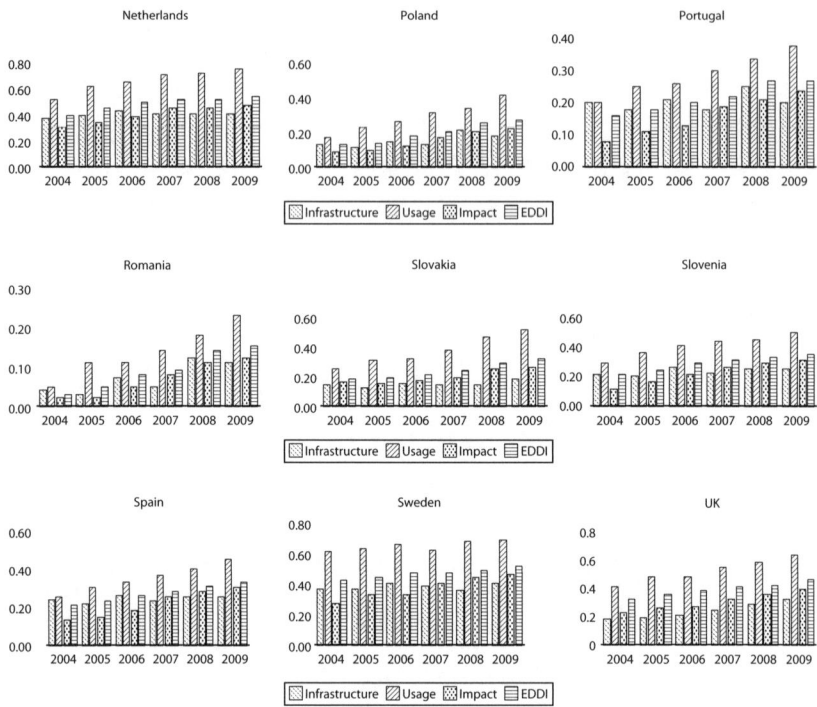

Figure 3.5   (continued)

a delay in the computerization of society. It is no coincidence that most of the greatest increase in the infrastructure dimension was registered in countries with a 'structural' weakness in ICT (Bulgaria, Romania, Poland, Latvia, and Lithuania).

On further perusal of the table, we can see for example that Poland also registered increases in the dimensions of usage (24 points) and impact (13 points). This 'internal' structure of the increase of EDDI (equal to 14 points) reveals a trend towards the strengthening of the technological infrastructure, the enlargement of the catchment area, greater intensity/ability to use the Internet and, to a lesser extent, the implementation of individual and collective empowerment processes resulting from the use of ICT. This 'internal' structure is counterbalanced by Denmark, which registered a particularly high value in EDDI growth (11 points), but also a 22-point increase in the impact dimension.

In a nutshell, this means that when a certain threshold is reached in technological infrastructure development and in the diffusion of usage and skills among the population, the new frontier for digitalization is the

Table 3.7 Change in values of EDDI, infrastructure, usage and impact (2004–09)

	Change in values of EDDI 2004–09	Change in values of infrastructure 2004–09	Change in values of usage 2004–09	Change in values of impact 2004–09
Austria	0.12	0.01	0.19	0.18
Belgium	0.11	0.01	0.23	0.11
Bulgaria	0.11	0.07	0.21	0.08
Cyprus	0.08	−0.01	0.16	0.10
Czech Republic	0.14	0.04	0.23	0.15
Denmark	0.11	0.03	0.12	0.22
Estonia	0.15	0.03	0.23	0.19
Finland	0.14	0.04	0.19	0.18
France	0.14	0.03	0.21	0.18
Germany	0.12	0.03	0.17	0.14
Greece	0.09	0.02	0.16	0.11
Hungary	0.16	0.03	0.30	0.16
Ireland	0.14	0.03	0.22	0.17
Italy	0.04	−0.02	0.11	0.02
Latvia	0.18	0.06	0.29	0.19
Lithuania	0.19	0.06	0.28	0.17
Luxembourg	0.16	0.06	0.25	0.18
Malta	0.09	−0.02	0.14	0.12
Netherlands	0.15	0.04	0.23	0.17
Poland	0.14	0.06	0.24	0.13
Portugal	0.11	0.00	0.18	0.16
Romania	0.12	0.07	0.18	0.10
Slovakia	0.14	0.04	0.27	0.10
Slovenia	0.14	0.04	0.21	0.19
Spain	0.12	−0.01	0.20	0.17
Sweden	0.10	0.03	0.08	0.19
United Kingdom	0.14	0.02	0.23	0.17
EU27	0.13	0.03	0.21	0.15
EU15	0.12	0.02	0.16	0.15

online performance of all those activities which make up people's daily lives. In countries such as Denmark, Finland, Luxembourg, Sweden and the Netherlands, the impact dimension is the only one to register high values, owing to the ever-greater range of services available and the willingness of citizens to use them.

NOTE

1. For each year, four groups of countries have been aggregated on the basis of the score
    obtained in relation to the EDDI. After ranking the countries in a decreasing order, three
    quartiles have been calculated to construct four groups. The first quartile divides the first
    25% of the distribution from the remaining 75%; the second quartile divides the distribu-
    tion into two equal parts; the third quartile divides the 75% of the distribution from the
    last 25%. Therefore, in the first group there are 25% of the countries with the highest
    values of the EDDI Index; in the second there are the following 25% of the countries with
    middle-high values; in the third there are 25% of the countries with middle-low values;
    in the fourth group there are the countries with the lowest values of the distribution.
    Finally, the arithmetic mean and standard deviation have been calculated inside each
    group.

4. Digital inequalities in Europe

4.1 OLD AND NEW FORMS OF DIGITAL INEQUALITIES

Although digital inclusion is proceeding all over Europe – even if not to the same extent – we are still far away from the knowledge-based economy and society hypothesized by the Lisbon conference. To hasten the realization of the concept and to recover the damage caused by the economic crisis that wiped out years of economic and social progress in Europe, the main principles of the Europe 2020 Strategy (CEC, 2010a) were launched by the European Commission in March 2010. Within the seven flagship initiatives of the Europe 2020 Strategy, the Digital Agenda for Europe's objective is to

> chart a course to maximize the social and economic potential of ICT, most notably the internet, a vital medium of economic and societal activity: for doing business, working, playing, communicating and expressing ourselves freely. Successful delivery of this Agenda will spur innovation, economic growth and improvements in daily life for both citizens and businesses. (CEC, 2010b, p. 3)

However, in order to ensure economic growth and significant improvement in the daily life of citizens it is vital that digital inclusion proceeds without establishing new forms of marginalization and exclusion. Unfortunately, data on the state of digitalization in Europe clearly show a scenario where 'high-performing' states, where a high percentage of people are digitally included, such as Denmark, Finland, the Netherlands, and Sweden, coexist with 'low-performing' states, where the majority of people are digitally excluded (Bulgaria, Greece, Poland, Portugal, and Romania). This kind of inequality not only prevents economic growth in parts of Europe but is often accompanied by an internal inequality among the different groups of people in the individual states.

This new form of exclusion manifests itself not only in technology, as has been convincingly stated, but in the sociological environment as well (Witte and Mannon, 2010). It is claimed that 'the digital divide is not a technological problem, but a social problem and the consequence of the underlying societal inequalities' (Fuchs, 2009). On the other hand, available empirical data confirm the existence of a link, showing how social indicators (the Gini coefficient, for example) have a significant role in explaining eventual digital exclusion (ibid.). For other scholars, the digital divide is a new form of social divide and represents only a small fraction of all the inequalities of social and economic development (Trémembert, 2010).

An approach that assures a strong and direct connection between social and digital exclusion takes into consideration the role of certain economic, social and cultural variables in determining the conditions of distance from the world of the Internet. One of the first variables considered is the generational one, which testifies to the significant distance of the 'silver generation'. Their outsider status appeared in the first monitorings of the composition of Internet users (Chen et al., 2002; Katz and Rice, 2002), so much so that it was called the 'gray gap' (Chen et al., 2002). Gender and educational variables also matter, as manifested in the following profile from the late 1990s: '[Internet users] are predominantly male (54 percent), over 30 (mean of 37 years), . . . have at least an undergraduate university education (58 percent), a full time job (59 percent)' (Chen et al., 2002, p. 86). In a nutshell, according to this profile, the typical Internet user was a youngish, well-educated and employed male.

Since the first profile outlined at the initial diffusion of the Internet, several significant changes have taken place: women gained ground while 'digital migrants' followed and imitated 'digital natives' to avoid the increase of distance between them. There is now more balance between the sexes and an advancement in favour of the older generation in the field of Internet usage. Despite these changes, technological appropriation is a phenomenon that still varies from one group to another in society. This diversity hinders the possibility of exploiting the advantage of digitalization in order to offer European citizens 'a better quality of life through, for example, better health-care, safer and more efficient transport solutions, cleaner environment, new media opportunities and easier access to public services and cultural content' (CEC, 2010b, p. 3)

Awareness of the costs connected to the varying acquisition of the Internet by the European population helps understanding of the 'rhythm' of the acquisition of technology by groups that potentially risk becoming digitally excluded. The Ministerial Declaration signed by the Ministers of the European Union in Riga on 11 June 2006 recognized that 'to convincingly address digital inclusion, the differences in Internet usage between current average use by the EU population and use by older people, people with disabilities, women, lower education groups, unemployed and "less-developed" regions should be reduced to a half, from 2005 to 2010' (Riga Ministerial Declaration, 2006, p. 3). The selection of groups taken as a basis for monitoring the diffusion of the Internet confirm a sociological interpretation that firmly links digital inequality to social inequality.

To support this approach, several groups have been selected for monitoring, to examine the functioning of the value of various indexes. The analysed groups are:

1. individuals aged from 55 to 64;
2. individuals aged from 65 to 74;
3. women;
4. individuals with no or low formal education;
5. unemployed individuals;
6. retirees and other economically inactive individuals;
7. individuals living in sparsely populated areas (less than 100 inhabitants/square km).

The reading of the values obtained from the so-called disadvantaged groups provides us with the possibility to particularize both the closing of the gaps that exist among the European population and, at the same time, the persistency of divides that threaten to become more and more structural.

4.2 DIGITAL USAGE DIVIDES

The objective of promoting a more inclusive information society implies that all individuals are to be given the possibility of gaining access to ICT. Data presented in the following pages give us a picture in which some are not well represented (Figure 4.1).

Looking first at Internet usage among older people, we immediately notice a huge negative difference between this group and the universe as a whole, which confirms that older citizens are consistently outsiders to the technological world. Despite this gap, however, in recent years the number of older people using the Internet rose. Data show a progressive growth in index values, which however remain below the European average for the group aged from 55 to 64; that is, the group poised between familiarization with technology, thanks to the fact that they are still employed, and their imminent retirement.

It is important to note that, in the case of the 'high-performing' group of countries, the index values for Internet diffusion and usage relating to the 55–64 age group are in fact higher than the European average. In this respect, we need only examine the data relating to the first year (2004) and the last year (2009) in the period considered: Denmark moves from

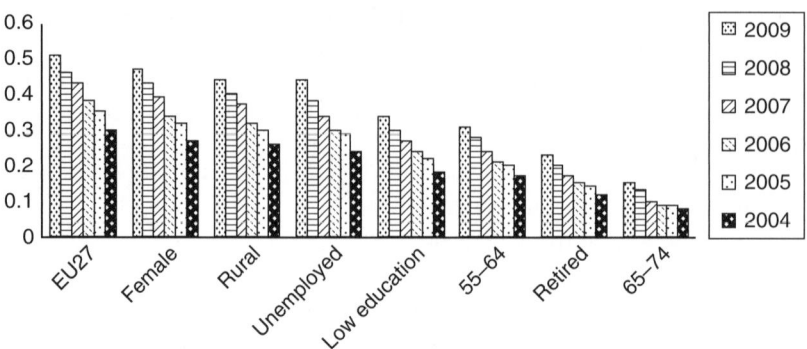

Note: * Groups according to the Riga definition: individuals aged from 55 to 64; individuals aged from 65 to 74; all women; individuals with no or low formal education; unemployed individuals; retirees and other economically inactive individuals; individuals living in sparsely populated areas.

Figure 4.1   Usage index in disadvantaged groups*

0.50 to 0.60, Finland from 0.36 to 0.49, the Netherlands from 0.38 to 0.63, Luxembourg from 0.30 to 0.63, and Sweden, finally, from 0.47 to 0.59. In addition to these cases of 'outstanding' performance, other countries performed above the European average: Germany (from 0.26 to 0.46), and the UK (0.27 to 0.53). Similarly to what occurs at European level, the countries ranking below average are still those of Eastern Europe, with the addition of Greece and Portugal. Finally, it is important to note that some countries have maintained a quasi 'stagnant' position over the course of several years, such as Italy, which moved from 0.14 to 0.22, and Malta, which fluctuated between 0.17 and 0.18.

In all countries, the final value of the usage index is greatly reduced by the low appropriation of skills. Even in technologically advanced and dynamic situations such as those characterizing the northern European countries, citizens in the 55–64 years age bracket registered low values. To sum up, in the usage subdimension, the lack of digital skills among citizens represents the 'ballast' preventing the index from registering much higher values.

With regards to the older age bracket, that is, from 65 to 74, which is more distant from the worlds of employment and technology, the index values indicate a gap of 22 points in 2004, 26 in 2005, 29 in 2006, 33 in 2007, 33 in 2008 and 36 in 2009. Over the course of time, the index values for this age bracket appear to be widening, rather than closing, the gap between this group and the average values. It follows that, in the European context, whilst the overall values of both Internet usage and diffusion increased in recent years, the older population is falling behind.

As in the younger age bracket, however, the lesser use of the Internet on the part of older people is not spread evenly across the various countries. On the contrary: there are countries that registered values in line with the European performance, and others which clearly underperformed the former cluster. On the other hand, one aspect which is common to all the countries examined is the deep gap between older people and the world of skills that are necessary to navigate on the Internet. An even wider gap in the older age category separates them from the skills necessary to make effective and profitable use of the web: compared to an average EU27 value of 0.46 in 2009, this age category registered a value of 0.12.

In summary, it can be stated that within the 55–64 age bracket we observe a positive trend that would suggest that the targeted intervention policies aimed at familiarizing individuals with the Internet – for those who still do not have access to the web – and at acquiring the skills necessary for a greater appropriation of the Internet – for those who already have a connection, have been very effective. Quite different is the situation concerning the 65–74 age bracket. The gap that exists between the average values point to a structural gap, at least starting from 2007. The data on the ageing of the European population and on its average life expectancy, which indicate a positive trend in Europeans belonging to this age bracket, impose the need to tackle the issue and find solutions which are fit to prevent the widening of the gap that separates older people from the rest of the population. In addition to the interventions implemented over the years, with the aim of improving and guaranteeing website accessibility at European level, there is a need to prepare plans designed to make the Internet 'appealing' to subjects who are culturally and technologically distant from that world. On the other hand, the good results obtained by a number of countries are raising hopes for the possibility of a significant widening of the Internet user base, and its use for the purpose of improving the daily life of individuals.

Proceeding with an analysis of the traditionally disadvantaged groups with respect to Internet diffusion and usage, it is interesting to note that women, who have been underrepresented in the Internet world for many years, performed nearly as well as the European average (Figure 4.2).

Over the course of the years considered in this research, women who use the Internet gained a position which, in 2009, was only four points away from the EU27 average: 0.47 versus 0.51. Countries which had an 'outstanding' performance were again those of northern Europe: Denmark (0.70), the Netherlands (0.70), Sweden (0.66),and Finland (0.54), with the addition of Luxembourg (0.66), UK (0.60) and Germany (0.55).

Some surprises emerge from a closer look at these data. If the women's group is disaggregated by age, it is possible to identify different trends. Taking as a reference the value achieved by the entire cluster of women

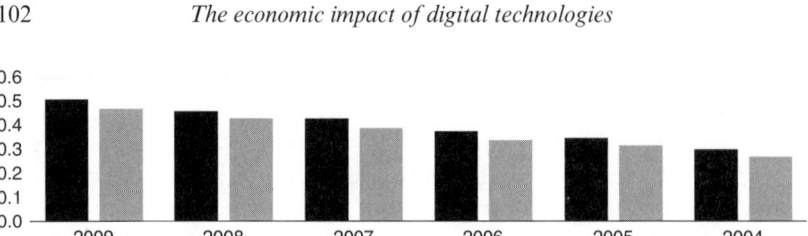

Figure 4.2   Usage index: women

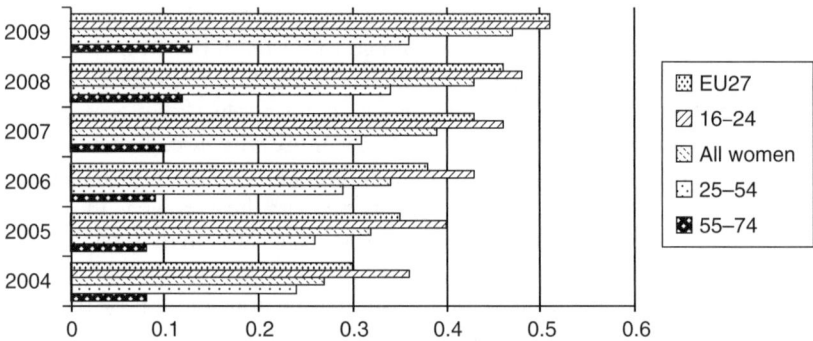

Figure 4.3   Usage index: women by age

and comparing it with that registered in the subcategories, we can see that the cluster of women aged between 16 and 24 years outperformed the average value and even the EU27 average. In 2004, the women's performance was in line with the EU27, namely 0.27 and 0.30 respectively, versus 0.36 for the group aged from 16 to 24 years; in 2009, compared to a value of 0.47 (female population) and 0.51 (total population), the same age group registered a value of 0.51. As we move up the age scale, the gap with the average values increasingly widens: in 2009, women aged between 25 and 54 years registered a 15-point gap with respect to the value registered by the total population, whilst women aged between 55 and 74 years underperformed the average value by as many as 34 points (Figure 4.3).

These data clearly show that the 'gender' variable in the use of the Internet needs to be reconsidered on account of the generational variable. Young women can be considered fully 'digital citizens' on a par with their male counterparts; adult and aged women, on the other hand, show once again that they are experiencing difficulties in appropriating the new technologies and in claiming their position. A third variable, that of education, could further contribute to enhance the different patterns that exist within

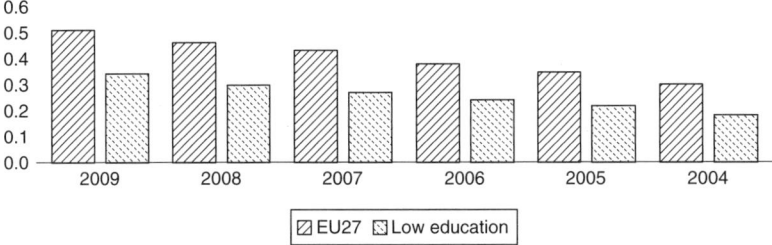

Figure 4.4   Usage index: individuals with low or no formal education

the female category. The generational variable, combined with the educational one, could very likely be the determining factors in the digital inclusion of women. Unfortunately, the Eurostat database does not provide sufficient data to disaggregate these variables further, and hence it is not possible to support this thesis with empirical evidence.

The group of subjects with low or no formal education[1] also showed a positive trend (Figure 4.4). In reality, this was only a partial improvement, given that the index continued to perform below the European average (in the EU27 in 2009, it was equal to 0.34). An increase from 0.18 in 2004 confirms a good technological dynamism.[2] At the same time, however, it is important to bear in mind that the gap with the European average value has increased rather than decreased over the years (4 points in 2005, 6 in 2006, 9 in 2007, 12 in 2008 and 17 in 2009), which confirms the difficulties encountered in keeping pace with the rest of the population. In this case too, disaggregation of the data by age shows interesting new aspects: in fact, the three age categories in which it is possible to disaggregate (16–24; 25–54; 55–74), show widely different values.

In the category of individuals aged from 16 to 24 years and having a low level of education, the usage index values are very close to those achieved by the population as a whole and much higher than those achieved by all individuals with a low level of education. This means that among young people – even though they have a basic education only – Internet usage and skills are common and widely distributed. This is not the case, however, for the older age groups. In fact, the pattern that emerges here shows that the higher the age bracket the less is the use of, and the ability to use, the Internet. In this case, we can assume that a low level of education in subjects belonging to the higher age brackets enhances the difficulties in their appropriation of the new technologies. In a young population, on the other hand, the difficulties connected with a low level of education are more easily circumvented and mitigated, thanks to participation in the numerous activities carried out on the web (downloading of music, downloading

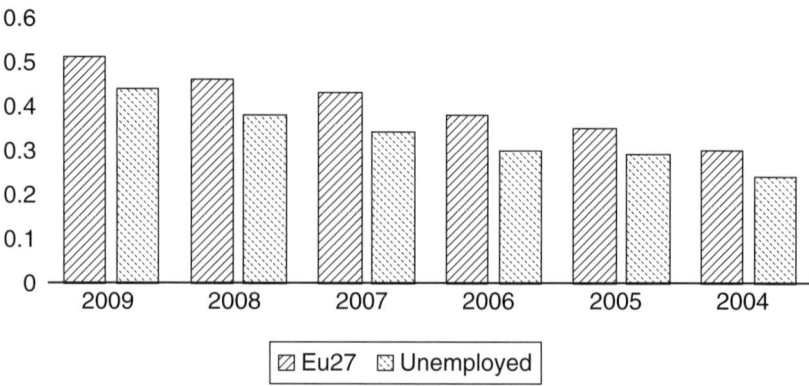

Figure 4.5   Usage index: unemployed

of films, videogames and so on). Furthermore, we should also consider the fact that many of the individuals included in this cluster are students, and hence, they are still undergoing an educational programme.

Conversely, individuals in the 'unemployed' group appear to be engaged in a slow but steady rise (Figure 4.5). Although the group's performance was not outstanding, it shows a gradual progression from a value of 0.24 in 2004 to 0.44 in 2009, with an annual increase of approximately 5 points. Such progress may be partially due to the presence in the group of a large number of young people, who face difficulties in entering the labour market; but this is only a hypothesis which requires separate data for each age bracket in order to be confirmed. It is self-evident that, should this hypothesis be confirmed, any provision aimed at developing professional skills, that is, at facilitating the search for employment, would act as a useful accelerator in the spread of Internet use.

Retired persons are definitely lagging behind: in 2004, the group's performance stood at 18 points below the EU27 average; in 2009, this gap had widened to 28 points (Figure 4.6). A comparison with EU15 values provides additional confirmation of the lagging behind of individuals who have retired from the labour market: in 2004, the gap stood at 21 points, in 2009, it had reached 25. It is evident that these data, together with those related to individuals aged between 65 and 74, confirm the difficult relationship that exists between older people and new technologies. It must be noted, however, that retired persons showed greater delays than those attributed to the group aged between 65 and 74. This difference is obviously attributable to the fact that the former group no longer has a place in the labour market, which is undeniably a driving force in the process of technological literacy for adult generations.

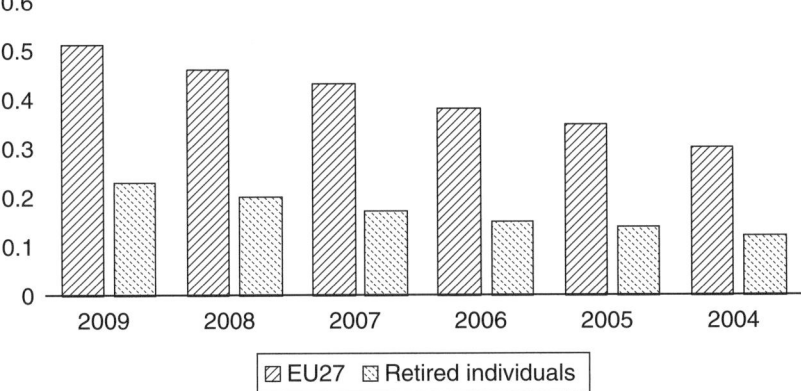

Figure 4.6   Usage index: retired

The last group of disadvantaged individuals considered in this paper is comprised of persons who live in sparsely populated areas (less than 100 inhabitants per square kilometre). This is the group that is most subject to the difficulties associated with poor technological infrastructures, with obvious consequences in terms of availability and quality of connection. The data show that the group is moving gradually closer to the European average: in 2009, for example, compared to the EU27 average of 0.51, the group's performance stood at 0.44. With respect to the average performance, however, large differences between countries clearly emerge: in 2008, Romania had a very low performance (0.13), as did Bulgaria (0.18), Greece (0.15), Cyprus (0.22), Portugal (0.29), Italy (0.34) and Poland (0.33). Not only are these values lower than the EU27 average, they are also lower than that of the group as a whole. As usual, the fact that Italy is among the countries that registered a large gap from the average group performance is alarming, and serves as the canary in the mine for the future of digital inclusion in the country.

In summary, from a reading of the usage index values in disadvantaged groups, in terms of digitalization development, the following considerations arise:

1. in more recent years, the women's group is close to the European average;
2. the position of the groups of individuals aged between 65 and 74 and of retired persons confirms major and long-lasting difficulties in the technological appropriation process, showing low performances and moderate increases compared to the European average;

3. the group of individuals aged between 55 and 64 shows a continuous growth pattern, although it still maintains a large gap as against the EU27 average;
4. the groups of subjects with low or no formal education and of the unemployed are still lagging far behind the European average, despite some improvements;
5. the group of individuals living in sparsely populated areas has recently had a very positive performance, ranking not far below the European average.

4.3 DIGITAL INEQUALITIES IN PERSONAL EMPOWERMENT: IMPACT INDEX

From the reading of the data above, major differences between the various European countries emerge, to the extent that we are once again reminded of the existence of multiple speeds, not only in the development of technological infrastructures but also in the use of the Internet. This new and, in fact, more insidious digital divide is felt even more deeply in traditionally disadvantaged groups, which, rather than benefiting from the new opportunities, are to various degrees being left out of the ongoing transformations. This may not be surprising, but in the light of the data examined above, its interpretation in empirical terms is striking, due to the width of the gaps that appear to exist.

Prior to delving further into an analysis of the individual groups, it is important to provide an overview of the impact index performance (Figure 4.7). The first detail that immediately captures our attention is the wide and constant gap separating the group of subjects aged between 65 and 74 years from the rest of the population. In contrast, women registered values which are close to the European average, confirming that they recovered ground over the course of recent years. Between these two extremes, we find – in decreasing order of impact index values – unemployed people, individuals living in sparsely populated areas, individuals aged from 55 to 64, individuals with no or low formal education, and retired people. The performances of the various groups in the index are very similar to those registered by the usage index: in both cases, women are positioned on the side closer to the European average, and individuals aged from 65 to 74 years are positioned farthest away from the average value. The other groups are distributed along the continuum in a similar way, thus confirming that there are different styles of Internet appropriation which can be found in the autonomy and ability to use the Internet as well as in its actual usage in daily life.

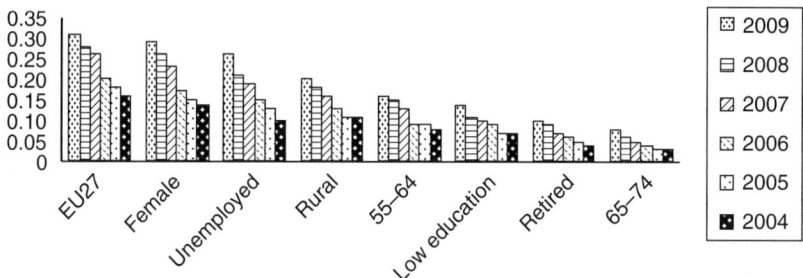

Note: * Groups according to the Riga definition: individuals aged from 55 to 64; individuals aged from 65 to 74; all women; individuals with no or low formal education; unemployed individuals; retirees and other economically inactive individuals; individuals living in sparsely populated areas.

*Figure 4.7   Impact index: disadvantaged groups**

A close look at the data related to the individual groups offers further elements for reflection. The data related to subjects aged between 55 and 64 years shows that, despite a constantly growing trend (about 2 points yearly), the group is unable to narrow the 15-point gap separating it from the EU27 average.

A careful examination of the rates achieved in each subdimension enables us to distinguish between the effect resulting from the subjects' stage in their lifecycle and that caused by the condition of not engaging with the Internet. Thus, a strong lack of interest in the opportunity to seek employment through the Internet on the part of already-employed individuals seems perfectly normal.[3] It is no coincidence that all the European countries, without particular exceptions, registered extremely low rates. In this case, the lifecycle effect clearly contributes to a strong and widespread lack of interest. The situation is not the same, however, in the case of the government subdimension, which is more relevant to adult subjects faced with complex and multi-form relations with public administrations. If we reconstruct retrospectively the diffusion of the management of such relations through the Internet on the part of the group of individuals aged between 55 and 64 years, we note that a 'progressive distancing' has occurred: in 2004, the divergence of the group's average performance from that of the EU27 was equal to 7 points, in 2006 it was 11 and, in 2009, 10. Rather than closing, the gap is gradually widening, and contributes to determining the overall impact index value. Another surprising element consists in the low performance shown by the economy subdimension. With a gap fluctuating between 7 and 10 points, the subjects included in this group show that they do not positively evaluate the benefits deriving from the online management of activities such as e-banking, the purchase of airline or railway tickets, or the trading of goods and services. However, it should be clarified that, unlike in the previous case of widespread low usage of e-government, we observe very different patterns: in 2009, for example, the value for the Netherlands stood at 0.40, that for Finland at 0.35, Sweden and Denmark at 0.40, Luxembourg at 0.40, the UK at 0.32 and Germany at 0.27. On the opposite side, the rates registered for Bulgaria and Romania stood at 0.1. Finally, limited interest is shown in the education, health and culture subdimensions. In all the cases, the divergence from the EU27 average fluctuated at around 15–20 points (2009), albeit with lower peak rates for the traditionally technologically advanced countries.

A case of even greater and more general divergence can be observed in the group of subjects aged between 65 and 74 years, with a gap as against the average performance which is constantly and gradually widening (from 13 points in 2004 to 23 in 2009). Among the disadvantaged groups, that of older people is positioned on an alternative trajectory to the main one, such as to preclude the possibility of a major recovery in the medium term. The rootedness of the condition of foreignness to technology proper to this group, an issue raised above with regard to the usage index, appears difficult to resolve with the traditional initiatives undertaken in recent years. In fact, the condition of 'digital foreigner', which is common to these subjects, appears so deeply rooted as to prevent the full benefits resulting from the adoption of technological practices in daily life from being achieved: from the acquisition of health information to the completion of bureaucratic procedures, from the management of online accounts to the reading of daily newspapers. Despite such difficulty, various interesting initiatives can be identified, albeit still limited and at the experimental stage, aimed at favouring ICT take-up by the aged. In Sweden, for example, the SeniorNet project was launched with the aim of diffusing new technologies among the aged by means of the following: creating a virtual community of older people interested in the potential of ICT as a service and communication instrument; launching and supporting the SeniorNet club as an ICT training centre; and setting up projects involving the aged.

Very similar values can be found in the group of retired people. The slightly higher rates (2 points in 2009) that distinguish this group from that of the older people are perhaps attributable to the opportunities for technological familiarization that were presented to them in the past, when they still had a place in the labour market. Nevertheless, this group is also positioned outside the main trajectory, suggesting that it will not recover in the medium term.

An opposite trend can be observed, on the other hand, in the women's group. With a very small gap (2 points) as against the EU27 average, as

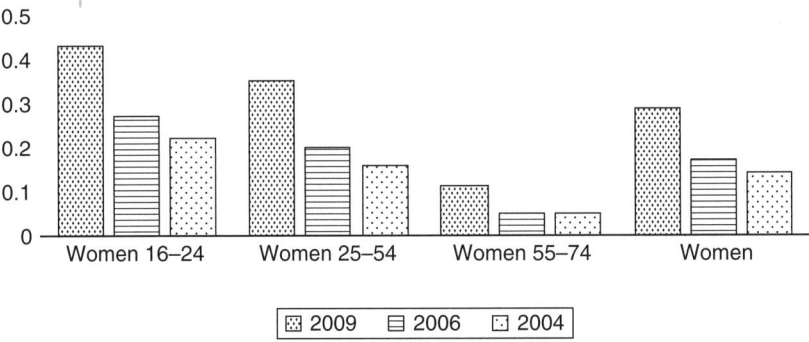

Figure 4.8   Impact index: women by age

we have already observed in the usage dimension, this group has qualified for promotion and is poised to leave the so-called disadvantaged groups. Its performance on the impact index, moreover, can be attributed to what is considered standard practice for all the subdimensions considered. Over the course of 2009, for example, women registered the same values as those obtained by the population as a whole in the education and government subdimensions, whilst they obtained nearly identical values in the economy and culture subdimensions. As regards the health subdimension, women performed even better that the overall rates (0.26 versus 0.20), perhaps because so many women are carers. Only in the labour subdimension did women register much lower rates than those achieved by the population as a whole (0.15 versus 0.27), indicating differences in the work patterns of women and men. In this case too, the disaggregation of the group into three age categories makes it possible to identify significant differences (Figure 4.8): in fact, young women are progressing at a faster pace than the EU27 average. In 2004, for example, women aged between 16 and 24 years registered a value of 0.22 versus the value of 0.16 in the EU27; in 2009, young women reached the 0.43 mark whilst the EU27 stopped at 0.31. Women in the next age category (25–54) are also progressing, albeit at a slower pace. In 2004, their performance was in line with that of the EU27 (0.16), but in 2009 they outperformed, albeit only slightly, the European value – 0.35 versus 0.31. Women aged 55 years and over performed differently: in this case, there is a large gap from both the female universe as a whole and the EU27.

If we then proceed to analyse the data related to the female group disaggregated by age in the individual subdimensions, new and interesting differences emerge. In this respect, there is almost a 'specialization' of uses, where young women are mainly engaged in activities related to the education, employment and culture/communication/recreation spheres, whilst older women appear to be more involved in activities related to the search for information on health, interaction with public administrations and the management of economic matters. In brief, the interests associated with the lifecycle clearly emerge: personal improvement and major attention to communicational and recreational activities in the early life span; instrumental use for the purpose of managing daily life in the adult age. This difference of interests, moreover, emerges from the first year examined and is strengthened over time. In the case of the economy sub-dimension, for example, since 2004 young women have registered lower values than those of older women (0.18 vs. 0.20) and this remains constant over time (in 2009, the values were equal to 0.36 and 0.39). Conversely, in the education subdimension, young women registered higher values, probably as a result of their stable position within the world of education. An interesting detail worthy of note relates to the subdimension of government: in 2006 and in 2009, women aged from 25 to 54 years outperformed the EU27 values: 0.29 versus 0.26 and 0.38 versus 0.32. This dramatic reversal of trend with respect to the male universe confirms the progressive appropriation of technology by women, including the traditionally male-dominated sphere of management of relations with public institutions. Lastly, and unfortunately, aged women are clearly excluded from the world of technology, with the partial exception in the case of activities related to the search for health information.

Generally speaking, a similar performance to that of women was observed in the group of unemployed persons: they showed a 16-point recovery over a six-year period and a 5-point gap as against the EU27 average in 2009. A precise analysis of the values in all subdimensions provides us with a very interesting picture. In the values related to 2009, for example, we observe a strong interest on the part of these individuals in using the Internet in a work context (0.41 vs. 0.27). Given the unemployed status of the subjects, it appears evident that the indicator which measures the employment-seeking activity through the Internet prevails. Moreover, we observe a fairly strong interest (0.34 vs. 0.25) in using the Internet for communication, recreational and cultural activities. All these factors contribute to outlining the profile of the unemployed as 'young' individuals, well familiarized with technology, and capable of utilizing it as a tool. This hypothesis, however, can only be confirmed by data on age bracket and employment status breakdown, which are presently not available.

On the other hand, a completely different situation is observed with regards to individuals with no or low education. With a gap fluctuating between 9 and 17 points – which, moreover, is expected to increase rather than decrease – these subjects testify to a great cultural distance from the world of technology. Such a distance prevents them from exploiting the educational opportunities presented by the web and, at the same time, from interacting with public administrations, carrying out business activities, and gaining access to the cultural and recreational facilities made available by the web. However, the disaggregation of data by age helps to identify significantly different lines of trend. Subjects aged from 16 to 24 years, for example, take up the educational opportunities offered by the Internet, to an even greater extent than the EU27 population as a whole: in 2004, this category registered a value of 0.14 vs. 0.07, in 2009 the value reached 0.49 vs. 0.37. For these subjects, the Internet offers a real opportunity to fill gaps and acquire additional knowledge and skills. On the other hand, it should be borne in mind that many of the individuals included in this category are 'students', that is, they are still a part of the educational institution. Their use of the Internet for educational purposes, therefore, is supplementary to the training programme. A completely different picture emerges, on the other hand, with respect to older subjects: in both the 25–54 year and the 55–74 year age categories, the values were far lower than those registered in the EU27 and in the population overall with a low level of education. Proceeding with the analysis of the subdimensions, young people in the group use the Internet to a large extent to search for information on health and, especially, to carry out communicational and recreational activities. Individuals belonging to the 25–54 year age bracket, on the other hand, outperformed, albeit only slightly, the younger generation in e-government procedures and trail closely behind the latter as regards economic and financial activities. Lastly, individuals belonging to the 55–74 years age bracket with a low level of education registered very low values with respect to all the subdimensions. For this cluster, the generational and educational variables are real 'predictors' of digital exclusion.

Lastly, the group of subjects living in sparsely populated areas continues to gain ground, showing a gap as against the EU27 average of approximately 7–10 points. In the analysis of the rates for the year 2009, first of all it is important to note the diffusion of economic activities carried out on the web by the subjects considered (0.21 vs. 0.25). Geographical and environmental constraints probably contribute to the adoption of these practices, which provide access to what would otherwise be inaccessible. The rates which measure the diffusion of the activities included in the health subdimension (0.27 vs. 0.32) point in the same direction. As usual, the countries showing the best performances are the Netherlands (0.42 for the economic subdimension, 0.38 for the government subdimension), Finland (0.43 and 0.34), and Denmark (0.43 and 0.46).

Following our analysis of the impact index values in the so-called dis-advantaged groups in terms of digital inclusion, we can summarize the existing situation as follows:

1. the group of women (especially the group of young women) is poised to leave the group of disadvantaged subjects in terms of digitalization;
2. the group of individuals aged between 55 and 64 years continues to recover slowly, although it is still performing far below the EU27 average;
3. the group of individuals aged between 65 and 74 years and that of retired subjects continue to experience great difficulties in gaining access to the digital world, although they show limited growth over time;
4. the group of subjects with no or low education has difficulties in utiliz-ing the Internet to complete specific activities, which is reflected in the modest growth measured over the course of the years;
5. the group of unemployed subjects, like that of women, gains ground on the EU27, with approximately a 2-point growth annually;
6. the group of individuals living in sparsely populated areas, finally, shows modest growth, which, however, brings it closer to the EU27 value.

4.4   BETWEEN DIGITAL INCLUSION AND DIGITAL EXCLUSION IN EUROPE

After the analysis of the usage and impact indexes in disadvantaged groups we can now consider the interpretation of the European Digital Development Index (EDDI). A close look at the data related to the indi-vidual groups offers further elements for reflection (Figure 4.9).

First, there are great inequalities among the population with respect to the generational variable: in the higher age brackets, the Internet's impact on people's daily lives gradually diminishes, thus annulling the benefits of all the numerous applications aimed at improving the quality of life and establishing self-sufficiency and constant control. In the age bracket from 65 to 74 years, for example, the EDDI value is constantly below European average and shows no sign of improvement: from 2004 to 2009, only a 7-point increase was registered (from 0.10 to 0.17) compared to an average European increase of 13 points. Thus, compared to an average EDDI value of 0.36 achieved in 2009, the 65 to 74 age bracket registered a value of 0.17, or approximately half. If, however, we analyse the performance of individual countries, we can see other elements of differentiation: in 2004,

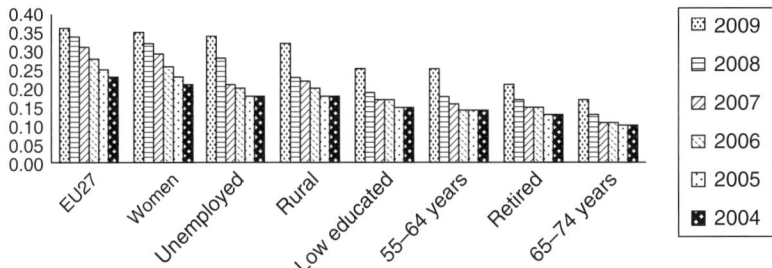

Figure 4.9   EDDI: disadvantaged groups

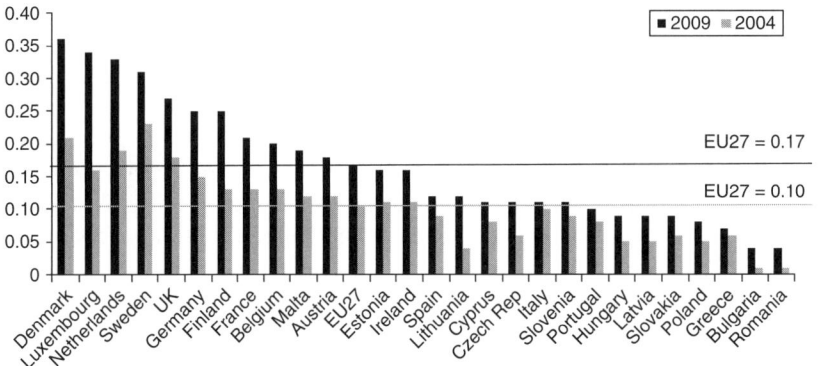

Figure 4.10   EDDI: 65–74 age group by country

for instance, when the average value was 0.10, some countries registered much higher values (Sweden 0.23; Denmark 0.21; the Netherlands 0.19; the UK 0.18), and others far lower values (Bulgaria and Romania 0.01; Poland and Hungary 0.05; Greece 0.06) (Figure 4.10).

After a five-year period, the situation does not appear any different: both the leading squadron (Sweden, Denmark, the Netherlands, Luxembourg, Finland, the UK and Germany), and the trailing group (Bulgaria, Romania, Greece, Latvia, Hungary) are still populated by the same countries. To sum up, the group of subjects aged between 65 and 74 years has progressed at a slower pace than the European population in some countries but not others.

If we compare these data with those related to the policies implemented by individual Member States, we can see that there is a positive relationship between best practices and high EDDI values in subjects aged between 65 and 74 years. Countries that have invested in lifelong and

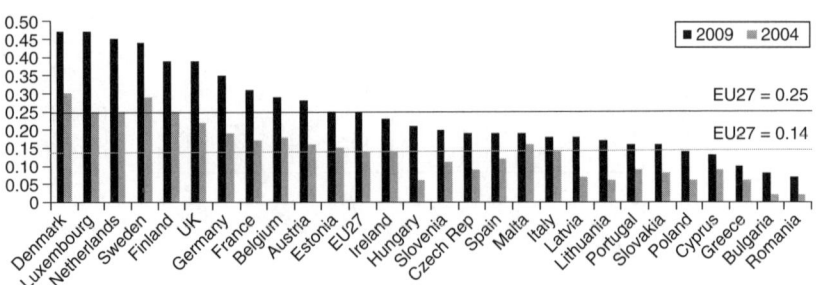

Figure 4.11   EDDI: 55–64 age group by country

regular re-skilling programmes have been able to widen their catchment area of aged people. Sweden's SeniorNet plan (www.seniornet.se) aims to support access to technologies, promote widespread technological literacy, improve the quality of life by creating virtual communities and ICT training centres, and foster technological innovation geared toward meeting the needs of the elderly. Several other countries have paid special attention to the needs of this particular population by setting up ad hoc interventions designed to speed up the process of technological literacy among the aged. Despite the cases of excellence that can be found, however, it may be stated that, in many European countries, subjects aged between 65 and 74 years live in a condition of 'double' disadvantage as a result of their personal status and geographical position.

Among the disadvantaged groups are also subjects aged between 55 and 64 years. Unlike the older group, this group has performed not very far below the average (0.25 versus 0.36 in 2009), and shows a positive upward trend. This 'better' performance can be ascribed to an increasing number of individuals aged between 55 and 64 who use the Internet to interact with public administration offices and conduct business activities. The picture that emerges from an analysis of the data shows that the subjects included in this age bracket use the Internet mainly as an instrument, which is in many ways typical of those who, as 'digital migrants', seize new opportunities to achieve goals. If we then compare the data for each country, we can see that the performance of a number of countries is in line with the European performance, whilst others are clearly lagging behind. By way of example, compare the values achieved in 2009 by Denmark and Luxembourg (0.47) and the Netherlands (0.45), with those achieved by Bulgaria (0.08), Romania (0.07) and Greece (0.10) (Figure 4.11).

The women's group, on the other hand, performs nearly as well as the European average: after years of lagging behind with a 2-point difference, in 2009 the gap finally narrowed to 1 point, suggesting that it may close

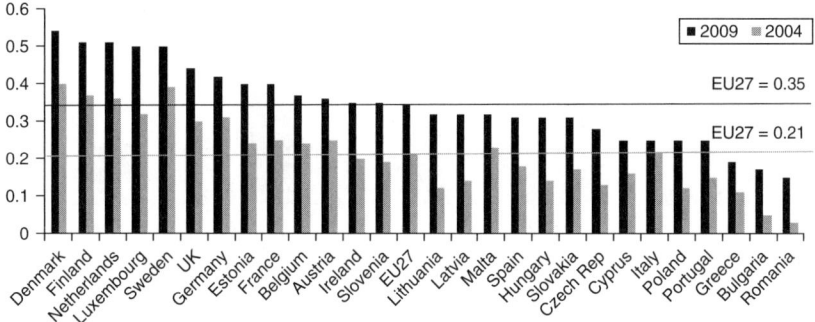

Figure 4.12   EDDI: women by country

in the near future. Similar signs emerged from the analysis of women's online activities, which showed a progressive decrease in the traditionally female specialization of personal care (Boneva and Kraut, 2002) and management of personal relations (Boneva and Kraut, 2002; Kennedy et al., 2003) in favour of the construction of a more varied mix comprising also instrumental and recreational, traditionally male-dominated sectors. Before we look at the barriers to equality of Internet appropriation, we should 'read' the EDDI value for each single country. As expected, there are still large differences characterizing women's relationship with the Internet: if, on the one hand, countries such as Denmark (0.54), Finland and the Netherlands (0.51), Luxembourg and Sweden (0.50) have produced noteworthy results, on the other hand, there are countries such as Romania (0.15), Bulgaria (0.17) and Greece (0.19) that are still far from bridging the gap (Figure 4.12).

If we analyse in greater detail the presence of women on the web, we can see further specifications. If, for example, we introduce the age variable, we see a very interesting breakdown of Internet usage by women: in 2009, young women, that is, those aged between 16 and 24 years, greatly overperformed the EDDI average in the EU27 as well as the women's overall value; adult women, aged between 25 and 54 years, on the other hand, registered slightly higher values than both the EU27 average and those related to the entire female universe, whilst women aged between 55 and 74 were the only ones to register much lower values (Figure 4.13).

This breakdown of the female group based on the generational variable establishes the distance that definitively separates the young women's group from the disadvantaged groups and sets them perfectly in line with the population as a whole. It is only in higher age groups that we find women among the disadvantaged groups, thus confirming the situation of

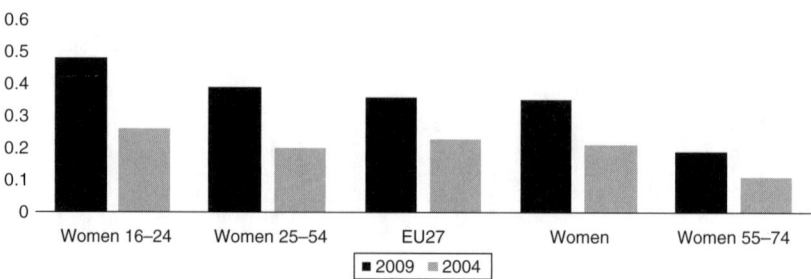

Figure 4.13 EDDI: women by age

social exclusion as the consequence, in numerous cases, of exclusion from the labour market (housewives and retired women) (Figure 4.13).

One last factor worthy of note is the breakdown of the group based on education level: women with a low level of education cannot keep pace with the Internet population as a whole. When such difficulties arise for women (especially in Romania, Bulgaria, Greece, Cyprus, Spain and Italy), the cause is likely to be found in a general situation of limited opportunities for women, which concerns the world of labour, education, culture and technology alike. In brief, women with a low level of education who live in these countries are practically cut out of the technology appropriation process, thereby falling into a vicious circle which perpetuates a pattern of female exclusion.

As regards the group of subjects with a low level of education, their performance indicates a slow but constant recovery after a longstanding gap. Over the six-year period analysed, the EDDI value increased from 0.15 to 0.25. This constant recovery does not suffice to bridge the gap which separates this group from the European average (0.25 versus 0.36 in 2009), but it is certainly an indication of an upward trend. As usual, we can see a number of irregular behaviours compared to the average: in Denmark, the index value exceeds the EU27 value (0.46 vs. 0.25), as in the case of Luxembourg (0.41), the Netherlands (0.41), Sweden (0.39), Finland (0.38) and Germany (0.36). Below-average performances include Bulgaria (0.08), Romania (0.08), Greece (0.10), Cyprus (0.13) and Italy (0.16) (Figure 4.14).

Due to the lack of data structured by age groups, no further analyses can be conducted, as much as that would be desirable to give us a better understanding of the weight that the education variable has on technological literacy and on the overall use of ICT. It is very likely that the group gained ground thanks to young people, who, although they lack formal education, appropriate technology by participating in communities of

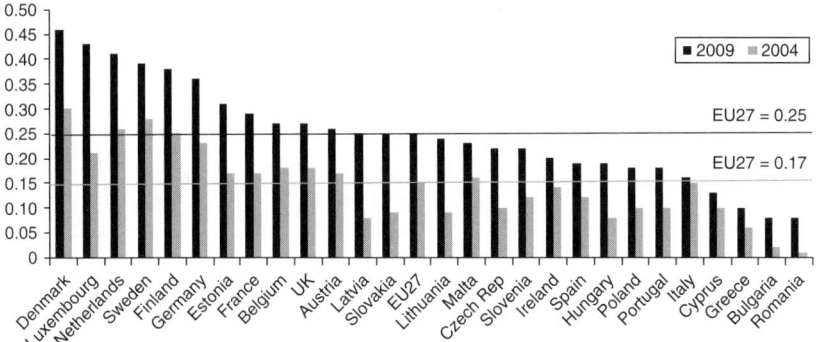

Figure 4.14   EDDI: individuals with no or low formal education, by country

interest, and by sharing the most common forms of multimedia consumption popular among the young. The validity of this hypothesis is indirectly confirmed by the values registered in the culture and communication sub-dimension over the years 2007–09: these values are constantly higher (0.14; 0.15; 0.18 compared to the impact dimension values, namely 0.10, 0.11 and 0.14). Conversely, it is evident that a starkly different situation can be found in adults and in the aged. The presence of diametrically opposite subjects within the same group is probably reflected in the size and slow growth of the EDDI value.

The group of retired subjects, on the other hand, shows difficulties in recovering ground over the population as a whole. Despite the constant, albeit limited, growth registered by the group, it stands at 15 points below the EU27 value of 2009. Together with the group of subjects aged between 65 and 74, this group has the greatest difficulties in recovering ground to position itself on the same trajectory as the rest of the population. Despite this evident technological exclusion, some countries show more widespread technology appropriation by retired subjects: once again, retired subjects living in Denmark (0.41), Luxembourg (0.40), the Netherlands (0.40), Sweden (0.35), Finland (0.34), United Kingdom (0.33) and Germany (0.30) have shown their ability to gain access to opportunities on the web and of performing above the average EU27 value (Figure 4.15).

The group of unemployed subjects slightly underperformed the average value of the European population as a whole (a 5-point gap in 2004 was narrowed to 2 points in 2009). As in the case of the subjects with a low level of education, it is very likely that these results were achieved thanks to the presence of young subjects within the group, familiar with the

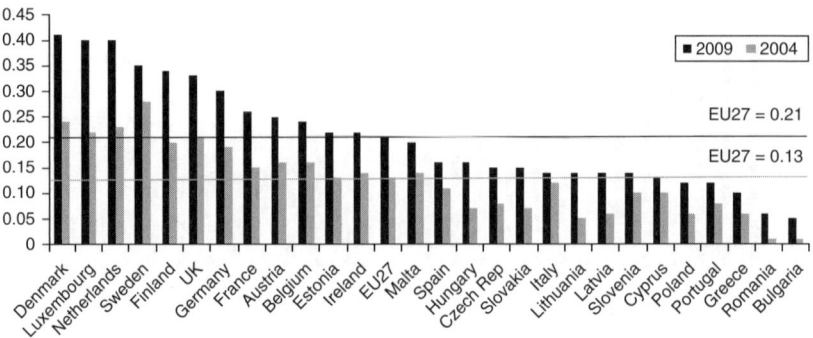

Figure 4.15   EDDI: retired individuals by country

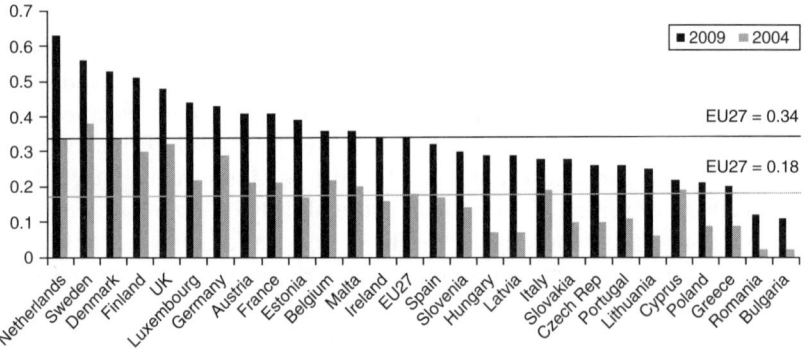

Figure 4.16   EDDI: unemployed individuals by country

new technologies, in search of their first job or, more generally, seeking employment. This is shown indirectly by the values registered in the cultural and communication and employment subdimensions: in 2009, for example, the former stood at 0.25 and the latter at 0.41. The presence of young people in the group appears to provide an explanation of the truly 'exceptional' values that were registered by a number of countries: Denmark (2004: 0.34; 2009: 0.53); the Netherlands (2004: 0.34; 2009: 0.63) and Sweden (2004: 0.38; 2009: 0.56).

Finally, the group comprising individuals living in scarcely populated areas performed just below the European average, achieving a score of 0.32 in 2009 compared to 0.36 by the EU27. As always, if we take a closer look at the latest data (that is, those related to 2009), we can see that numerous countries performed well above average: Luxembourg (0.55),

Denmark (0.52), the Netherlands (0.51), Sweden (0.49), Finland (0.48), United Kingdom (0.48) and Germany (0.40).

Having analysed the EDDI values, we may draw some general conclusions, confirming and identifying old and new inequalities. As regards the objectives set by the Riga Conference with respect to the so-called disadvantaged groups, the data presented offers useful material for redefining such groups.

Women, individuals living in scarcely populated areas, and the unemployed have significantly narrowed the gap that separated them from the population as a whole. In some countries, these groups registered even higher values than those of the EU27. In this respect, therefore, they achieved excellent results. This was not the case, however, for the aged and the retired, for whom large gaps still remain that need further interventions to be bridged. Finally, the values obtained by individuals aged between 55 and 64 and by subjects with a low or no formal education show a slow but steady recovery.

To sum up, the picture that emerges from these data shows a Europe in which digitalization progresses and develops unevenly, with large areas being excluded from the ongoing process. In brief, a Europe progressing at differing speeds and along trajectories that hardly ever intersect each other, at least not in the short term.

NOTES

1. This category includes all individuals with no or low formal education, corresponding to level 0–2 in the Isced classification: level 0 corresponds to pre-primary education; level 1 to primary education or first stage of basic education; level 2 to lower secondary or second stage or basic education.
2. This value, although obtained through different indicators and by applying a different method, is consistent with that obtained through the computation of the index of Internet use in at-risk groups which was calculated in the annual report (CEC, 2009): both showed an improvement within the group.
3. When the data were broken down into the various disadvantaged groups, it was not possible to keep the three indicators selected for the labour subdimension.

5. The economic impact of e-inclusion: a review of the literature

5.1 ASSESSING THE ECONOMIC IMPACT OF E-INCLUSION: OPEN ISSUES AND CHALLENGES

The idea that the emergence and diffusion of ICT represent a paradigmatic change potentially similar, in scale and scope, to previous technological revolutions that have shaped and fuelled long cycles of economic growth, is widely accepted. Over the last two decades a substantial body of empirical literature has tried to assess such an impact precisely. Until recently, the basic conceptual and methodological framework used in this stream of empirical research has been rooted in a neoclassical-type production function setting. The underlying idea was that ICT could be treated as any other capital input, ignoring the pervasive and general-purpose nature of this new bunch of technologies able to re-shape almost any aspect of the way in which society and economies are organized and function.

In the last decade a more complex and holistic way of looking at ICT, and at its potential contribution to economic and social life, has progressively emerged. This literature has developed within a policy-oriented framework along two main themes concerns: the emergence of new phenomena of social exclusion associated with an uneven capacity (both within society and the economy) to access and benefit from ICT (digital divide literature); and the recognition of the potential benefits brought about by ICT, seen as an extraordinary means to facilitate social and economic inclusion and through this to achieve greater and more widespread wealth (CEC, 2007a). Both themes are very much empathetic with the Lisbon agenda and the Europe 2020 strategy and their underlying idea that 'broad based growth' is the only way to obtain real and solid prosperity. As stressed in other parts of this book, concepts such as digital inclusion/exclusion or e-inclusion/exclusion reflect this enlarged perspective.

What is important to stress in the context of the survey presented in this chapter, is that this change of perspective implies a new view on the relevant dimensions and mechanisms governing the relationship between ICT and the economy. In an e-inclusion perspective, this relationship becomes less strictly technological in nature, less linear and direct, and mediated by a variety of contextual (cultural-socio-economic) factors affecting the ways, and the extent to which, the new opportunities offered by ICT can be actually appropriated and exploited by individuals, organizations, economies and societies at large. Such a change of perspective raises severe difficulties on both a theoretical and a measurement ground. These difficulties are related to various and intertwined factors, the most important being: the length, the indirect and the 'two-ways' nature of the causal chains linking the access and use of ICT to their very final economic outcomes; the plurality of socioeconomic domains affected by ICT; the fact that most of the economic effects of ICT take place outside the production boundaries of firms and involve a wide set of relationships that are not mediated by market transactions and can hardly be measured in monetary terms and with the traditional tool-kit used in economic studies; the recognition that individuals are the most direct beneficiaries and relevant actors of e-inclusion processes, which implies that the final economic outcome of e-inclusion is first and foremost obtained through a process of empowerment of human capital that in turn positively affects the economic performances of communities/institutions/organizations they are involved in; and the fact that a good deal of the economic effects of e-inclusion take place in the public sector affecting the overall efficiency of the public administration and the cost/quality dimension of services delivered. These effects are however difficult to estimate because of the lack of data on costs and productivity parameters and the fact that most public services have a social rather than a market value/output.

These theoretical and methodological difficulties clash against an increasing demand, especially by policy makers, for sound data and evidence on costs and effects of e-inclusion policies. In fact, both in the Riga Declaration and the i2010 policy agenda, explicit references are made to the need of governments to commit themselves to clear, bold and measurable targets as well as to demonstrate tangible final impacts of these policies (CEC, 2007a).

Over the last few years some steps have been taken in order to start broadening the analysis of ICT and its impact. This is particularly visible in the area of data collection and production of statistics, which are increasingly covering the diffusion, usage and impact dimension of ICT.[1] However, these data have so far been used only in a rather descriptive fashion with very little systematic effort to connect them to the e-inclusion research agenda.

As pointed out and demonstrated in other parts, of this book, a major objective of this research has consisted of making a tangible effort in such a direction. In particular, the provision of data and synthetic indicators able to grasp the infrastructure, usage and impact dimensions of e-inclusion processes can be seen as a successful attempt at synthesizing and operationalizing in empirical terms a great deal of conceptual and theoretical work on e-inclusion. With reference to the empirical assessment of the economic impact of e-inclusion, this research has made some significant steps ahead, highlighting the differentiated effects that the specific dimensions of infrastructure, usage and impact of ICT have on various types of economic performance indicators (see the next two chapters, on the economic impact of e-inclusion).

The purpose of this survey is to further emphasize the added value provided by this research, reviewing the scant empirical literature which has dealt (directly or indirectly) with the economic impact of e-inclusion. Accordingly, in the following sections three main bodies of literature have been selected and reviewed.

The first one is the very rich literature on digital divide/inclusion (Section 5.2). Although it investigates the causes (rather than the economic effects) of the processes of digital inclusion (or exclusion) it nonetheless provides several hints and useful indications for a better understanding of both the e-inclusion phenomenon and (indirectly) its potential economic impact.

Section 5.3 reviews the standard econometric literature assessing the economic impact of ICT, picking up those contributions that have (explicitly or implicitly) taken into account phenomena and variables related to e-inclusion processes and their final economic effects. This is particularly the case of the microeconomic literature exploring the impact of ICT on employability and wages and the most recent empirical attempts to assess the economic impact of broadband and Internet (Section 5.4).

Section 5.5 focuses on the few quantitative exercises that have tried to obtain proper quantitative/monetary figures on the impact of e-inclusion in a selected number of economic areas.

5.2   THE LITERATURE ON DIGITAL EXCLUSION: HINTS AND LESSONS FOR MEASURING THE ECONOMIC IMPACT OF E-INCLUSION

As already anticipated, the move toward a more complex and multifaceted perspective of ICT and its impact on the economy and society owes much to the literature on the 'digital divide' and more generally to the literature on ICT diffusion. It could also be argued that the e-inclusion concept is the natural outcome of the large amount of theoretical and empirical work carried out within this stream of multidisciplinary empirical research. What is argued here is that although this literature looks at the determinants and obstacles of ICT diffusion (rather than at its economic effects), it conveys a series of important insights and lessons which can be useful for identifying areas of investigation, mechanisms and outcome variables to be used for assessing the economic impact of e-inclusion.

While the traditional economic literature was dwelling on the so-called Solow paradox using a linear and deterministic view of ICT, a parallel stream of literature started to challenge the narrow and optimistic view implicit in these approaches. Most contributions started to suggest, and show on the basis of wide and robust empirical evidence, that the paradigmatic nature of ICT, far from paving the way to a smooth and homogeneous process of digitalization, was producing – or producing new types of – economic and social fractures (Norris, 2001).

Initially, this literature too was characterized by the adoption of a strict technological/infrastructural/access perspective, the digital divide phenomenon being defined as a gap between those who have access to ICT and those who do not. This literature has progressively evolved towards a more complex and multifaceted perspective on both ICT and the dimensions and factors characterizing the process of ICT diffusion and use. The terminological shift from the term 'digital divide' (implying a binary vision of the digitalization processes) to terms such as 'digital inclusion/ exclusion', 'digital inequality' (DiMaggio and Hargittai, 2001; Hargittai, 2003) and finally 'e-inclusion/exclusion' synthesizes this change of perspective. DiMaggio and Hargittai (2001) were the first two scholars to introduce the term 'digital inequality', which describes not just differences in access (labelled as the first-level, or basic digital divide), but autonomy of use, skill, social support and the purposes for which the technology is employed (labelled as the second-level digital divide).

The evolution of the empirical literature on digital inequality or exclusion reflects this change of perspective. It has in fact advanced from examining the extent and causes of differences in IT access and use, to differences in intensity and types of use. While early research studied, for example, digital divides by sex, race, and income in computer ownership and Internet access (for example, Hoffman and Novak 1998; Bikson and Panis 1999; Kominski and Newburger 1999; Ono and Zavodny 2003), subsequent studies emphasize differences in frequency of use, types of applications used, and access to emerging technologies such as broadband (for example, Robinson, DiMaggio and Hargittai 2003; US Department of Commerce 2004; OECD, 2007b). The most common ICT variables used in this later stream of literature (the number of Internet hosts per capita, computer per capita, Internet connection per capita, Internet users, mobile phones per capita, and so on) are in fact rather coherent with an e-inclusion perspective being more closely related to a usage dimension.

The evidence provided by this very rich literature is worth a short review since it provides further support on the variety of factors influencing ICT diffusion and also conveys a series of important messages for assessing the economic outcome of e-inclusion. These can be synthesized as follows.

In most studies digital divide has been conceptualized and empirically estimated as a cross-country asymmetry in the diffusion and adoption of ICT. Probably one of the strongest empirical stylized facts emerging from these studies is that the digital divide is mostly due (associated) to differences in the economic wealth of countries. Caselli and Coleman (2001), Baliamoune-Lutz (2003), Pohjola (2003) and Chinn and Fairlie (2007), by analysing a sample including both developing and developed countries, provide empirical evidence showing that income per capita is in fact positively and significantly related to different ICT rates of adoption. Hargittai (1999b) introduces another important element characterizing digital divide, which has direct implications for e-inclusion and its macro-economic effects. By estimating a model on a sample of OECD countries, he argues that income per capita is not per se sufficient to explain the digital divide, and suggests that income distribution has a relevant role in the diffusion of Internet.

Most of the contributions assessing the macroeconomic determinants of digital divide are affected by a typical endogeneity problem. This means that the causality links addressed in these studies could be read and interpreted the other way round, providing indications to the effect that many digital divide/exclusion dimensions (which in some cases overlap with typical e-inclusion variables) have on macroeconomic performance variables. Leaving aside the econometric technicalities, what these studies are likely to reflect is the existence of a two-way, cumulative and self-reinforcing mechanism, linking economic growth to e-inclusion. Such a mechanism should be properly taken into account and modelled in the empirical literature assessing the macroeconomic impact of e-inclusion.

Another factor that has been widely covered in this literature, both at the macro and at the micro level, is the central role of human capital. From a theoretical point of view, the argument is that skilled (that is, educated) workers are more capable of learning how to use new technologies and that they are more flexible with respect to their job assignment. The adoption of ICT often requires a reorganization of the firm, and a firm with a high percentage of skilled workers can implement information technologies more easily. However, when tested in a macro cross-country framework the empirical evidence has not produced univocal results. Those authors who analyse samples including both developed and developing countries find mixed evidence (Baliamoune-Lutz, 2003; Chinn and Fairlie, 2004), whereas those who analyse OECD countries find a significant influence of the level of human capital on ICT adoption (Hargittai, 1999b; Gust and Marquez, 2002; Luciani and Padoan, 2007).[2] Studies at the micro level, on the other hand, find a positive relationship between the general level of employee qualification and ICT use (Bayo-Moriones and Lera-Lopez, 2007; Haller and Traistaru-Siedschlag, 2007).

Demographic factors such as the age structure of the population and the size of the urban population have also been taken into account. The idea is that ICT has larger diffusion among younger people[3] and that urban populations tend to adopt more ICT (Internet and computers) because of network economies. Nevertheless, the empirical evidence is mixed. Regarding population age, Chinn and Fairlie (2004) argue that if the developing countries had the same population age composition as the US, the divergence in personal computer and Internet penetration would have been even larger; on the other hand Bayo-Moriones and Lera-Lopez (2007) find no relationship between workforce age and ICT at the firm level. With respect to urban population, Dasgupta et al. (2001) find a positive elasticity with ICT adoption and Chinn and Fairlie (2004) find it negative.

As shown in other parts of this book, this research has provided new and more detailed evidence on the extent and nature of the socio-economic factors affecting e-inclusion processes in Europe, highlighting differences and gaps both across and within the main European economies and societies in the infrastructure, usage and impact dimensions of e-inclusion. Concerning the position of the more disadvantaged groups (older people, women, unemployed persons and those with low or no education), this study has shown a rather variegated picture. Taking into account the impact dimension of e-inclusion (that is, the extent to which people are actually able to exploit the opportunities offered by the network in several economic and social areas) the data reveal both a clear capability of women to progressively close the gap and the persistence of severe barriers to use, for the elderly, the retired and those with low levels of education (see Chapter 4).

The economic structure of a country has also been shown to be relevant for ICT adoption, and it is therefore likely to play an important role also in explaining the economic impact of digital inclusion. The empirical analysis in this area tries to answer two questions, namely: (a) what are the firm's specific characteristics that influence the adoption of ICT, and (b) whether, and if so to what extent, the sectorial composition of a country plays a role in terms of ICT performance. Many contributions have found that firm size is a relevant variable for ICT investment decisions (Haller and Traistaru-Siedschlag, 2007): the larger the firm, the higher the probability of adopting new technologies. Not only firm size matters though:

the organizational structure has been shown to be relevant as well (Caroli and Van Reenen, 2001). Hollenstein (2004) suggests that team working and horizontal structure are organizational characteristics that encourage ICT adoption. The answer to the second question is also positive: given that some sectors use more ICT than others, different sectorial compositions determine different rates of investment in ICT. The literature emphasizes how the higher the share of the service and manufacturing sectors, the higher the ICT investment rate will be, while an inverse relation exists with agriculture and the public sector (Caselli and Coleman, 2001; Gust and Marquez, 2002; Guerrieri and Padoan, 2007).[4] All in all these contributions seem to suggest that similar e-inclusion policies and processes might have quite different economic effects depending on the structural characteristics of the economy.

Over the last few years the issue regarding the impact of regulation on ICT adoption has also received increasing attention. In general, it has been argued that all kinds of restrictions, regulations or constraints that somehow limit the set of decisions of an economic agent may drive the economy to a sub-optimal equilibrium. The question is whether they also negatively influence the adoption of ICT. Gust and Marquez (2002) demonstrate that regulation in the labour market negatively affects ICT expenditure; Luciani and Padoan (2007) show that barriers to entry are one of the major restraints in diffusion of ICT within Europe; Dasgupta et al. (2001) emphasize how competition policy matters for Internet density, while Hargittai (1999b) focuses on the influences of the structure of the telecom market (monopoly vs. competition). Some authors, analysing the digital divide, have also included indices of property rights and/or of civil liberties that have proved to be important variables as well (Caselli and Coleman, 2001; Baliamoune-Lutz, 2003; Chinn and Fairlie, 2004). Both regulations and institutional factors might not only facilitate or hamper the diffusion and adoption of ICT but also influence the extent to which the latter produce final economic outcomes. So far, the issue regarding the potential relevance and role of these factors for e-inclusion and its economic impact has not been properly addressed on either a conceptual or an empirical ground, and this represents another relevant research area to be explored.

In conclusion, the digital divide literature has not only significantly contributed to the development of the e-inclusion concept but has also identified a broader set of determinants, preconditions and complementary factors hampering (in a negative sense) and facilitating (in a positive one) the diffusion of digital skills and ICT practices. These are all factors worth taking into account when one aims at conceptualizing, modelling and empirically assessing the economic impact of e-inclusion.

5.3 THE ECONOMETRIC LITERATURE ON THE ECONOMIC IMPACT OF ICT

Over the last two decades a large body of empirical research has tried to assess the specific contribution provided by the diffusion of ICT to economic and productivity growth. At a macro level such an impact has been measured either through growth-accounting exercises or through country-level econometric studies. In both cases (in the growth accounting tradition by definition and in the other studies by common practice) the impact of ICT on the economy has been assessed within a neoclassical methodological setting, using as basic measurement tools the production function and the total factor productivity (TFP). Results and methodologies, as well as strengths and limitations of this stream of literature, have been effectively synthesized by several reviews (OECD, 2004; Draca et al., 2006; Dunnewijk et al., 2007; Guerrieri and Padoan, 2007). For the purpose of this survey it is enough to recall that the linear, deterministic and simplified view of ICT contained in this type of literature is rather at odds with the complex, indirect and multifaceted mechanisms through which these technologies are affecting almost any sphere of socioeconomic behaviours.

The use of micro-level data, along with increasing the econometric robustness of the estimates of the economic impact of ICT, has conveyed a broader perspective of ICT and its economic effects, highlighting factors and drivers of ICT diffusion which get closer to dimensions and variables highlighted by the e-inclusion literature. The most recent micro-based contributions assessing the effects of ICT on firms' performances has contributed, in fact, to diffuse a less deterministic, auto-referential and simplified reading of the relationship between the adoption of ICT and productivity gains. These new microeconomic studies have challenged the idea that ICT has an economic impact 'per se', showing that this impact is dependent on parallel changes in the organizational structure of firms and in the level and type of skills and competencies (Brynjolfsson and Hitt, 2000, Bresnahan et al., 2001; Hughes and Scott Morton, 2005; Crespi et al., 2007; Codagnone, 2009).[5] Other firm-level studies have stressed the indirect nature of the effects of ICT on firms performance, showing that productivity gains are obtained through the positive impact that these technologies have on the capability of firms to innovate (Koellinger 2008, OECD, 2008). In particular broadband is expected to function as a powerful leverage for innovation, increasing the speed and amount of knowledge circulating in the network (especially in a global context), enhancing absorptive capacity of individuals and firms, and improving the organization and efficiency of R&D and innovation activities (Venturini, 2008; Hanna, 2010).

E-inclusion has something to do with the mechanisms and effects ana-lysed in these studies in two main respects. First, this literature suggests that there is an e-inclusion dimension which specifically involves firms as organizations (that is, integrated sets of technological assets, organiza-tional routines and competencies). The processes of digital empowerment can in fact be extended also to firms and take the form of an increased capability to be part of, and play an active role in, the network economy. This is the reason why, in this book, a distinct set of infrastructure, usage and impact e-inclusion indicators, specifically referring to firms, have been identified and used for analysing the processes of digital empowerment involving the business sector. Second, in all these studies a large part of the positive effects of ICT on firms' performance takes place through a process of empowerment of human capital, and this is an essential element (and outcome) of any e-inclusion process. In this latter perspective such a process of empowerment has two intertwined economic effects: a direct effect, on labour productivity, employment perspectives, wages and incomes of digitally skilled workers; and an indirect effect on the overall innovation and competitive performance of firms.

In the case of micro-level studies, data constraints have for a long time limited the possibility of exploring the impact of ICT in a more compre-hensive way. Most of the micro-level literature uses mere indicators of ICT expenditures which are not able to grasp any quantitative and qualitative dimension of ICT usage and the ways in which these different modalities are combined with organizational settings and skills.

However, over the last few years, some countries have started to collect and use in empirical research data on the use of, rather the mere access to, ICT. Varian et al. (2002) have looked at the effects of the use of the Internet on cost savings and productivity, using firm level data for the US, UK, Germany and France, finding in most cases a positive and significant impact. Arvanitis (2004) analyses, in the case of Switzerland, the relation-ship between labour productivity, organizational variables, and various ICT indicators measuring the intensity of use of Internet and intranet by firms' employees. Maliranta and Rouvinen (2004), using Finland's Internet Use and E-commerce in Enterprises Survey, look at the impact of various ICT related technologies (computers, Internet, local area net-works) on firms' productivity. Clayton et al. (2004) analyse the economic impact of e-commerce in the UK. The collection of data on the diffusion and use of online services by firms and individuals represents a further step that statistical offices are making in order to assess the real impact of ICT. Studies making use of these data to assess the impact of ICT on firms' performance include Atrostic et al. (2004) with reference to the US, and Rincon-Aznar et al. (2005) with reference to the UK. Atrostic and Nguyen

(2006), in a study covering Denmark, Japan and the USA, have analysed at the firm level the impact of different types of networks (wireless, Internet, intranet and electronic data interchange) on labour productivity, finding that (in the case of Japan and US manufacturing sectors) firms using networks showed higher levels of labour productivity, and both intra-firm and inter-firm networks were found to be associated to TFP.

Data collected by Eurostat through the Community ICT use survey represents in this respect a unique and – at least at a micro level – still largely unexploited data-source. These data could in fact be effectively used to broaden the analysis of the economic impact of ICT at a micro level, bringing into the picture a wide range of qualitative and quantitative aspects related to the use and economic exploitation of ICT. Furthermore, in each EU country, data from this survey can (at least in principle) be matched with production, labour and innovation survey data, making it possible to shed light on the determinants and economic effects of a wide range of ICT practices and skills. This research avenue is currently explored by a project titled 'ICT impact on productivity/growth assessment by linking data across countries and sources' funded by Eurostat and involving 13 EU countries (Clayton, 2009) and by an OECD (OECD/WPIA project) initiative consisting of linking (in a selected number of countries) individual data on education, income, sex and age to firm level economic data (sales, capital stocks, value added, labour productivity, multifactor productivity) and innovation and ICT surveys (R&D, CIS, e-business, patent data and trade statistics). Both these projects indicate a possible methodological path to shed new light on the micro effects of e-inclusion policies as well as on the complex channels through which e-inclusion measures affect the economic and innovation performances of firms, sectors and economic systems as a whole.

The micro-level econometric literature assessing the impact of ICT on labour market variables (employability and wage differentials) deals with issues and bears results which are closely related to e-inclusion and its economic impact. Improving employability conditions and raising individual wages and family incomes are in fact fundamental dimensions and targets of social inclusion policies. It is clear therefore that insights on the extent to which, and the modalities by which, the increasing digitalization of economies and societies impacts on the skill requirements of employment and wages are highly relevant to shedding light on the potential benefits (both to individuals and to society at large) of e-inclusion.

The main research hypothesis underlying all this large body of empirical literature is the supposed skill-biased nature of ICT. This stream of research started by simply associating the rise of wage differentials between skilled and un-skilled workers (more pronounced in the USA and UK than in continental Europe) to the widespread diffusion of ICT. The interpretation of this correlation is based on the idea that not only do these technologies tend to substitute low-qualified labour routines, but also that labour's (or total factor) productivity gains can be obtained only if the adoption and use of ICT are complemented with qualified skills and competencies. The increase of wage differentials observed over the last two decades is therefore interpreted as the result of a strong increase in the demand for qualified (digitally skilled) labour, which has not found in the labour market, or in the education system as a whole, a corresponding capacity for supplying these sets of competencies and skills. As in the case of the literature assessing the ICT–productivity linkage, this stream of empirical research originated in the USA – at the end of the 1980s, and then expanded to other major OECD countries.

One of the first contributions showing the existence of a significant wage premium associated to the use of ICT is the seminal work by Krueger in 1993. Using a cross-sectional dataset (combining different data sources for the period 1984–89), this study showed that workers using PCs were paid much higher salaries (in a range of 14–17 per cent) than the rest of the labour force. Similar estimates (10–15 per cent) have been found by Bikson and Panis using US Current Population Survey data referring to the second half of the 1990s (Bikson and Panis, 1999). Other studies have tried to assess the impact of ICT on wages going beyond a pure ICT binary variable (use of PC or Internet access). Using data drawn from an ad hoc survey on ICT use, Cooper distinguishes between three different categories of Internet users: Internet users who are 'fully connected' (with Internet Service Providers or high speed Internet access at home); the 'partially connected' (workers with basic Internet or email service at home), the 'potentially connected' (workers with no home Internet service, but who do have a home computer or cell phone); the totally disconnected workers (no Internet service, computer, or cell phone). This study found that the disconnected earn less than half the income of the fully connected ($25.5K vs. $45.2K), are much less likely to have a college degree (13 per cent vs. 46 per cent), are more likely to be black (12 per cent vs. 7 per cent), older (53 vs. 44 years), and have smaller households (2.1 vs. 2.8). Each of these significantly predicts differences across the four levels of connectedness, with income being the most powerful predictor (Cooper, 2000 as reported in Rice and Katz, 2003).

The cross-sectional nature of data used in these first exercises and the omission of variables able to capture differences in the 'individual ability' of workers – which are on their own potential sources of wages differential and factors explaining the likelihood of a worker to use a PC – have been identified as the two main important flaws of the empirical exercises reviewed above (Di Nardo and Pischke, 1997; Entorf and Kramarz, 1997). These caveats have been somewhat tackled by later contributions using longitudinal datasets, more detailed indicators on ICT use and digital skills, and by controlling for several types of fixed individual effects, especially those associated to the level of education and overall ability of the labour force (Entorf and Kramarz, 1997; Dolton and Pelkonen, 2007; Dostie and Jayaraman, 2008).

Although the dispute about the skill-biased nature of ICT is still at the centre of a lively debate, the empirical research produced over the last two decades seems to provide overall support to the idea that ICT has contributed, along with other factors, to the increasing wage polarization and income inequalities observed over the last two decades.

5.4 EVIDENCES AND SCENARIOS ON THE ECONOMIC IMPACT OF BROADBAND AND THE INTERNET

Since the end of the 1990s the collection and release of data on broadband has provided new opportunities for a more comprehensive assessment of the economic impact of digitalization. It is widely acknowledged that the availability, access and use of broadband represent a fundamental 'enabler' of e-inclusion policies as well as an important precondition for an effective appropriation of the potentialities offered by a digital society. The existence of a strong relationship between the diffusion of broadband and the intensity of Internet usage has been shown by several empirical studies (Hitt and Tambe, 2007; Horrigan, 2007; OECD, 2008, 2009). Over the last decade several studies have tried to estimate the effects of broadband penetration on aggregate economic variables such as GDP, employment, and the growth of new business. These contributions can be divided into two main categories: the 'econometric studies' estimating the macroeconomic impact of broadband using 'real' available data; and 'forward looking studies' aiming at drawing scenarios or making simulations in order to highlight the long term potential economic impact of broadband. Both these streams of contributions are coherent with an e-inclusion perspective of ICT and its economic impact, putting a great emphasis on the use dimension of this technology as well as assuming a plurality of social and economic domains affected by broadband penetration.

One of the first studies trying to assess the economic impact of broadband on the basis of real data is the one commissioned in 2006 by the US Department of Commerce, Economic Development Administration and carried out within the National Technical Assistance, Training,

Table 5.1   Estimated magnitude of broadband impacts (NTATREP study)

Economic indicator	Results
Employment (jobs)	Broadband added about 1–1.4% to growth rate, 1998–2002
Business establishments (proxy for the number of firms)	Broadband added about 0.5–1.2% to growth rate, 1998–2002
Housing rents (proxy for property values)	More than 6% higher in 2000 in zip codes where broadband was available by 1999
Industry mix	Broadband reduced share of small (<10 employees) establishments by about 1.3–1.6%, 1998–2002
	Broadband added about 0.3–0.6%, to share of establishments in IT-intensive sectors, 1998–2002

Source: NTATREP (National Technical Assistance, Training, Research and Evaluation Project), 2006.

Research and Evaluation Project (NTATREP, 2006). The essence of the study was to differentiate US geographic areas (both at the state level and for 22,390 zip codes) by their availability and use of broadband, and then to compare economic indicators for these areas over a long enough period (1998–2002) to see if consistent deviations from the secular trend were observable (also controlling for other factors known to distinguish among the areas (regulation, education, income, urban vs. rural)). The dataset used is the result of a matching of ICT data drawn from the US Federal Communication Commission and other economic data drawn from the US Population Census and Business Establishment Surveys. The level of broadband availability and use is measured respectively through the number of high-speed Internet providers and the number of lines in service. The first message conveyed in this study is that broadband access does impact on a wide set of economic performance dimensions and that such effects are real and can be measured. In particular, the evidence presented shows that broadband exerts a positive impact on GDP and employment, on the growth of businesses (overall and in the IT-intensive sectors) and on the dynamics of property values (see Table 5.1). Contrary to what was found by the ICT-wage premium literature, this study does not find any significant impact of broadband on wages. A second, more conceptual, message stemming from this study is that for most of these economic effects to be tangible and measurable, broadband has to be used rather than just being available. The implication that the study draws for economic development professionals, and which is relevant also in an e-inclusion perspective, is that 'a portfolio of broadband related policy interventions that is reasonably balanced (i.e., also pays attention to demand-side issues such as training) is more likely to lead to positive economic outcomes than a single-minded focus on availability' (NTATREP, 2006, p. 3).

An exercise very similar to the one reviewed above, is contained in the Crandall, Lehr and Litan study published in 2007 in the Brookings Institution *Issue in Economic Policy* journal. In this case too, the aim is to assess the extent to which differences in the level of broadband penetration across the lower 48 states of the US were able to explain cross-state differences in GDP and employment growth in the period 2003–05. Data on broadband are drawn from the US Federal Communication Commission and the indicator used is the broadband lines/population ratio. The results of this study confirm the positive impact exerted by broadband on employment: in the non-farm private sector, for every 1 per cent increase in broadband penetration, employment is estimated to increase by 0.2 to 0.3 per cent per year, which amounts to an increase of about 300,000 jobs. Services, and in particular health care and financial services, are the sectors which seem to benefit the most from broadband penetration.

There are also some econometric studies which have found more ambiguous and counter-intuitive relationships between broadband and GDP. Thompson and Garbacz (2007 and 2008) find a negative and statistically significant cross-(US) state relationship between broadband deployment and economic output. A possible explanation of this puzzling result might be based on the so-called 'delay hypothesis' (existence of a time lag between the introduction of ICT and the evidence of economic effects) or (more worryingly) on the presence of a negative time-wasting effect on labour productivity accompanying the first introduction of these technologies. Another possible explanation of this counter-intuitive result is the existence of a threshold level above which broadband penetration starts to produce tangible effects. The presence of such an effect has also been found by Koutroumpis (2008) in one of the few empirical studies covering the European continent.

The presence of a threshold effect in the economic impact of broadband, this time referred to the existence of appropriate levels of PC diffusion and digital skills, has been found in a more recent cross-country study covering the whole OECD area (LECG, 2009). The paper distinguishes between low and high 'broadband environments' and finds that a positive impact of broadband is found positive and statistically significant only in the case of the most favourable ICT environments ('ICT eco-systems'). In the case of 'medium or high ICT countries' the econometric model predicts that a 1 per cent increase in the number of broadband lines per 100 individuals increases productivity by 0.1 per cent, while in countries characterized by low ICT diffusion (namely most southern European countries) such a positive impact is not found. More generally this study shifts the emphasis from purely supply side and technological factors (broadband penetration) to factors facilitating the exploitation of the potentiality of this technological infrastructure and, above all else, the skill level of the workforce and of total population. The results presented in this study are the outcome of a broader research agenda carried out by the LECG within the so-called Connectivity Scorecard project (Waverman and Dasgupta, 2010; www. connectivityscorecard.org). The aim of this project is to use a wide range of data on ICT to rank countries on the basis of the level and quality of broadband connectivity. The approach followed by the Scorecard is again rather coherent with an e-inclusion framework, deliberately taking 'a broad and holistic look at many aspects of ICT – not just the development of infrastructure but also the usage levels of key technologies, and ICT skills in the workforce and the general population' (LECG, 2009, p. 2).

Crandall and Jackson (2001) have made one of the first attempts at assessing 'The potential economic benefit associated to a widespread diffusion of broadband access'. The methodology used in this study is very much grounded in the standard (welfare) economics and as such deviates strongly from the econometric literature reviewed above. The potential impact of broadband is estimated by making projections on the demand function for high-speed access (ADSL, cable modems, satellites, 3G, wireless, and so on) and then measuring the 'consumer surplus' on the basis of specific assumptions regarding the evolution of the price and the demand elasticities as well as the rate of broadband penetration. An alternative and additional methodology used in this study consists of estimating the increase of the consumer surplus stemming from efficiency gains, cost savings and price reductions brought about by broadband diffusion in areas such as shopping, entertainment, commuting, telephone services and telemedicine.

The MICUS study (Fornefeld et al., 2008), commissioned by the EU DG Information Society, is perhaps one of the most ambitious attempts to provide a quantitative evaluation of the potential impacts of broadband technology on the European economy as a whole, to draw long term scenarios on the diffusion of broadband and to assess the impact of the latter on productivity, employment, GDP and on the process of structural change (that is, process of tertiarization and growth of knowledge intensive business services, or KIBS). One of the added values of this study (in an e-inclusion perspective) is that it proposes three composite broadband indicators covering respectively: (a) the diffusion of the broadband infra-structure; (b) the broadband readiness of the users (skills); and (c) the extent to which the potentiality of this technology is exploited through the use of online services. Each indicator combines information and data drawn from Eurostat and OECD.

The study provides estimates of the impact that broadband has had during the period 2004–06, and draws three different scenarios for the period 2006–15. In both cases three main types of economic effects of broadband are taken into account and estimated, namely the effects on: (a) productivity (positive) and employment (negative in the short run and pos-itive in the long run in presence of high growth rate of economy); (b) GDP growth (positive, largely based on the growth of services and KIBS); and (c) structural change (outsourcing, tertiarization and growth of KIBS).

The main results of these estimates are the following:

- The macroeconomic broadband-related productivity improvement in Europe has been on average 0.29 per cent during the period 2004–06. This is considered a rather modest result due to a slow adoption of broadband-based value added services especially among SMEs (3 per cent per year on average as emerging from the broadband-usage composite indicator built on the basis of Eurostat data);
- The diffusion of broadband has driven a substantial structural shift with a displacement of 725,000 jobs from traditional economic sectors to the business services sector;
- The diffusion of broadband has fostered innovation in knowledge-intensive sectors and this has been crucial for the development of new markets and economic growth. The model has estimated that (in 2006) broadband-related innovations have generated 440,000 new jobs in the business services and 549,000 jobs in other sectors. The net impact of broadband on employment (difference between the jobs displaced by the introduction of broadband and new ones generated by the innovation-induced growth) is positive and equal to 105,000 jobs.

Despite the use of a rather ad hoc and somewhat discretional methodology this study has the indisputable merit of combining in a macroeconomic framework different types of data sources (micro, meso and macro) and matching a wide set of variables related to both ICT use and to other key economic variables.

The OECD study on the economic impact of optical fibres (OECD, 2009) carries out a sort of cost/benefit analysis of large-scale broadband investment programmes in various sectors. More particularly the study compares the costs of building the most forward-looking broadband network possible (optical fibres) with the short-term cost savings that could be achieved with the use of this technology on a selected number of areas and sectors: namely electricity (production, management and consumption) and health, transport and education, accounting for roughly a quarter of GDP in the USA. Benefits are expected and foreseen both through the efficiency gains which can be obtained in the production/delivery/management of the services provided in these different areas/sectors and through changes in the behaviours and consumption practices of the final users (that is, individuals or households).

The approach is deemed to be particularly appealing since it does not have the ambition of estimating the future demand of broadband services as well as their specific impact on the economy; more simply it aims at showing 'how much of a cost savings would be required in various sectors to justify the large up-front investment of a new broadband network'. Despite this low-profile statement the study turns out to provide not only estimates of the 'break-even points' justifying the broadband investment in the different areas but also approximate figures of the total amount of cost savings which could be achieved.

The results obtained in this study are rather clear-cut indicating levels of 'required cost savings' which are very low (between 0.5 per cent and 1.5 per cent), and that are in any case much lower than the most pessimistic estimate of the economic benefits brought about by the investments in this technology. The study indicates that the cost savings which could be obtained in the health sector could justify the whole cost of rolling out a network, and this would occur if health costs were to fall between 1.4 per cent and 3.7 per cent as a direct result of having the network in place. These are deemed to be rather underestimated values of the potential economic effects of e-health.

All in all, even if this exercise too is built on rather ad hoc and discretionary methodologies, it provides interesting evidences, and proposes a methodological framework for an ex ante cost-benefit assessment of ICT related policies which could be extended to other types of e-inclusion policy schemes. The study raises another very relevant policy issue, namely the existence in the ICT sectors of potential market failure, with important policy implications within an e-inclusion perspective. The evidence presented in the study clearly shows the existence of a potential gap between the social value of ICT and the private returns deriving from investments in this expensive infrastructure. Private returns are in most cases much lower than the wide social and economic benefits that this infrastructure, and the related services, could provide to the community as whole. This type of argument is highly relevant to e-inclusion, since broadband represents an essential infrastructure needed to implement a wide range of e-inclusion policies.

A very grand and ambitious attempt at defining the long term socioeconomic scenarios connected to the full development of an Internet-based society is contained in the report on 'Trends in connectivity technologies and their socio economic impacts' (Cave et al., 2009). The report synthesizes the results of an EU funded project titled 'Policy options for the ubiquitous Internet society'. The socioeconomic impact of the emergence of an 'ubiquitous Internet society' is assessed following three distinct (though interconnected) analytical steps: a first one in which the major technological trends linked to the ubiquitous properties of the Internet are identified; a second one identifying three possible broad 'world scenarios' differing from each other on the basis of the ways in which the technological trends will interact with market forces and the governance level (public vs. private governance; open vs. closed technologies; competitive vs. collusive markets). These are named respectively 'Scattered world' (closed, private, competition), 'Connected world' (open, public, competition) and 'Borderless world' (open, private, competition). A third stage in which these scenarios are modelled uses the International Futures (IFs) model in order to generate a range of long term socioeconomic impacts (taking into account the period 2005–20 and different economic areas: EU15, EU27, North America, Japan and Korea, and the BRICs).

On the basis of (assumed) long term changes in some broad 'framework variables' (network/telephone infrastructure, networked population, globalization, government effectiveness, and so on) and some basic input and productivity drivers (government. expenditure, private investment as per cent of GDP, basic multifactor productivity (MFP) growth, human and physical capital contribution to MFP growth), the IFs model makes projections on the long term dynamics of key macroeconomic variables such as GDP (total and per capita) and income distribution (both within and across countries). The model simulates four different scenarios and economic impacts, one corresponding to a 'base case' (invariance of all the relevant input variables/framework conditions) and the other three corresponding to the emergence respectively of a scattered, a connected and a borderless world.

5.5 EXPLORATIVE EVIDENCES FROM CASE STUDIES AND SIMULATIONS

In this section we review the contributions which have moved (often as a result of a pressing demand by policy makers) towards a more pragmatic

and direct estimation of the economic impact of e-inclusion. These contributions are rather heterogeneous in terms of both ICT indicators used
(and dimensions of e-inclusion taken into account) and economic areas
affected by ICT. We have identified five such empirical exercises. The
methodology and main results of these studies are briefly presented below.

Probably the first empirical assessment of the economic impact of
e-inclusion is the one contained in the EU 'impact assessment' (IA) document accompanying the Communication on the European i2010 initiative
on e-inclusion (CEC, 2007b). The exercise was part of a broader research
agenda aiming at exploring the policy challenges, options and scenarios
connected to the implementation and achievement of the e-inclusion Riga
targets (CEC, 2007b, p. 2). Along with providing quantitative figures on
the potential economic impact of e-inclusion, the IA document contains an
in-depth discussion of the main conceptual and methodological challenges
underlying the measurement of e-inclusion and its effects on the economy.
The document proposes 'an e-inclusion positive impacts framework'
(eIPIF) identifying a rather detailed set of micro, meso and macro mechanisms through which ICT are expected to exert an impact on several types
of economic areas and indicators. As admitted in the EU study, an empirical estimation of all these mechanisms and effects represents an almost
prohibitive task. The potential impact of e-inclusion is therefore estimated
at an aggregate level (at the EU level) taking into account three basic
channels though which e-inclusion is expected to affect GDP: through
an increased take-up of transactional e-government services, which are
expected to improve the productivity of the public sector; through an
increased level of human capital, increasing skills, health and employability; and through the growth of the ICT producing sector, fuelled by an
increasing demand for ICT services and products. In addition a set of cost
saving opportunities, obtained by reducing the problems caused by social
exclusion, health and care needs, are also taken into account.

For each 'area of impact' two distinct estimates are provided: one more
optimistic, under the assumption of a complete fulfilment of the Riga
targets ('Riga scenario'); and one more pessimistic, based on the assumption that ICT disparities get reduced by only 25 per cent ('slow adoption
scenario'). The estimates are obtained by combining real data on ICT use,
earnings and social welfare expenditures with a set of assumptions and
projections regarding the effects of training programmes and e-inclusion
policies on skills, employability perspectives, wage increases and the
demand for ICT related services and products (CEC, 2007b, pp. 132–33).
As stressed in the EU IA, the estimates are affected by several methodological caveats and their main purpose is to provide only a tentative idea
of the potential impact of e-inclusion policies.

The research objectives of the EU funded Vienna study were rather ambitious, aiming at analysing the role of 'inclusive innovation for growth and cohesion' and at 'modelling and demonstrating the impact of e-Inclusion' (Codagnone, 2009). The first part of the study contains an effort to define, on a purely conceptual and methodological ground, 'the big picture' of e-inclusion processes and their socioeconomic effects. The study identifies four distinct dimensions of e-inclusion processes, namely inputs, outputs, outcomes and impacts, and indicates for each of these domains the most appropriate (or available) data and methodologies to be used in the empirical research (Codagnone, 2009, p. 22).

Like the EU IA, the Vienna study identifies a set of key economic areas and mechanisms of e-inclusion: (i) ICT and entitlements; (ii) ICT and online services; (iii) ICT and health; (iv) ICT matching functions and network effects; (v) ICT and consumer welfare; (vi) ICT industry output effect; and (vii) ICT supported community building. The same study also proposes a detailed list of potential benefits provided by ICT in the public sector area. Various types of benefits and economic returns are examined, referring to various types of administrative functions, service delivery processes, and the final users (Codagnone, 2009, p. 48).

The empirical section of the study falls short of covering all the areas, mechanisms and effects listed above. The main empirical contribution of this project consists of a detailed review of the existing e-inclusion policy initiatives across Europe and of a set of econometric firm level estimations on the effects of ICT on employment, wages and productivity. The case-study part of the project on e-inclusion policies, besides showing the presence of a heterogeneous picture of objectives, tools and initiatives, points out the absolute lack of impact measurement capacities among e-inclusion practitioners. Only in very few cases (out of the 1000 cases of e-inclusion initiatives reviewed) were these policy actions accompanied by some demonstration of the tangible outcomes and some kind of cost-benefit monetized analyses.

The 'Champion for digital inclusion' report by PricewaterhouseCoopers (2009), referring to the UK, makes a more pragmatic attempt at operationalizing in empirical terms some of the mechanisms described in both the EU IA study and the Vienna project, and seeks to get quantitative/monetary figures on the economic benefits of digital inclusion. The potential benefits of digital inclusion are estimated in four main areas: consumers, education, employment and government efficiency. The quantification of the final economic benefits of digital inclusion ('digital dividends') in each area is carried out by first identifying the 'logic chains' linking digital inclusion to the different types of economic outcomes, then importing into the model a set of parameters (concerning the impact of several types of digital inclusion measures in the four economic areas) 'borrowed' from previous studies largely based on the UK experience.

If e-inclusion and digital exclusion are two sides of the same coin, then the economic impact e-inclusion can also be assessed by estimating the costs of digital exclusion, that is, costs that could be saved by raising the level of e-inclusion. Such an exercise has been commissioned by the US Federal Communications Commission (FCC), and carried out by two consultancy firms, Digital Impact Group and Econsult (DIG-Econsult, 2010). The DIG-Econsult study is very similar in scope to the one carried out by PricewaterhouseCoopers. The study proposes a general conceptual framework identifying the main types of groups and national purposes affected by digital exclusion, and a set of mechanisms by which benefits from remedying digital exclusion are realized.

The report identifies six main areas of impact (corresponding to a set of broad national policy targets): health, education, economic opportunity, government/civic engagement, energy, and public safety. The main mechanisms through which cost savings can be obtained include: personal gains, reduction in opportunity costs, network effects.

As in the case of the PricewaterhouseCoopers study, the DIG-Econsult report draws upon previous studies and policy documents related to the many facets of the digital exclusion issue. As with the other exercises reviewed in this section, the estimates provided by this study should be considered as preliminary and tentative and best viewed – using the Report's own words 'as an approximation of the scale of economic impact and as offering guidance on concepts worth further elaboration, analysis, and quantification'.

Outside Europe there have been several more limited attempts at assessing the economic impact of e-inclusion. One of these studies has been carried out by a management consulting firm (Infoxchange–A.T. Kearney, 2009) within the context of the Australian 'Digital Inclusion Initiative'. This initiative is coordinated by the non-profit organization Infoxchange, and is designed to 'eradicate digital divide by providing access to computer hardware, software, affordable Internet and user support for residents of public housing'.

These policies have been implemented in two Australian regions. In 2002, in the Atherton Gardens Estate in Fitzroy approximately 800 properties have been wired up, 1500 residents trained and over 900 computers installed. A specific attempt has been made to assess, through a 'robust model' the economic impact of this initiative. The methodology is not described in detail and is based on the use of both official statistics and quantitative and qualitative data collected through an ad hoc survey directed to the residents of the region involved in this initiative. The study has estimated strong economic effects of this initiative on four main areas: (i) employment; (ii) communication and connectivity; (iii) transactional efficiencies; (iv) health and well-being.

The research has shown that e-inclusion policies can be very effective in enhancing social inclusion and reducing anti-social behaviours (such as drug and alcohol abuse, domestic violence, and juvenile delinquency), which also have indirect negative economic effects.

All in all, this study represents the classic case in which very relevant research/evaluation objectives are combined with somewhat loose and/or apache quantitative methodologies, with results often relying upon rather ad hoc anecdotal evidences.

5.6 FUTURE PERSPECTIVES

The survey presented in these pages has confirmed that assessing the economic impact of e-inclusion is a complex and ambitious task, requiring the availability of data on the use and appropriation of ICT, as well as models able to take into account the complexity of the mechanisms and variables at work in the numerous spheres of social and economic life where ICT is likely to have an impact.

The state of the art of the economic literature on the economic impact of ICT can in fact be depicted as one characterized by a gap between, on the one hand, a conceptual framework on the socioeconomic effects of ICT (that is, e-inclusion) which has become increasingly complex and multidimensional, and, on the other hand, empirical models which are able to grasp such complex effects only to a very limited extent. The review has nonetheless shown that over the last few years some progress has been made, and in particular in three main directions: in the area of data collection and production of statistics – which are increasingly covering the diffusion, usage and impact dimension of ICT; in the use of these data in the standard econometric literature; and in the efforts made to obtain direct estimates of the economic benefits of e-inclusion in terms of GDP growth, employment, wages and other relevant economic indicators.

The main purpose of our research has been to contribute to closing the gap between theory and empirical practice in this new and challenging research field, by providing a meaningful set of indicators distinguishing between different dimensions of e-inclusion (infrastructure, usage and impact) and assessing their differentiated economic impact. The provision of a new set of data and indicators on the infrastructure, usage and impact dimensions of ICT can in fact be seen as a first successful attempt at synthesizing and operationalizing in empirical terms a great deal of conceptual and theoretical work on e-inclusion. With reference to the empirical assessment of the economic impact of e-inclusion, this project has made some significant progress exploring the differentiated effects that the specific dimensions of usage and impact of ICT have on various types of economic performance indicators (see the following two chapters). These are rather encouraging results which further confirm the robustness of the e-inclusion metrics proposed and their potentiality to be further exploited for a thorough assessment of the economic impact of e-inclusion.

In the next few years research in this area will probably proceed in a rather exploratory way continuing to follow different approaches and methodologies. This is not only fully coherent and physiological with the infant phase of this new research field but is also likely to be (at least at this stage) the most fruitful path to follow.

All that said, three broad methodological indications can nonetheless be drawn.

The first relevant issue has to do with the level of the analysis. This review has clearly shown that e-inclusion has many dimensions and affects very different socioeconomic domains, through different and long-chained mechanisms. Here a sort of dilemma emerges: is the idea of capturing long term effects of e-inclusion on the economy at an aggregate level both meaningful and feasible, or is it rather too ambitious a goal in terms of both model designs and availability of data? Probably it is too early to provide a final answer to this question, and it is very likely that this is an issue which will remain open for some time ahead. Nonetheless the empirical analyses conducted at the macro level in this project, providing consistent results in various economic areas, seem to suggest that investigating the effects of different dimensions of e-inclusion on different macroeconomic variables can provide interesting and policy relevant results. What seems reasonably clear is that the heuristic value of a traditional approach based on the growth-accounting methodology and on the use of production function models is rapidly becoming exhausted. More eclectic econometric and multivariate statistical approaches (such as the ones adopted in this project) seem to be, at least at this stage, more appropriate and fruitful tools to search for preliminary stylized facts and empirical regularities across countries and regions. The evidence presented in this project clearly supports this methodological approach.

The use of newly released data on the usage dimension of ICT by firms and individuals is likely to be a second particularly fruitful research path to follow, in order to shed light on the many sources of heterogeneity characterizing both the processes of e-inclusion and their economic effects. Within the micro-based literature on the economic impact of ICT, the literature looking at the impact of these technologies on employment, and more generally on the performance of the labour market at large, is perhaps the more closely related to e-inclusion. Besides these econometric contributions, we have come across a large number of anecdotal contributions highlighting the positive impact of various e-inclusion initiatives in the employment/labour market area. This literature needs however to be complemented and further supported by more robust evidence, matching existing labour survey data with the new micro-level data on ICT use and digital skills.

Finally, the more inductive and pragmatic approach of estimating the impact of digital inclusion in specific areas and contexts also represents a fruitful (and complementary) avenue to follow. As shown in this survey, so far we have only a limited number of tentative and explorative exercises, which are highly heterogeneous in terms of sectors covered, methodologies used and overall robustness of the analyses. These types of studies need to be further strengthened and carried out, as much as possible, in a cross-country comparative framework. On the other hand, adding up these different effects in order to get an overall macroeconomic estimate of the impact of e-inclusion does not seem to be (at present) a valuable methodology to follow, and this is because of the numerous caveats affecting these exercises and the many areas of impact left uncovered. These studies could nonetheless help to shed light on the mechanisms and effects of e-inclusion in specific economic areas and, thus, help researchers to better understand and model the complex link between e-inclusion and aggregate economic performance, as we have done in this project.

NOTES

1. Surveys collecting data on the ways and the extent to which ICTs are used in the daily life of households, individuals and firms, are spreading all over the world, although often in a rather spontaneous fashion and with little international standardization and methodological validation. In this new scenario, probably the most robust, large scale and comprehensive survey on ICT-use by firms, households and individuals is the one coordinated by Eurostat and carried out from 2003 on (Eurostat, 2009, 2010).
2. By starting from the consideration that the language of most websites is English, some of these authors have also tested that, in addition to an education variable, English proficiency is a further explanatory variable for ICT adoption. However, other empirical results do not support this hypothesis (Hargittai, 1999b; Caselli and Coleman, 2001).
3. Barth et al. (1993) argue that older workers, given that they are less flexible, may either directly slow down the process of innovation, or make it harder to implement those organizational changes necessary to fully exploit ICT (see Skirbekk, 2004, for a review of the literature and evidence on the impact of age on productivity).
4. The rationale for this result is that the public sector often lacks the incentive to obtain high productivity standards, and thus to innovate, and so adopt ICT.
5. All these studies seem to converge in pointing out that at least three components are needed to produce the full benefits of higher productivity growth from ICT: higher

ICT capital, higher investment in the complementary skills, and adjustment of the organizational structure of firms. The effect of ICT on firms, productivity, as well as the level of complementarity with organizational innovation and skills, have been found to vary across countries, industries and firm size. This emerges from the results of the EU Sectoral e-Business Watch project (which has looked at these effects using the EU KLEMS database and at a micro level using data collected through an ad hoc survey (SeBW project, www.ebusiness-watch.org).

6. The economic impact of digital technologies: an empirical analysis on European countries

6.1 ASSESSING THE ECONOMIC IMPACT OF E-INCLUSION: A BRIEF SUMMARY OF THE RELEVANT LITERATURE

The economic benefits of e-inclusion are difficult to estimate. In fact on the macroeconomic quantification of the inclusive potentials of ICT and its impact on economic performance (productivity, consumer welfare, employability and economic growth) there is almost no or only anecdotal evidence in the current socioeconomic literature (see literature review, Chapter 5). The analysis carried out in this part of the book aims at moving a step ahead in the direction of quantifying the economic impact of e-inclusion by relating the set of indicators of e-inclusion developed in the first part of the project with a set of economic variables that should be affected by the diffusion of ICT. We will also highlight the possible transmission mechanisms between the various proxies of e-inclusion and the 'performance' variables.

The analysis asks whether the different dimensions of ICT diffusion identified in the first part of the study (infrastructure, usage and impact) exert different impacts on performance variables. In this framework we also aim at assessing the extent of interdependencies between the goals defined in the Riga Ministerial Declaration (2006) in terms of e-inclusion and the economic targets defined formerly in the Lisbon Strategy and now in the strategy Europe 2020, concerning in particular the overall employment rate and that of disadvantaged categories (women and older workers).

In particular the strategy Europe 2020 aims at bringing to 75 per cent the employment rate for women and men aged 20–64 and to favour a greater participation of youth, older workers and low skilled in the labour market.[1] We will see later in the chapter that European countries show highly differentiated levels of the above mentioned indicators and that differences are particularly high when one considers disadvantaged people (women, older workers). For these categories of workers the gap between northern countries and Mediterranean countries is much higher than for the overall employment rate. We will assess whether a movement towards achieving the Riga objectives in terms of e-inclusion may help with reducing such gaps.

Before showing the results of the empirical estimations, we will briefly review the relevant literature on the economic impact of e-inclusion. This literature has been thoroughly reviewed in the previous chapter, here we will only briefly recall some of the results that are particularly relevant for our empirical estimations, namely the impact of ICT on the labour market and on disadvantaged groups, and the macroeconomic impact of broadband.

There have been several studies showing that both the access to and the ability to use ICT affect employability conditions along the entire lifecycle of individuals, being able to influence the decision to enter the labour market (the labour participation decision), the likelihood of getting a job (the transition from unemployment to employment) (Codagnone, 2009), the likelihood of losing a job (the transition from employment to unemployment) (Friedberg, 2003) as well as decisions on early retirement (Bartel and Sicherman, 1993; Schleife, 2006).

Although these findings cannot be regarded as proper estimates of the economic costs of digital exclusion or of the economic impact of digital inclusion, they nonetheless provide useful insights in this direction, identifying a specific area (labour market) and specific dimensions affected by ICT (employability, wages, lifelong earning perspectives), which can be used as a methodological basis for assessing the impact of e-inclusion policies. As we have shown in Chapter 5, this literature and its findings have in fact inspired (and have been used as inputs in) several empirical exercises aiming precisely at assessing the aggregate and long-term potential economic effects brought about by an increased level of digital skills and e-inclusion policies.[2]

A relevant e-inclusion issue in this respect emerges when the highly uneven distribution of digital skills across age classes is taken into account. Several studies as well as the recent figures released by OECD and EUROSTAT show that the shortage of ICT skills is concentrated among the older generations (Miniaci and Parisi, 2005, 2006; OECD, 2008; CEC, 2009). There is a large amount of empirical evidence showing that this is a particularly vulnerable component of the labour force which is more at risk of getting laid off during periods of downturn, and of experiencing long-lasting periods of unemployment. The structural nature of these processes creates severe problems of social exclusion, destroys a large amount of human capital, and jeopardises the long-term sustainability of welfare systems, especially in demographic contexts characterized by ageing populations. These are all relevant areas and variables of concern for any attempt at assessing the economic impact of e-inclusion.

A contribution in this direction is provided by a recent study which, within the context of the Vienna study (Codagnone, 2009), has looked at the impact of ICT on labour market variables. The impact of digital skills on employability (probability of getting a job) has been investigated using a micro-level longitudinal dataset (2000–06) drawn from the Bank of Italy survey of Household Income and Wealth. This study has used a robust econometric technique controlling for a large number of fixed effects. Using a longitudinal analysis and controlling for education variables the study clearly shows that the ICT revolution is penalizing especially older workers via a depreciation of their human capital.

With regard to the impact of e-inclusion on employment, this chapter provides new and interesting evidence which supports and further qualifies – at macro level and through the use of more robust and comprehensive data on e-inclusion – the findings of the micro-level literature reviewed above. In the regression analysis (Section 6.4) we will investigate whether there are differentiated effects of the infrastructure, usage and impact dimensions of e-inclusion on the employment rate in general, and in particular on the employment rate of 'disadvantaged groups'.

Another strand of literature that is directly related to the empirical analysis carried out in this chapter consists of econometric studies on the economic impact of broadband at the macro level. Over the last decade several studies have tried to estimate the effects of broadband penetration on aggregate economic variables such as GDP, employment, and productivity, mainly finding a positive significant effect. These contributions are rather coherent with an e-inclusion perspective of ICT and its economic impact, putting a great emphasis on the use dimension of this technology as well as assuming a plurality of social and economic domains affected by broadband penetration. These studies have been reviewed in Chapter 5. Here we only report the main conclusions and explain the similarities and differences with our approach.

Most of the studies assessing the macroeconomic impact of broadband focus on the USA and find a positive impact on employment (NTATREP, 2006; Crandall et al., 2007; Connected Nation, 2008) and on GDP (NTATREP, 2006; Crandall et al., 2007).

There are also some econometric studies which have found more ambiguous and counter-intuitive relationships between broadband and GDP. This is the case of a couple contributions by Thompson and Garbacz (2007 and 2008). In these studies a negative and statistically significant cross-(US)state relationship between broadband deployment and economic output has been found. A possible explanation of this puzzling result might be based on the so called 'delay hypothesis' (existence of time lag between the introduction of ICT and the time the economic effects show up) or (more worryingly) on the presence of a negative time-wasting effect on labour productivity accompanying the first introduction of these technologies. Another possible explanation of this counter-intuitive result is the existence of a threshold level above which broadband penetration starts to produce tangible effects. The presence of such an effect has also been found by Koutroumpis (2008) in one of the few empirical studies covering the European continent.

The presence of a threshold effect in the economic impact of broadband, this time referred to the existence of appropriate levels of PC diffusion and digital skills, has been found in a more recent cross-country study covering the whole OECD area (LECG, 2009). The paper distinguishes between low and high 'broadband environments' and finds that a positive impact of broadband is found only in the case of the most favourable ICT environments ('ICT-eco-systems').

Beyond the positive relationship found in the majority of these studies between broadband and important macroeconomic variables such as GDP and employment, a second more conceptual message stemming from some of these contributions is that in order to reach most of these economic effects, broadband has to be used rather than just being available.

This is an important point that we will investigate in our empirical analysis aiming at capturing the differentiated affect of infrastructure, usage and impact (empowerment) dimensions of e-inclusion on performance variables. Moreover, making use of the rich results available from the literature (including the case studies reviewed in Chapter 5) we will make some a priori assumptions on the expected effect of the different dimensions of e-inclusion on GDP, employment and productivity, thus building a conceptual framework that will then be tested using the data and indicators presented in the first part of this book (together with other statistics provided by the Eurostat).

6.2   THE THEORETICAL FRAMEWORK

In order to theoretically devise the possible transmission mechanisms between each of the different dimensions of e-inclusion and the performance variables selected in the empirical analysis it is useful to briefly recall the meaning of the indicators of infrastructure, usage and impact.

As far as 'infrastructure' is concerned it should capture the degree of development of the infrastructure available in a given country – or in the whole of Europe – for disseminating and developing the use of the internet.

Infrastructure is, therefore, a precondition for the effectiveness of the more sophisticated measures of e-inclusion, namely usage and impact. In the absence of a sufficiently developed infrastructure there would be no possibilities to increase the usage and the impact of information technologies.

Overall, we expect that among EU countries the minimum level of infrastructure that is a necessary precondition for the usage and impact dimensions is guaranteed. If this is the case the most important determinants of differences in performance variables should be found when looking at differences in the usage and impact (empowerment) dimensions.

Usage and impact may well affect economic variables differently. In fact the first index captures the extent to which individuals 'use' and 'know how to use' the web, while the second index captures many different areas of application of the new technologies providing information on the structural changes that are taking place with the diffusion of the new technologies.

Going back to what is included in the two indexes allows the formulation of hypotheses on how they are expected to affect economic variables. The 'usage' index captures the autonomy, intensity and skill in the use of the new technologies, thus measuring the intensity and competence with which people have access to the new technologies. For the same level of infrastructure (as captured by the 'infrastructure' index) a more intense use is expected to have a positive impact on labour productivity through the increasing competence of the labour force. However this is not the only possible economic outcome. In fact, the Riga Ministerial Declaration (2006) identified and proposed a set of well-defined parameters that can help to monitor the state of progress of the digital inclusion process: 'to convincingly address e-Inclusion, the differences in Internet usage between current average use by the EU population and use by older people, people with disabilities, women, lower education groups, unemployed and "less-developed" regions should be reduced to a half from 2005 to 2010'.

Based on these considerations a higher 'usage' index with reference to certain disadvantaged groups (women, older workers, long-term unemployed, and so on) may allow these groups to bridge their gaps with the rest of the population, favouring a higher participation in the labour market and a higher employment rate.

Finally the 'impact' or 'empowerment' dimension captures the whole area in which the positive effects of individual and social empowerment resulting from the technology appropriation process are felt. As discussed, the impact dimension has been subdivided into six subdimensions, which can help to shed light on the different areas in which empowerment effects can be felt at both individual and social level. More specifically, the

Table 6.1   Transmission mechanisms from the subdimensions of impact to economic variables

Area/subdimension	Transmission mechanisms	Variables affected
Economy	Development of new services Competition/cost savings	Economic growth Total factor productivity
Labour	Better matching Job flexibility (encouraging part-time)	Employment and participation rates Employment and participation rates for women and older people
Education	Increases in human capital Lifelong learning	Labour productivity, employment rate Employment rate of older and long-term unemployed
Health	Cost savings	TFP
Government	Cost savings, efficiency gains	TFP
Culture, communication and recreation	Creation of new markets	Economic growth

subdimensions are: economy; employment and labour; education; health; government; and culture, communication and entertainment.

How are these different measures expected to affect economic performance variables? Table 6.1 summarizes some possible transmission mechanisms and the main economic variables that are likely to be affected.

In the case of the economy subdimension, the Internet changes everyday life. In particular the use of the Internet for banking, for buying and selling goods, and for arranging travel and accommodation are just three examples where it increases competition, leads to cost savings, and by these means, also stimulates the growth of different service activities.

The second subdimension that we have selected comprises indicators that are connected to the complex world of labour, with respect to both those who already have a place in it and those who seek employment. For the latter subjects, especially the young ones, the Internet is an opportunity for research and application. Rather than limiting their job search to a limited geographical area, Internet users can take as a reference point an independently selected universe to offer their services or evaluate what it has to offer. For those who, on the other hand, already have a place in the labour market, the Internet represents an instrument which becomes part of the work routine, that is, it enables one to carry on a business activity away from the office or company premises. In the first case the use of the Internet allows a better matching between employers and employees thus reducing the frictional rate of unemployment. In both cases – even with all the obvious differences – the quality of the work performed changes significantly, new forms of more flexible jobs are made possible with again possible positive consequences on the employment rate also of disadvantaged people (women and old workers).

The education subdimension comprises all the indicators that contribute to determining 'human capital', that is, that valuable asset which is becoming increasingly significant for the development of the information society. Human capital, understood as the whole of knowledge, skills and information, is closely connected to the education dimension, which extends throughout the lifespan of individuals. In this context, the opportunities offered by the Internet acquire significant relevance: from online university to courses on specific subjects of interest, from professional courses to post educational programmes. The main economic consequence should be increases in labour productivity and in the employment rate.

In the case of the health and the government areas, the use of the Internet should mainly lead to efficiency gains, cost savings and, therefore, increases in total factor productivity (TFP).

Finally the culture, communication and recreation area comprises the most common communication opportunities, such as electronic mail and chat rooms, the consumption of radio and television on alternative platforms, downloading of games, music, magazines and software, and the reading of newspapers free of charge or on payment. In summary, these are some of the many activities that Internet users carry out over the web, and which constitute the contemporary forms of communication and cultural consumption. The main economic impact of these activities is expected to be the creation of new markets and, consequently, economic growth.

Overall, the complex and variegated subdimensions of the 'impact' index should capture the extent to which the use of the new technologies leads to a transformation of the society and the economy that involves a paradigmatic change. In this respect, if the opportunities offered by this change are appropriately exploited, increases in empowerment should favour a higher growth à la Schumpeter, that is, involving a process of structural change.

Summarizing, we expect that 'usage' should mainly affect labour productivity and eventually also the employment rate, while we expect the main economic effects of 'impact' to be found in stimulating economic growth, total factor productivity growth and the employment rate. These hypotheses are tested in the remaining part of the study. Before that, we present the data used in the empirical analysis, the methodology, and some descriptive statistics on the variables used in the regression analysis.

6.3   DATA AND ESTIMATED EQUATIONS

The purpose of the empirical analysis is to test how different dimensions of e-inclusion (infrastructure, usage and impact) affect countries' economic performance. With this purpose, we start by decomposing per capita GDP into two main components: the employment rate and labour productivity:

$$\frac{GDP}{POPULATION} = \frac{GDP}{EMPLOYEES} \frac{EMPLOYEES}{POPULATION} \qquad (6.1)$$

We then estimate the impact of e-inclusion variables separately on the rate of growth of labour productivity, the employment rate and on the rate of growth of per capita GDP. In the case of the labour market we also focus on e-inclusion targeted categories, namely women, older workers and long-term unemployed. Unfortunately data on TFP (from EUKLEMS database) were available only for 12 countries with only two years overlapping with the e-inclusion indexes (2004 and 2005); this did not allow us to directly test the impact of e-inclusion on TFP. However evidence of such effects may be indirectly taken from the estimation of countries' rates of growth.

When estimating the impact of e-inclusion on the employment rate we control for labour costs (which are expected to negatively affect the employment rate), human capital (which should have a positive impact), and the rate of growth of demand (also with an expected positive sign). The estimated equation is, therefore, the following:

$$EMPR_{it} = a_0 + a_1 LC + a_2 HC + a_3 DEM + a_4 INCL + e_{it} \qquad (6.2)$$

where $EMPR_{it}$ denotes the employment rate of country i at time t, LC is labour costs (measured as total employees remuneration in constant prices), HC is human capital (measured as either the percentage of the population aged 25 to 64 having completed at least upper secondary education, or the share of lifelong learning where 'lifelong learning' refers to persons aged 25 to 64 who stated that they received education or training in the four weeks preceding the survey (numerator); the denominator consists of the total population of the same age group, excluding those who did not answer the question on 'participation to education and training'), *DEM* is the rate of growth of demand (measured as the rate of growth of GDP at constant prices) and *INCL* denotes e-inclusion variables.

When estimating the impact of e-inclusion on the rate of growth of labour productivity, we control for human capital and for the investment rate:

$$LPROD_{it} = a_0 + a_1 HC + a_2 INV + a_3 INCL + e_{it} \qquad (6.3)$$

where $LPROD_{it}$ is the rate of growth of labour productivity (measured as the ratio of GDP at constant prices to the number of employees) and *INV* is the share of gross fixed capital formation on GDP.

Finally, when estimating the impact of e-inclusion on the rate of growth of per capita GDP, we control for human capital, for the investment rate and for the rate of growth of population:

$$GDPPC_{it} = a_0 + a_1 HC + a_2 INV + a_3 POP + a_4 INCL + e_{it} \qquad (6.4)$$

where *GDPPC* denotes the rate of growth of per capita GDP (measured as the ratio between GDP at constant prices and total population) and *POP* denotes the rate of growth of total population.

Data for all these variables are obtained from Eurostat and cover 27 EU countries over the period 2004–08 for a total of 108 observations (one time period is lost due to the computation of growth rates). Equations are estimated in rates of growth in a repeated cross-section time-series using generalized least squares with heteroschedastic robust standard errors.

Figures 6.1 and 6.2 report summary statistics. Figure 6.1 reports variations across countries as an average over time in at-risk groups (women, people aged 55–64, long-term unemployed) in the employment rate and in usage and impact indexes, while Figure 6.2 reports mean changes over time in the same variables for each country.

Summary statistics (not reported) show that per capita GDP has grown at an average yearly rate of 3 per cent over the period 2004–08 in EU27 countries, labour productivity at the rate of 2 per cent and the employment rate at the rate of 1 per cent. Looking at at-risk groups we find that the employment rate of women has grown as the average (1 per cent) while among people aged 55–64 employment has grown at a significantly higher rate (3 per cent). Finally long-term unemployment has decreased at an average rate of 12 per cent (from 3.89 in 2004 to 2.27 in 2008). Looking at e-inclusion indicators the infrastructure index shows the lowest increase (0.01) followed by the impact index (0.03) and the usage index (0.04). Distinguishing among groups, usage has increased less than the average

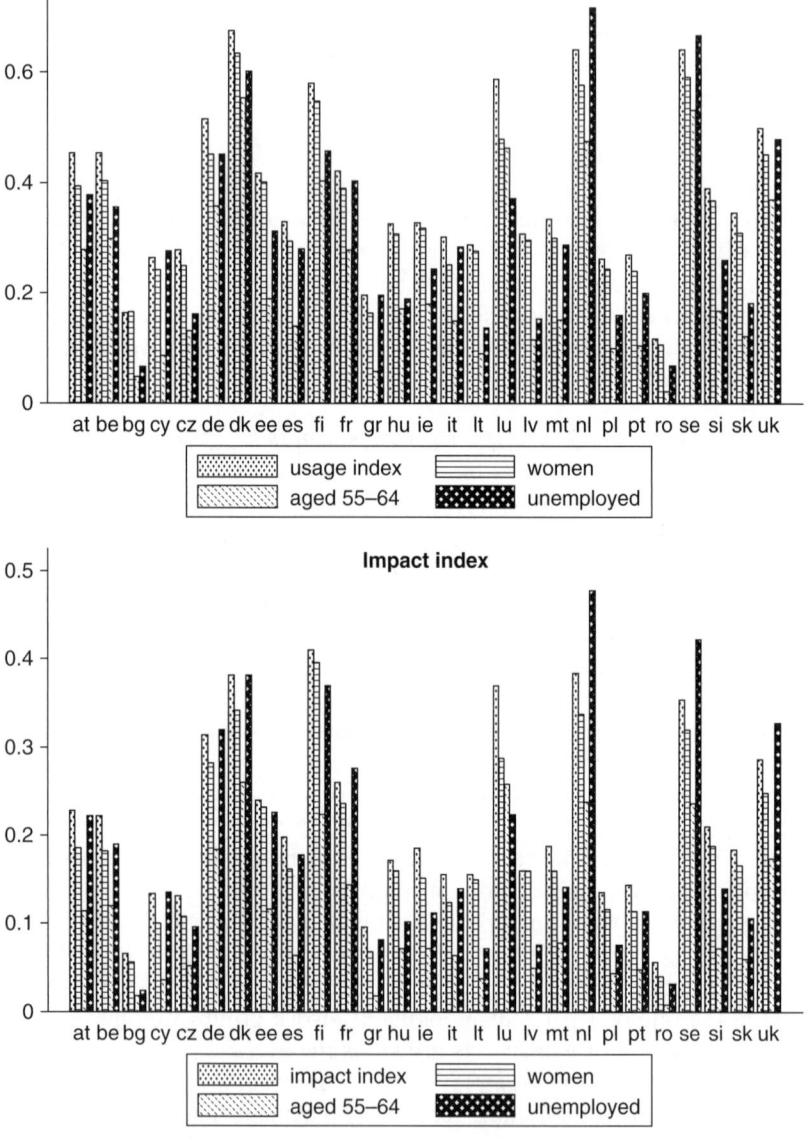

Figure 6.1   Average over time (2004–08) for EU27 countries in the usage and impact indexes and employment rate, by groups

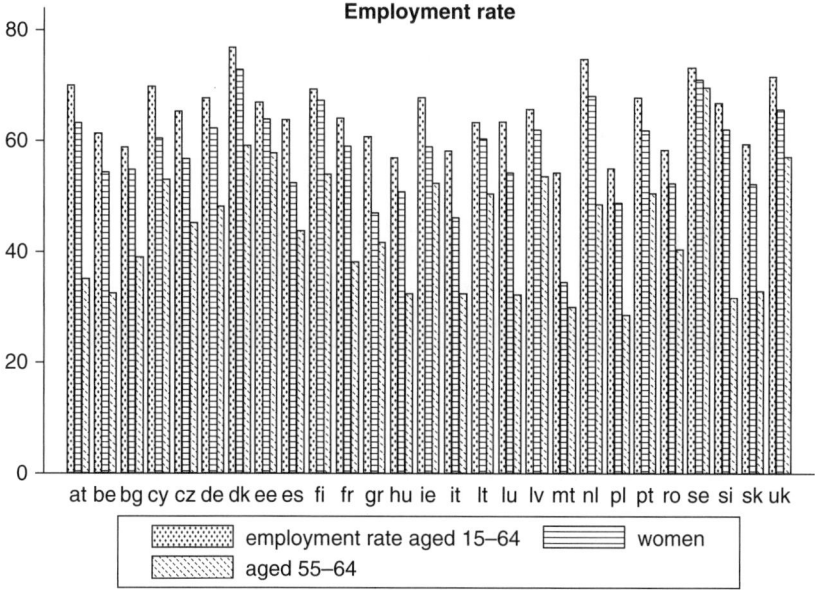

Figure 6.1   (continued)

for older people and for unemployed while for women it has increased as the average. The impact index has increased as the average for women and unemployed but less than the average for older people. Overall it does not appear to be a significant convergence trend in disadvantaged groups in the period under analysis, as shown in other parts of our study.

Looking at Figure 6.1, we can observe that northern countries (Sweden, Finland and Denmark), Luxembourg, the Netherlands and the UK perform well in both the usage and impact dimensions. Among these countries there are however differences in the position of 'at risk' categories. In fact, while in northern countries, in the Netherlands and the UK the difference between men and women is not too large and the group of unemployed performs sometimes even better than the other groups (as in the Netherlands, Sweden, the UK and Finland), by contrast in Luxembourg women and unemployed have significantly lower values than the average. In all countries the gap with people aged 55–64 is large. The countries with the lowest values of the usage and impact indexes are Bulgaria, Greece and Romania.

Looking at the employment rate, we can observe that several countries meet the Lisbon target value of 70 per cent, and some meet and others are close to the Europe 2020 target of 75 per cent (Austria, Cyprus, Denmark, Finland, Netherlands, Sweden and the UK). Moreover, in the case of

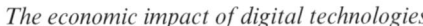

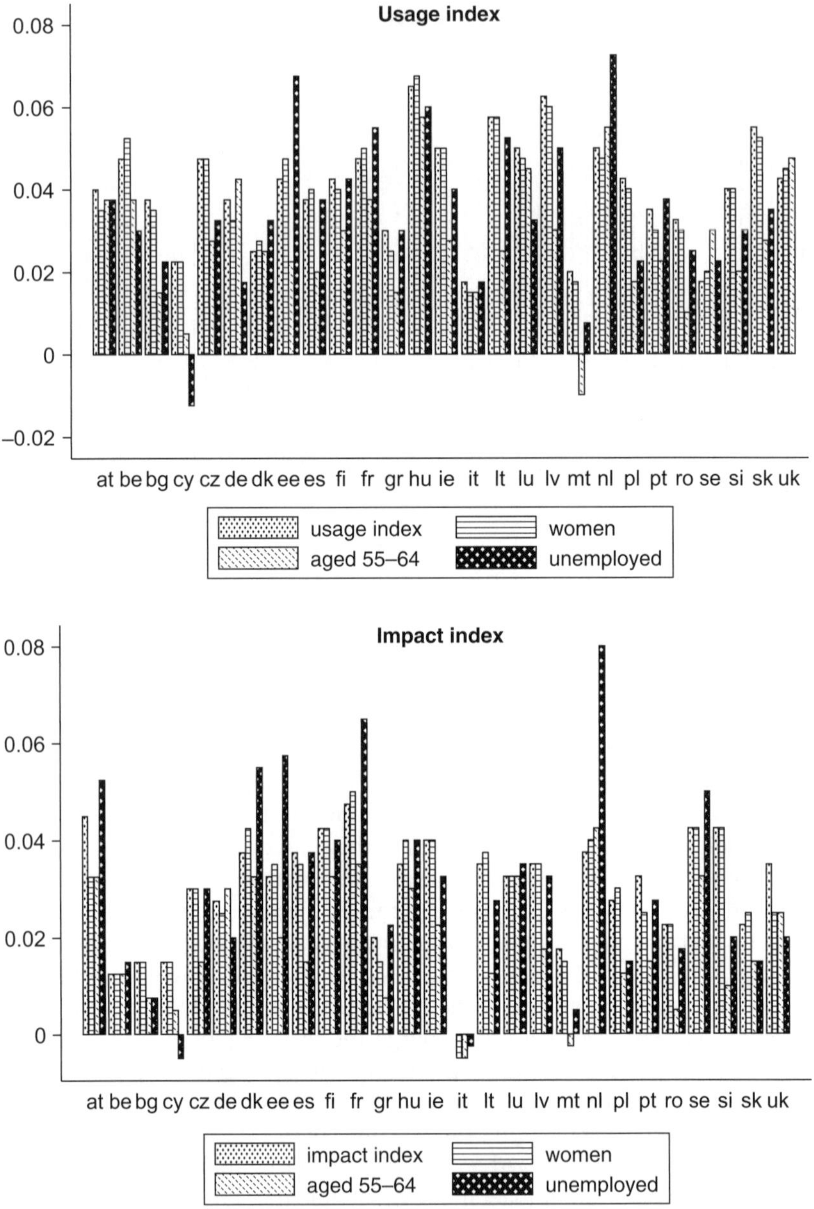

*Figure 6.2   Average change in the usage and impact indexes and
employment rate by groups in EU27 countries: 2004–08*

Figure 6.2   (continued)

Denmark and Sweden, the target is also met for the female employment rate, and, in the case of Sweden, for the population aged 55–64 (for these groups the Lisbon targets were respectively 60 per cent and 50 per cent, therefore these countries are well above the targets, although they do not meet the new target of 75 per cent). The Netherlands and the UK are also very close to the 70 per cent target for the female employment rate. It is interesting to observe, when looking at at-risk categories (in particular the case population aged 55–64), that there are enormous differences across countries in the employment rate. In particular the employment rate of population aged 55–64 is below 40 per cent in numerous countries (Austria, Belgium, Bulgaria, France, Hungary, Italy, Luxembourg, Malta, Poland, Slovenia and Slovakia) some of which have overall employment rates above 60 per cent (Austria, Belgium, France, Luxembourg and Slovenia).

Looking at changes over time (Figure 6.2) it appears that over the period 2004–08 the indexes capturing the usage and the impact dimensions of e-inclusion have both increased. The only exceptions are usage and impact among the unemployed in Cyprus, usage and impact among people aged 55–64 in Malta, and all impact indicators in Italy. Moreover there does not appear to be a convergence trend across countries: in fact some of the countries with already high values also experience high increases (the Netherlands, Luxembourg and the UK for usage; the Netherlands, Sweden and Denmark for impact). Among countries lagging behind, many new entrants experience large changes (Estonia, Hungary, Lithuania and Slovakia for usage; Estonia, Hungary and Slovenia for impact) but this is not the case for other laggard countries (Italy and Greece).

The performance of the employment rate appears on average positive. Exceptions are the decrease in the employment rate among old people in Denmark, Malta and Portugal, and the decrease in the total and female employment rate in Hungary. The highest increases in the total employment rate are found in newcomers (Bulgaria, Estonia, Latvia, and Poland) while Spain also registers a high increase in female employment. The employment rate of older people registers very high increases in Bulgaria, Germany, Latvia and Slovakia.

6.4   REGRESSION RESULTS

Tables 6.2, 6.3 and 6.4 report the results of the estimation of equations (6.2), (6.3) and (6.4). The first table (6.2) reports the results of the impact

Table 6.2   *The effect of the composite indicator of e-inclusion on employment rate, labour productivity and economic growth: EU27 2004–08*

	Employment rate		Labour productivity		GDP growth	
	Coef.	z-value	Coef.	z-value	Coef	z-value
E-inclusion index	0.053 *	1.860	0.134 **	2.070	0.121	1.110
Wages	−0.036 ***	−4.100				
Demand	0.123 ***	3.110				
Secondary education	0.001	1.290	0.000 ***	3.020	0.230 **	2.080
Lifelong learning	0.002 ***	3.340				
Investment			0.046 ***	4.790	0.097 ***	7.770
Population					−1.690 ***	−3.910
Constant	0.005 **	2.330	−0.145 ***	−4.930	−0.255 ***	−6.410
Number of observations	107		108		106	

Notes: The z-values are based on heteroscedasticity consistent standard errors (using White's method); *, **, *** denote respectively significant at 10%, 5% and 1%.

Table 6.3   *The effect of various dimensions of e-inclusion on the*
employment rate, labour productivity and economic growth:
EU27 countries 2004–08

	Employment rate		Labour productivity			GDP growth		
	Coef.	z-value	Coef.		z-value	Coef.		z-value
Infrastructure	0.021	1.520	0.019		0.500	−0.079		−1.540
Usage	−0.004	−0.190	0.087	**	1.850	−0.091		−1.300
Impact	0.034 *	1.720	−0.036		−0.760	0.187	***	2.570
Wages	−0.036 ***	−4.140						
Demand	0.131 ***	3.120						
Secondary education	0.001 *	1.640	0.000	***	2.950	0.318	***	3.240
Lifelong learning	0.002 ***	2.710						
Investment			0.046	***	4.820	0.099	***	8.490
Population						−1.984	***	−4.810
Constant	0.005 **	2.140	−0.146	***	−4.910	−0.259	***	−6.950
Number of observations		107		108			106	

Notes: The *z*-values are based on heteroscedasticity consistent standard errors (using White's method); *, **, *** denote respectively significant at 10%, 5% and 1%.

of e-inclusion on the employment rate, labour productivity and per capita GDP growth using the composite indicator of e-inclusion, while Table 6.3 reports results including simultaneously all three dimensions of e-inclusion (infrastructure, usage and impact). Finally Table 6.4 reports the results of the impact of the different dimensions of e-inclusion on disadvantaged groups (the female employment rate, the employment rate of people aged 55–64, and the employment rate of long-term unemployed).

The results show that e-inclusion has a positive impact on the employment rate and on labour productivity. However different dimensions of e-inclusion have different impacts on various economic variables. In particular the 'infrastructure' dimension does not appear to discriminate. This result should not be interpreted to mean that this dimension is not important but that the level reached by advanced countries in this dimension is sufficient to allow more sophisticated dimensions of e-inclusion to play their positive role. Moreover it has to be taken into account that not a single low-performing country in the infrastructure index ranks among the best-performing countries in terms of Internet usage.

Regression results show that the usage dimension is the strategic one when we look at the rate of growth of labour productivity, while the

Table 6.4   *The effect of various dimensions of e-inclusion on the*
              employment rate of disadvantaged groups: EU27 countries
              2004–08

	Female		Employment rate aged 55–64		Long-term unemployed rate	
	Coef.	z-value	Coef.	z-value	Coef	z-value
Infrastructure	0.144	1.390	0.014	0.240	−0.395	−1.470
Usage	−0.066	−0.770	0.308 ***	3.350	0.183	1.010
Impact	0.260 **	2.520	−0.297 ***	−2.740	−0.560 **	−2.330
Wages	−0.076 *	−1.900	−0.063 **	−2.240	0.359 ***	2.560
Demand	0.615 ***	2.930	0.321 ***	3.010	−2.436 ***	−5.790
Secondary education	0.001	0.400				
Long life learning			0.003 **	1.940	−0.039 ***	−4.520
Constant	−0.013	−1.310	0.012 **	2.180	−0.003	−0.140
Number of observations		108		107		105

Notes: The z-values are based on heteroscedasticity consistent standard errors (using White's method); *, **, *** denote respectively significant at 10%, 5% and 1%.

empowerment (impact) dimension is what really matters for creating new jobs and for the rate of growth of the economy. This is consistent with our expectations. In fact the 'usage' index captures diffusion, autonomy, intensity and skills in the use of the new technologies, all aspects that are expected to change the familiarity with the new technologies, and, therefore, to make individuals more productive for the same amount of infrastructure provided. On the other hand, as we have stressed in Section 6.2, the 'impact' or 'empowerment index' contains various dimensions that capture the capability of the new technology to transform modes of production and consumers' everyday life in a Schumpeterian fashion. The expected consequence is the creation of new markets and, therefore, more jobs, higher TFP and a higher rate of growth.

   Results also show, as expected, that the employment rate decreases when wages rise while it increases with increases in demand and in the level of education (in particular lifelong learning). Labour productivity increases with the investment rate and with the share of educated people (people with secondary education). Finally the rate of growth of per capita GDP increases with the investment rate and with the share of educated people, and decreases with the rate of growth of population.

Finally it is interesting to assess the impact of infrastructure, usage and empowerment on 'at risk' groups. This analysis allows a more direct assessment of the 'inclusiveness' potential of the new technologies, with specific attention to participation in the labour market. Here the empirical analysis shows that empowerment is a strategic variable for allowing women and long-term unemployed to increase their participation in the labour market. On the other hand, when the focus is on people aged '55–64' what really matters for their inclusion in the labour market is their ability to use the new technologies. This is probably due to the fact that, for this part of the population, as the data have shown, 'usage' is still relatively low and, therefore, becomes a conditioning variable to grasp the inclusive benefits of the new technologies.

NOTES

1. Formerly the Lisbon Strategy had the following goals: (i) an overall employment rate of 70%; (ii) an employment rate of women over 60%; (iii) an employment rate of 50% among older workers; annual economic growth around 3%.
2. In the US empirical tests on the relationship between ICT skills on the one hand, and employability as well as the likelihood of remaining employed on the other hand, have produced significant coefficients (Friedberg, 2003), while for Germany the evidence is less clear-cut. Evidence on Italy (Codagnone, 2009) shows that there is a serious digital exclusion issue for older and less educated individuals and – among these – especially for women.

7. The impact of e-inclusion in Europe: a scenario analysis

7.1 THE CRITERIA FOR MODEL SELECTION

Differently from the econometric analyses carried out in the previous chapter, the methodology followed in this chapter consists in simulating (rather than estimating) the economic impact of e-inclusion policies by constructing several scenarios. The simulation exercises carried out are just examples of a larger set of possible analyses to be conducted with International Futures (IFs) and possibly other computable general equilibrium (CGE) models.

The most difficult task is to carry out the simulations with the aim of disentangling the different effects of the various dimensions of e-inclusion identified in this research (infrastructure, usage and impact, or empowerment) since in simulation exercises we cannot directly use the data and indicators presented in the first part of this book and used in the econometric analysis carried out in the previous chapter. The strategy that we follow is therefore different and is based on the choice of the parameters to modify in order to put into action the different dimensions of e-inclusion that emerged in the previous chapters. The key issues are related to the choice – and the motivation behind it – of parameters and their inclusion in one of three dimensions of e-inclusion.

Based on this choice, simulations will be structured into three steps aiming to disentangle the effects of: (a) higher infrastructure of e-inclusion; (b) higher infrastructure and usage of e-inclusion; and (c) higher infrastructure, usage and impact of e-inclusion.

Simulations include two sets of scenario analysis. The first one is devoted to the study of quantitative impacts of e-inclusion policies for EU27 countries as a whole. The second set of simulation exercises is devoted to the study of the ability of e-inclusion policies to determine different processes of divergence and/or convergence across European countries. The outcome variables included in the analysis are chosen taking into account that e-inclusion is an economic opportunity and should not be seen only as a problem, and referring to the rich, although not yet systematized results (causal links) available from the literature reviewed in Chapter 5.

An inclusive information society: (a) brings large market opportunities for the ICT sector, (b) contributes to productivity growth, and (c) reduces the costs of social and economic exclusion. Consequently, we concentrate our attention on the macroeconomic performance of countries, focusing mainly on those aspects that we expect to be influenced, namely productivity, consumer welfare, employability and economic growth. Nonetheless, we include in the analysis a series of variables as proxies of e-inclusion, to make clearer the direct effects of changes in the values of parameters chosen in each scenario. This also facilitates the reconstruction of the causal links among the highly complex networks of relationships existing in the model.

In order to select the model to be used in the simulations we use the following characteristics: (i) it has to be internationally used; (ii) it has to be able to assess e-inclusion policy initiatives in multiple dimensions (economic and social) and geographically within Europe, across Europe and in a global context.

To assess and compare existing models we also identified a set of reference parameters. Such parameters are related to: (a) methodological approach; (b) structural specification; and (c) performance variables. The way each of the parameters is considered has implications for the assessment of policy impact.

First, with respect to methodological approach, two classes of models can be identified in the policy analysis literature: (i) CGE models and (ii) macro-econometric models.

CGE models (such as WorldScan) are entirely constructed in accordance with economic theory: behavioural equations are derived from microeconomic principles (consumers maximize their utility while firms maximize profits), and at each point in time prices are such that all markets clear (both goods and production factors markets); that is, the system is in general equilibrium. Due to their commitment to economic consistency, parameters are not estimated. They are calibrated.

At the opposite end, macro-econometric models (such as NEMESIS and International Futures) are entirely estimated. They are not committed to some economic theory, but are on the other hand tested through statistical methods.

Both approaches have pros and cons. CGE models, thanks to their consistency with economic theory, allow for comparable policy scenarios. In addition, given that they do not require estimation, the cost in terms of data availability is smaller compared to macro-econometric models. On the other hand, their main quality (that is, theoretical consistency) is at the same time their main weakness: everything that is not consistent with the economic theory is ruled out a priori.

Macro-econometric models, given that they are estimated, are suitable for short- and medium-run forecasting/simulation, where they are undoubtedly superior compared with CGE. However, given that estimation is performed on a certain period of time, their long-run simulations are less reliable compared with short- to medium-run predictions, and they can be considered inferior compared with CGE in performing this task.

Secondly, with respect to structural specification we have: (i) exogeneity or endogeneity of the innovation process and technological change, and the ensuing problem of e-inclusion/exclusion; (ii) treatment of diffusion effects; (iii) technological and knowledge spillovers; (iv) aggregate or sectoral dimension; and (v) degree of flexibility in simulations of policy impact and other changes in the model structure and parameters.

It is necessary to explain why (i)–(iii) are structural specifications relevant for our project. In order to incorporate the analysis of e-inclusion in the model, it is necessary to understand what determines e-inclusion and what the economic effects of increasing e-inclusion are. The literature has not yet addressed the issue of the effects of e-inclusion on the economy. Hence, it is easily predictable that there is no model already equipped for analysing e-inclusion. Despite that, there are certain characteristics that a model needs to have in order to be considered for the analysis of e-inclusion.

The widespread diffusion of ICT has been favoured initially by the innovations in the ICT sector and the ensuing sharp decrease in their prices; in a second phase, the gain in terms of efficiency of the firms who adopt ICT and the differentiated usage of households have promoted a diffuse adoption of this technology throughout society.

It is therefore clear now, how the concepts of innovation, diffusion, and spillovers are fundamental when analysing ICT, no matter what the focus of the analysis is. We are therefore looking for a model that has an endogenous specification of the innovation process, and that allows modelling of both the diffusion effects of ICT, and the technological and knowledge spillovers.

1. Exogenous innovation does not allow taking into account feedback responses from economic performance. Modelling endogenous technical progress, however, requires a careful examination of the transmission mechanism from effort to outcome. Finally, endogenous innovation can provide for a better identification of the complementarity between innovation policies (including ICT spending), e-inclusion and other policies (for example, better and less intrusive regulation, investment in education, and so on).

2. The consideration of diffusion effects of ICT and knowledge accumulation efforts at both the national and EU level is relevant in assessing the impact of joint efforts in inclusive ICT and other policy action, such as the liberalization of the market for services (and hence larger service trade), better and more uniform regulation, and lower transport costs thanks to better EU-level infrastructure.

3. A detailed modelling of technological and knowledge spillovers (both positive and negative) while adding to the complexity of the model, improves the understanding of the effects of innovation. It also allows focusing on the effects of effort, including inclusive ICT, from the impact and their feedbacks (for example spillovers of a given effort can have different intensity according to different process innovation mechanisms).

4. Most existing models are still based on an aggregate structure. This has important drawbacks, including a less than satisfactory analysis of the transmission mechanism from ICT, e-inclusion and knowledge accumulation efforts to performance, at both the level of national economies and the EU level. One important aspect of a multi-sector approach is the identification of sectoral interactions that can play a relevant role in amplifying and transmitting the impact of policy. An important question in this respect is to understand what the complementarities are that generate the largest multipliers.

5. Finally, policy simulations should include the assessment of different policy scenarios as represented by alternative paths in (exogenous) policy variables, as well as changes in relevant model parameters reflecting changes in behaviour and/or structural characteristics. Most models assessing the impact of policy reforms on economic performance focus on the impact of single policy actions, usually neglecting systemic effects. The joint impact of reforms, however, is larger than the sum of each reform undertaken separately. This is very important for assessing the impact of e-inclusion policies, since they have very significant systemic effects and synergies. Therefore, the selected model should take into account the simultaneous impact of policy on several variables of interest to the policy maker (sustainable and cohesive growth, e-inclusion, and so on). Models have, therefore, to be judged also on the basis of their capability to take into account interactions and synergies among different policy actions.

With respect to the performance variable we have: (i) models where the performance variable is economic growth, employment effects and/or total factor productivity; and (ii) models that take into account measures of social inclusion and/or sustainable development. Furthermore, the selection will take into consideration those models that are able to cover the largest portfolio of options in terms of performance variables so as to include both economic growth and social cohesion variables.

To sum up, we identify the following features that any model should ideally include:

(a) Capability of identifying the impact of e-inclusive policy on a number of performance variables including economic growth, job creation, and social inclusion, and of assessing the impact of alternative policy strategies;
(b) Richness and variety of the structural characteristics of the economy, in terms both of structural details and of the interaction across sectors;
(c) Richness and detail of the treatment of transmission mechanism linking innovation, ICT diffusion, e-inclusion, and performance;
(d) Assessment of the impact at the level of individual countries and the EU as a whole, in order to take into account the impact of EU integration and diffusion effects;
(e) Flexibility to accommodate different policy scenarios, including different policy dynamics and sensitivity to changes in model parameters;
(f) Possibility of taking into account both short and medium/long run effects of policy.

7.2 THE CHOICE OF INTERNATIONAL FUTURES MODEL

For an assessment of a set of models that can be used to evaluate the effects of e-inclusion on, broadly speaking, the economy, with respect to an 'ideal benchmark' as identified by items (a)–(f) above, see the interim report of our research project (Bentivegna and Guerrieri, 2010) and Guerrieri and Padoan (2007). We include here the final model assessment and comparison table (see Table 7.1). It shows that the International Future (IFs) model better corresponds to our criteria and research goals and hence it has been selected for our simulation analysis.

IFs is a CGE model developed by Prof. B.B. Hughes of the Graduate School of International Studies (University of Denver). The first version dates back to 1980; we are currently using the fifth generation of the model.[1]

The basic idea behind IFs is strongly related to the world models of the 1970s, including those of the Club of Rome. In particular, IFs drew on the Mesarovic-Pestel or World Integrated Model (Mesarovic and Pestel, 1974). The author of IFs had cooperated with that project, including the

Table 7.1 Model assessment and comparison

Reference Parameters	WorldScan	NEMESIS	QUEST	MULTIMOD	International Futures	NiGEM
Performance variable						
Economic growth or total factor productivity	Economic growth	GDP	GDP	GDP	GDP	GDP
Employment effects	No	Yes	Yes	Yes	No	Yes
Social inclusion and/or sustainable development	No	No	No	No	Yes	No
Structural specification and detail						
Multi-equation vs. single equation	Multi-equation	Multi-equation	Multi-equation	Multi-equation	Multi-equation	Multi-equation
Exogenous vs. endogenous innovation process and technological change	Endogenous in the extension	Endogenous	Exogenous	Endogenous in the extension	Endogenous	Endogenous in the extension
Aggregate or sectoral dimension	Sectoral	Sectoral	Aggregate	Aggregate	Sectoral	Aggregate
Input-output linkages and/or technological spillovers	Technological spillovers in the extension	Yes	No	Technological spillovers in the extension	No	No

Table 7.1 (continued)

Reference Parameters	WorldScan	NEMESIS	QUEST	MULTIMOD	International Futures	NiGEM
Treatment of diffusion effects						
Microeconomic foundations	Yes	Yes	Yes	Yes	Yes	Yes
Flexibility in simulations of policy impact	Yes	No	No	No	Yes	No
Methodological approaches						
Non structural approach	No	No	No	No	No	No
Structural approach	Yes	Yes	Yes	Yes	Yes	Yes
Continuous time approach	No	No	No	No	No	No
Estimation vs. calibration	Calibration	Estimation	Calibration	Estimation	Calibration	Estimation

construction of the energy submodel. IFs is also consciously based on the Leontief World Model (Leontief et al., 1977), the Bariloche Foundation World Model (Herrera et al., 1976), and Systems Analysis Research Unit Model (SARU, 1977), following comparative analysis of those models by Hughes (1980). The project of the fourth generation was initiated in the early 2000s. It took into account comments arising from the usage of the model in an increasingly policy-analysis-oriented mode by several important organizations. First, General Motors asked for a specialized version of IFs named CoVaTrA (Consumer Values Trends Analysis). Second, the Strategic Assessments Group of the Central Intelligence Agency commissioned a specialized version named IFs for SAG. Third, the European Commission sponsored a project named TERRA that has led to another specialized version, called IFs for TERRA.

Nowadays, IFs has reached the fifth version, and appears to present a considerable improvement of both the theoretical features of model and of its usability. The latter has become easier because the software can be found online, due to collaboration with the National Intelligence Council (http://www.ifs.du.edu). Moreover, new scenarios were created for UNEP (focusing on environmental change) and Pardee (focusing on poverty). Finally, the largest change has been the incorporation of 182 countries into the base-case scenario used by IFs. The other CGE models reported in Table 7.1 usually do not allow a full understanding of the complex patterns through which ICT impacts economic performance. Although some transmission mechanisms can be identified in the various models, IFs works much better in this respect and ensures external validity.

Moreover, IFs was chosen because it includes an explicit definition of the ICT sector and allows ICT to exert its impact on the economy via different channels, not just as a simple input in a standard production function. The simulation exercises carried out in the following are examples of a larger set of possible analyses to be conducted with IFs and possibly other CGE models.

The scope of IFs is not limited to economics, as it is composed of seven interlinked modules dealing with economic, sociopolitical, population, energy, agriculture, environmental and technological aspects (see Figure 7.1).

Indeed, the use of the IFs platform offers two main advantages: (a) it allows the study of multi-dimensional aspects related to the diffusion of ICT and to e-inclusion; and (b) it entails a high degree of external validity; that is, it is widely used among experts to make forecasts (for example, Obama group) and it can be downloaded for free. The files that contain the set of parameters values can be easily exported so that the scenario analysis performed can be re-run by any user.

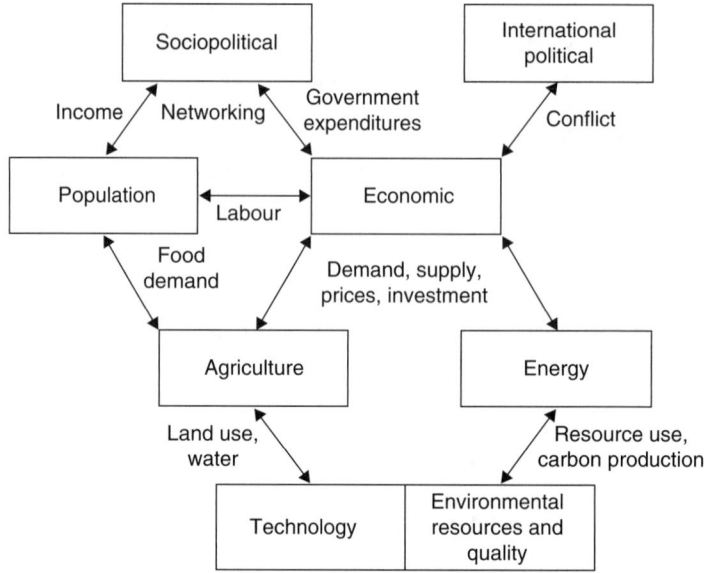

Source: Hughes and Hillebrand, 2006.

Figure 7.1   The blocks structure of IFs and their main linkages

On the down side, a shortcoming is the impossibility of modifying the source code without mining the external validity of the model. To put it differently, the source code can be modified, but such modifications may deeply alter the philosophy of the original model with the result that the customized model may entail a non-shared view about the causal relationships composing it.

Our key purpose is to strengthen the quantitative evidence on e-inclusion and to understand the relationship between indicators of e-inclusion and of economic and social performance in a wider sense. Moreover, we aim at proposing to policy makers a tool facilitating the benchmarking for monitoring the process of e-inclusion in Europe. More specifically, by adopting our multi-perspective and multi-dimensional approach (infrastructure, usage, impact on quality of life) our goal is to provide a quantitative evaluation of e-inclusion for all 27 EU Member States and other advanced countries. Obviously, it must be taken into account that there are a number of issues in defining and mapping e-inclusion dimensions, namely infrastructure, usage and impact, into IFs.

We propose to exploit the features of IFs to incorporate the properties of ICT in a satisfactory way. Indeed, ICT are general purpose technologies

(GPTs), whose impact on the economy cannot be understood in the framework of the simple production function and must be assessed taking into account, among other aspects, their interaction with the regulatory framework, the structure of the economy, and the evolution of skills and organizations.

In the following we provide quantified estimates of impacts of various forward-looking policy scenarios, and run policy simulations using different assumptions with regard to digital inclusion policies. Both short-term and long-term impacts of policy interventions will be quantified. The results of the simulations will be extensively analysed in order to highlight costs and benefits (that is, impact) of different policies and incentives. Furthermore, particular attention will be given to the explanation of the limitations and uncertainties of the policy simulations; we will also suggest possible ways of improving and further developing the models. These policy simulations should help to provide conclusions and identify policy recommendations that may be relevant for the future post-2010 strategic framework, keeping in mind the peculiar characteristics of ICT as a general purpose technology.

7.3 THE SETUP FOR THE SCENARIO ANALYSIS: CONCEPTS AND DEFINITIONS

By using the IFs platform for our scenario analysis we are able to infrastructure and modify the IFs model functioning through many channels via the tuning of many parameters. Such parameters are exogenous factors and can be tuned yearly within specific ranges of values. There are several parameter types that serve different aims. A complete list of these groups includes:

- *Multipliers* They have a normal value of 1;
- *Additive factors* Most have a normal value of 0, thereby leaving that to which they are added unchanged;
- *Exponents* For instance, many 'elasticities' raise something to a power. For these parameters the 'normal value' will vary greatly, but they will most often fall between −2 and 2, with many clustering around 0;
- *Reactivities* These are factors that relate growth in one process to growth in another. Although many range between −2 and 2 (with 0 eliminating linkage of the processes), some have very large values;
- *Growth rates* It is possible to force some processes to grow at specified rates;

- *Transforming coefficients* Some coefficients transform units of variables or link variables in other ways;
- *Initial conditions* These are not strictly parameters, but rather first-year values for variables subsequently computed by the model;
- *Switches* These parameters turn some parts of the model on or off. They generally take on values of 1 (on) or 0 (off).

Parameters in IFs can also be grouped along a second relevant dimension: the level of aggregation that can be used to customize their values. In particular, we find, at a more detailed level, those parameters that can be changed at country level. At a higher level of aggregation, we have sector-specific parameters. Finally, aggregate parameters can be adjusted to alter the behaviour of the model at the highest level.

We organize our exploration of the effects of e-inclusion policies as a multi-stage investigation. We first analyse the impact of empowered infrastructure to ICT in the system; secondly, we study how a more intensive use of the infrastructure made available in the system spans through the model and, finally, we investigate the modifications and quantitative effects of a higher impact of e-inclusion on different aspects of the socio-economic system.

The most difficult task we accomplished concerned the choice of the parameters to modify in order to put into action that the concepts emerged in the empirical part of the project. The key issues are related to the choice – and the motivation behind it – of parameters, and their inclusion in one of three groups singled out to quantify e-inclusion of a country, namely infrastructure, usage and impact.

We first singled out a set of parameters of interest given the scope of our project. Secondly, we reclassified the parameters into the categories related to infrastructure, usage and impact of e-inclusion (Table 7.2).

The parameters used as proxies of infrastructure to ICT are the following:

1. *Ictbroadm* ICT broadband multiplier. The parameter has a multiplicative impact on **ICTBROAD** that represents the percentage of population with broadband infrastructure technology. Note that **ICTBROAD** is directly linked to **ICTINDEX**, that is an index of ICT physical capacity in the system (Figure 7.2). **ICTBROAD** is determined through an s-shaped function whose exogenous parameters are: *ictbroadhighr*, *ictbroadlowr* that are, respectively, the higher and the lower limits, and *ictbroadinflection* that governs the steepness of the transition between the two. Moreover, the ICT spending as a percentage of GDP is important.

Table 7.2   A taxonomy of IFs parameters into proxies of e-inclusion

Dimensions	Parameters					
Dimensions of infrastructure	ID	Name	Description	Type	Level	Base value for EU27
Quality	A1	Ictbroadm,	ICT broadband multiplier	MU	Country	1
Quality	A2	ictspendm,	ICT spending multiplier	MU	Country	1
Dimensions of usage						
Intensity	U1	Infranetm	Infrastructure, Internet density, multiplier	MU	Country	1
Intensity	U2	numnwpgrm	Number of networked persons, growth rate multiplier	MU	Country	1
Dimensions of impact						
Economic	I1	Mfpadd	MFP growth additive factor	AF	Country	0
Economic	I2	mfpinfict	Elasticity of MFP to ICT index	EL	Aggregate	0.02
Economic	I3	mfpinfrnt	Elasticity of MFP to infrastructure, electronic network	EL	Aggregate	0.025
Cultural, Communication	I4	Numnwpgrinc	Number of networked persons, impact on growth	AC	0.01 (for all sectors)	0–0.2

2. *Infranetm*   Infrastructure, Internet density multiplier. It has a direct effect on the internet density use in the system (INFRANET) according to the relationship:

$$\text{INFRANET} = \frac{NUMNWP}{POP} \cdot 100 \cdot \text{infranetm}$$

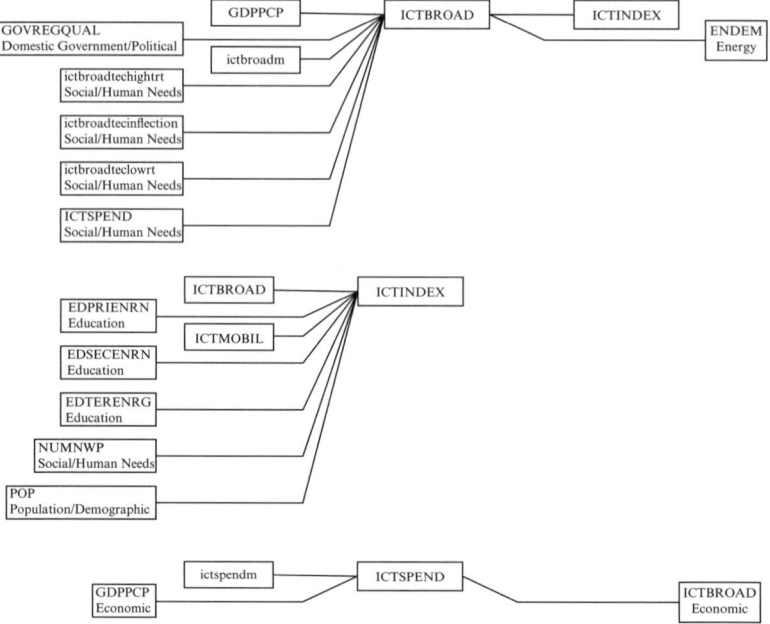

*Figure 7.2   Causal charts for the variable ICTBROAD: percentage
              of population with internet infrastructure with broadband
              infrastructure technology*

where *POP* represents the population and *NUMNWP* is the overall
number of networked persons in the country.

As Figure 7.3 shows, INFRANET has a direct effect on other variables of the technological block of IFs: GLOBALIZ (globalization
index), INFRAMOID (modern infrastructure index) and MFPPC,
which represents the MFP contribution of physical capital (including infrastructures). INFRAMOID is defined as a function of three
variables measuring the level of infrastructures related to: electronic
networks, telephonic network and the internet density use.

3. *ictspendm*   ICT spending multiplier. This parameter allows improve-
    ment of the effectiveness of ICT investments in the system;
4. *numnwpgrm*   Number of networked persons, growth rate multiplier.
    The parameter enhances the growth rate of the number of the net-
    worked persons;
5. *Mfpadd*   MFP growth additive factor. An exogenous component of
    MFP used to simulate an additional stimulus coming from other com-
    ponents of the model, namely ICT;

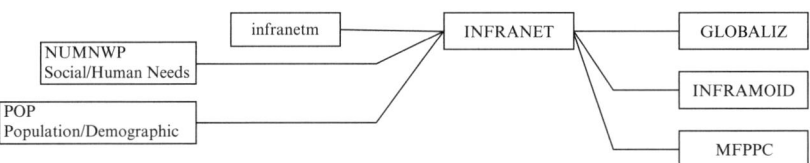

Figure 7.3   Causal chart for the variable INFRANET (internet network density of usage)

6. *mfpinfict* Elasticity of MFP to ICT index. Gives the degree of reaction of MFP to ICT index defined as a function of all the ICT different aspects existing in the platform;
7. *mfpinfrnt* Elasticity of MFP to infrastructure, electronic network. Gives the degree of reaction of MFP to the existence of infrastructure network;
8. *Numnwpgrinc* Number of networked persons, impact on growth. Modifies the impact on growth of MFP of the number of networked persons in the system.

7.4   THE SETUP OF THE ANALYSIS: TIME AND SPACE SCOPE AND TARGET VARIABLES

The time period of the simulations is 2005–25. The starting year is determined by the availability of data. We recall that IFs is based on a very large collection of time series coming from different sources (see Hughes and Hillebrand, 2006). The current version allows us to feed in historical data until the year 2005. After that year, many of the time series are still lacking and/or not sufficiently robust to be used. In other words, the model works as if the year 2005 is the last year observed in the real world and from that year on starts to provide forecasts for all the time series involved in the calculation of the year by year equilibrium configurations.

The scenario analysis proposed covers twenty years so that it is possible to provide short- and medium-run results. It will be clear from the presentation and from the comments we provide in the following sections that some of the impacts take time to diffuse in the model. At the same time, such a time window enables us to make insightful considerations as a counterpart to the policy scenarios we propose that refer to different lengths of the periods. In doing so we are aware of the fact that we potentially may be sceptical about on those policies of e-inclusion that do not present any result in the short- and medium-run, but that may have a long-run effect.

The focus of the analysis will be on the differential effects of e-inclusion policies on EU27 countries. More specifically, we study the effects of alternative e-inclusion policies in EU27 countries on different economic and socio-demographic variables, other things being equal in other countries.

We organize our simulative investigation in two sets of scenario analysis. The first one is devoted to the study of quantitative impacts of e-inclusion policies for EU27 countries as a whole. This part of the analysis (effect of different intensity of e-inclusion policies on EU27 countries), is in turn, structured into three steps aiming at disentangling the effects of: (a) higher infrastructure of e-inclusion, (b) higher infrastructure and usage of e-inclusion; and (c) higher infrastructure, usage and impact of e-inclusion, where the terms infrastructure, usage and impact have the meaning recalled above.

The second set of simulation exercises is devoted to the study of the ability of e-inclusion policies to determine different processes of divergence and/or convergence across European countries.

The second part of the study as stated above is devoted to the evaluation in the EU27 countries of within-country effects of e-inclusion policies. To do so we group the EU27 countries into four groups:

- Northern Europe: Denmark, Finland, Iceland; Norway, Sweden (*EU_North*);
- North-west Europe: Austria, Belgium, France, Germany, Ireland, Luxembourg, Netherlands, UK (*EU_NorthWest*);
- Eastern Europe: Bulgaria, Czech Republic, Estonia, Hungary, Latvia, Poland, Lithuania, Romania, Slovak Republic, Slovenia (*EU_East*);
- Southern: Cyprus, Italy, Greece, Malta, Spain, Portugal (*EU_South*).

This part of the scenario analysis focuses on the comparative futures of the EU countries. Hence, it represents a way to deepen our knowledge about more disaggregated effects of e-inclusion in differential conditions.

The outcome variables included in the analysis are chosen taking into account that e-inclusion is also an economic opportunity and should not be seen only as a problem. An inclusive information society: (a) brings large market opportunities for the ICT sector, (b) contributes to productivity growth, and (c) reduces the costs of social and economic exclusion. Consequently, we concentrate our attention on the macroeconomic performance of countries focusing mainly on those aspects that we expect to be influenced, namely productivity, consumer welfare, employability and economic growth. Nonetheless, we include in the analysis a series of variables as proxies of e-inclusion to make clearer the direct effects of changes in the values of parameters chosen in each scenario. This also facilitates the reconstruction of the causal nexuses among the highly complex networks of relationships existing in the model.

Hence, we propose a protocol for the analysis of the results articulated in two sets of variables. Final impact variables included are the following:

1. Gross Domestic Product (GDP), and GDP per capita;
2. Value Added (VA) of ICT sector as a percentage of GDP;
3. R&D spending as percentage of GDP (RANDDEX);
4. Multifactor productivity contribution from physical capital (MFP PC);
5. Multifactor productivity contribution from knowledge creation and diffusion (MFP KN);
6. Multifactor productivity total growth rate (MFPTOT);
7. Consumption per capita (CONPC);
8. Investments by sector: 1: agriculture, 2: materials, 3: energy, 4: manufacturing; 5: services, 6: ICT (IDS[1], ...,IDS[6]).

Direct e-inclusion impacts are measured by the following proxies:

1. Internet use density (INFRANET);
2. Infrastructure index, modern (INFRAMOID), 0-100 (better);
3. Number of networked persons per 1000 of population (NUMNwper1000);
4. ICT broadband percentage of population (ICTBROAD);
5. ICT index of physical capacity (ICTINDEX);
6. Knowledge Society index (KNOWSOC), 0-100 (better); defined as a function of the R&D level in the system and the level of tertiary education in the system.

7.5   THE ROLE OF E-INCLUSION IN THE DEVELOPMENT OF EU27 COUNTRIES

We conduct our investigation by means of scenarios that assess particular e-inclusion policies at the EU27 aggregate level. The first set of parameters takes into account a policy aiming at providing the system with the necessary infrastructures related to e-inclusion (A). The second one considers also the effort at stimulating the use of the infrastructure (AU). The last two are dedicated to an additional effort from a policy point of view aiming at favouring the transmission of e-inclusion into the system so as to exploit all the potential behind the e-inclusion concept. In particular, we

*Table 7.3   Parameter settings for the analysis of aggregate effect of
            infrastructure, usage, low impact and high impact policies of
            e-inclusion in EU27*

Par. id	Name	Benchmark values for other countries		EU27 parameter setups			
		AUILow	AUIHigh	A	AU	AUILow	AUIHigh
A1	Ictbroadm	1.2	1.2	1.1	1.2	1.2	1.2
A2	ictspendm	1.2	1.2	1.2	1.2	1.2	1.2
U1	Infranetm	1.2	1.2	1	1.2	1.2	1.2
U2	numnwpgrm	1.2	1.2	1	1.2	1.2	1.2
I1	Mfpadd	0.05	0.07	0	0	0.05	0.07
I2	mfpinfict	0.1	0.1	0.02	0.02	0.1	0.1
I3	mfpinfrnt	0.08	0.1	0.025	0.025	0.08	0.1
I4	Numnwpgrinc	0.08	0.1	0.01	0.01	0.08	0.1

assume a scenario with a low degree of impact (AUILow) and another one
that allows for a high impact of e-inclusion dimensions (AUIHigh). See
Table 7.3 for details of parameter values.

Based on these sets of values we define four scenarios in which we
assume that the countries not belonging to EU27 implement an e-inclusion
policy of the type AUIHigh:

1. Lagging behind 1 (LB1). In this scenario EU27 enhances only the
   dimension of infrastructure of e-inclusion.
2. Lagging behind 2 (LB2). In this scenario EU27 enhances the dimensions of infrastructure and use of e-inclusion.
3. Catching up 1 (CU1). In this scenario EU27 implements a policy looking
   at the dimensions of infrastructure, use and low impact of e-inclusion.
4. Catching up 2 (CU2). In this scenario EU27 implements a policy
   looking at the dimensions of infrastructure, use and high impact of
   e-inclusion.

In all the scenarios considered we obtain an increase in the number of
networked persons in the EU27. All the e-inclusion policies in the EU27
enhance the number of networked persons in the EU countries. The bigger
effect is obtained when EU27 countries implement CU2 policy (Figure 7.4).

Moreover, analysing the scenarios CU1 and CU2 we see that the EU27
percentage of networked persons increases over time by around 3 percentage points, irrespective of the policy implemented.

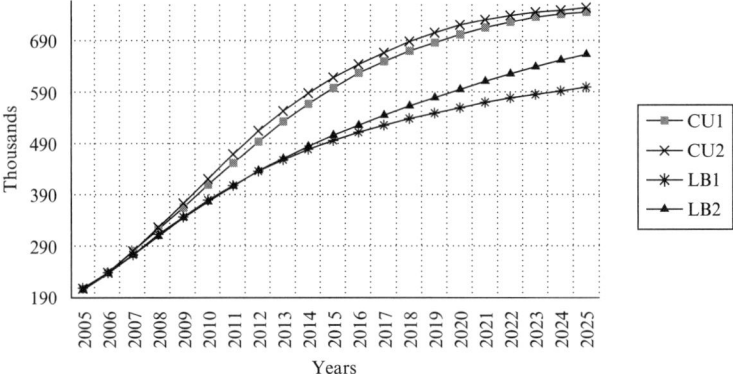

Figure 7.4   Number of networked persons in the EU27 in the different scenarios

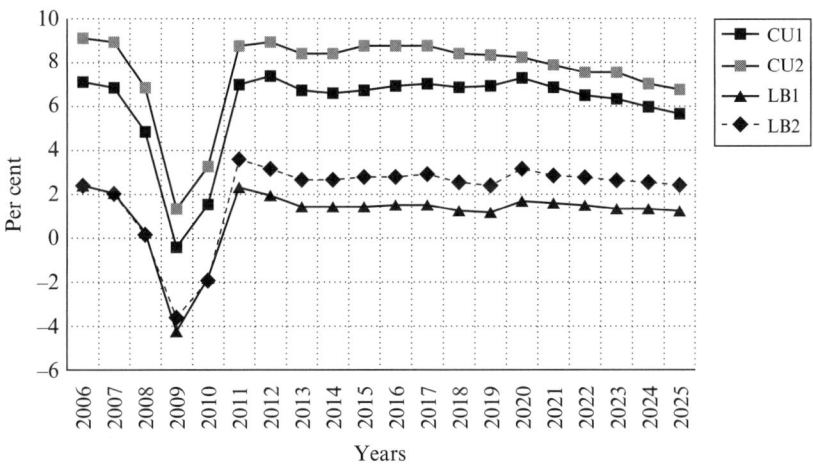

Figure 7.5   Growth rate of GDP per capita in EU27 in different scenarios

Figure 7.5 shows the evolution of the growth rate of GDP per capita over the 20-year horizon of the simulation in the EU27. The impact of scenario CU2 is relevant, as the corresponding growth rate is the largest one over the whole time horizon. This shows that the earnings of the EU27 in terms of disposable income are non negligible if the EU27 decides not to lose ground in terms of e-inclusion policies with respect to the other groups of countries that implemented high intensity e-inclusion policies (CU1 and CU2). Meanwhile, we can observe that a reduced e-inclusion

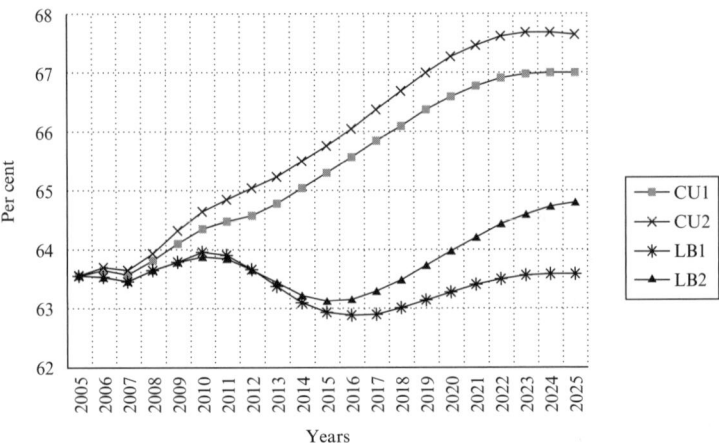

*Figure 7.6   Percentage of services value added with respect to GDP in
EU27 in different scenarios*

effort leads to a mild increase of GDP per capita in the EU27 countries:
the opportunities of growth are captured by the other countries.

The dynamics of GDP is explained by the role and the dynamics across
scenarios of the services sector in the economy. The value added (VA)
of the ICT sector as a percentage of GDP constantly increases in CU1
and CU2, whereas it decreases until 2015 in the other scenarios. If we
compare the CU1 and CU2 scenarios, we note that from the early years
of implementation of high effort policy the share of services VA follows
a steeper path of growth. At the end of the period under analysis, the
gap between the two scenarios is stable in favour of the CU2 scenario.
In general, VA of services increases everywhere after 2015, so that in
year 2025 all the corresponding values are higher than the initial values
(Figure 7.6).

Another piece of the story comes from the role played by ICT technologies in the economic system. The impact on ICT is significant and bigger
for impact scenarios: Figure 7.7 shows a steady increase, especially for the
CU2 scenario.

The final aspect that accounts for the pattern emerging with regard to
GDP has to do with the dynamic features of R&D spending. There is a
significant impact in the first few (five, say) years. Later on, R&D spending as a percentage of GDP stabilizes in CU1 and CU2 (the inflection
point is observed sooner for CU1 and later for CU2), whereas it significantly increases in the remaining scenarios (see Figure 7.8). In this case,
the timing makes the difference: if an area starts to implement e-inclusion

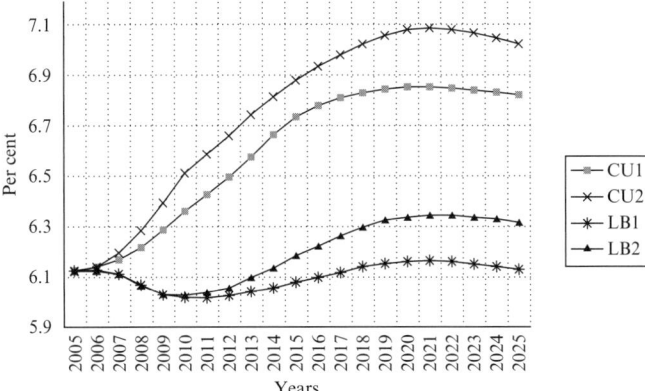

Figure 7.7   Percentage of ICT value added with respect to GDP in EU27 in different scenarios

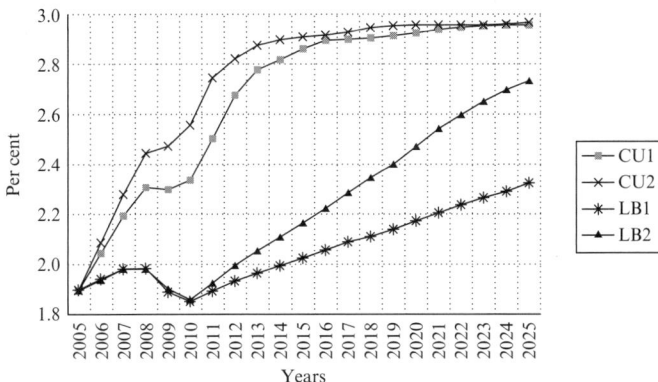

Figure 7.8   R&D spending as percentage of GDP in EU27 in different scenarios

policies earlier, then it will accumulate an advantage with respect to the others that is stable over time.

An analysis of the time series of consumption per capita (Figure 7.9) reveals a considerable increase over time for scenario CU2, which maintains a growth rate larger than scenario CU1. This evidence confirms the intuition that the gains – in terms of additional production for the system – ensured by e-inclusion policies are then distributed among citizens of EU27 countries, leading to a higher growth rate of per capita consumption.

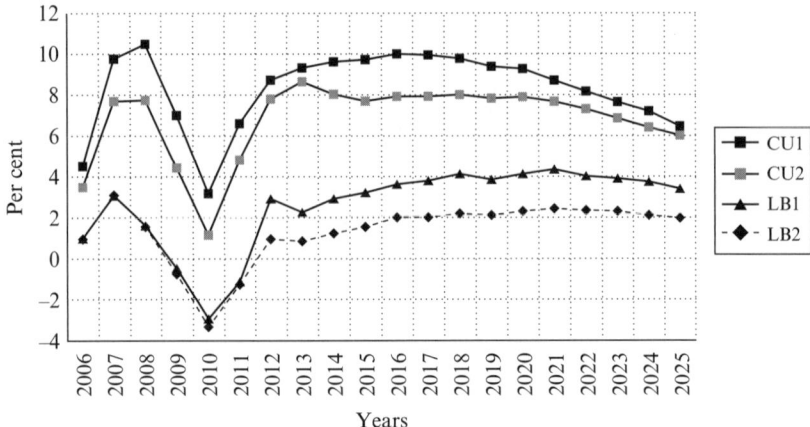

Figure 7.9   Growth rate of consumption per capita in EU27 in different scenarios

7.6   DISAGGREGATED E-INCLUSION EFFECTS IN EU27

The analysis proposed in this section aims to disentangle the effects of e-inclusion policies at a more disaggregated level. The scenarios are used to explore the effects, at country level, on the process of convergence and divergence across countries in EU27.

First we introduce a set of scenarios aiming to investigate the role of disaggregated e-inclusion policies in determining growth and controlling for inequalities dynamics. Secondly, we propose a scenario that studies the effects for EU27 of an e-inclusion policy that enhances the degree of infrastructure, usage and impact of all countries and implements a high effort policy for EU_South in order to enable such countries to bridge the gap, with respect to e-inclusion, with the high e-inclusion European countries.

In Table 7.4 we summarize the set of parameter values used in the different scenarios taken into account. We study four different possible situations (Table 7.5). The first one is dedicated to a scenario in which EU27 decides a unified common policy of e-inclusion looking at infrastructure, usage and impact (scenario DIV1). The second one takes into account a bigger effort of e-inclusion policies on slower countries (EU_East and EU_South countries).[2] This scenario proposes a first way to cope with divergence among EU countries: concentrate a given level of aggregate effort on slower countries (DIV2). The third scenario adds to the DIV2

Table 7.4   Parameter settings for the analysis of convergence–divergence across countries in Europe

Par. id	Par. name	Base value for EU27	High INC+	High INC++	AUI Low	High INC
A1	Ictbroadm	1	1.2	1.4	1.2	1.2
A2	ictspendm	1	1.2	1.2	1.2	1.2
U1	Infranetm	1	1.2	1.2	1.2	1.2
U2	numnwpgrm	1	1.2	1.2	1.2	1.2
I1	Mfpadd	0	0.09	0.09	0.05	0.07
I2	mfpinfict	0.02	0.1	0.1	0.1	0.1
I3	mfpinfrnt	0.025	0.1	0.1	0.08	0.1
I4	Numnwpgrinc	0.01	0.1	0.1	0.08	0.1

Table 7.5   Scenario definition for the analysis of aggregate effect of infrastructure and usage low impact and high impact policies of e-inclusion in EU27 and groups of countries

ID	Scenario	Notes:	EU_ North	EU_ North West	EU_ East	EU_ South
DIV1	Divergence 1	High e-inclusion for all countries	High INC	High INC	High INC	High INC
DIV2	Divergence 2	Working on divergence of EU countries: more effort on slower countries	AUI Low	AUI Low	High INC	High INC
DIV3	Divergence 3	Working on divergence of EU countries: additional effort on slower countries	AUI Low	AUI Low	High INC+	High INC
DIV4	Divergence 4	Working on divergence of EU countries: bursting slower countries	High INC	High INC	High INC++	High INC

scenario an additional effort on the impact of e-inclusion in slower countries. The last scenario is based on the DIV1 scenario which, as we will demonstrate, ensures the highest growth rates for the EU27 countries and adds an enhanced attention for infrastructures and impact of e-inclusion

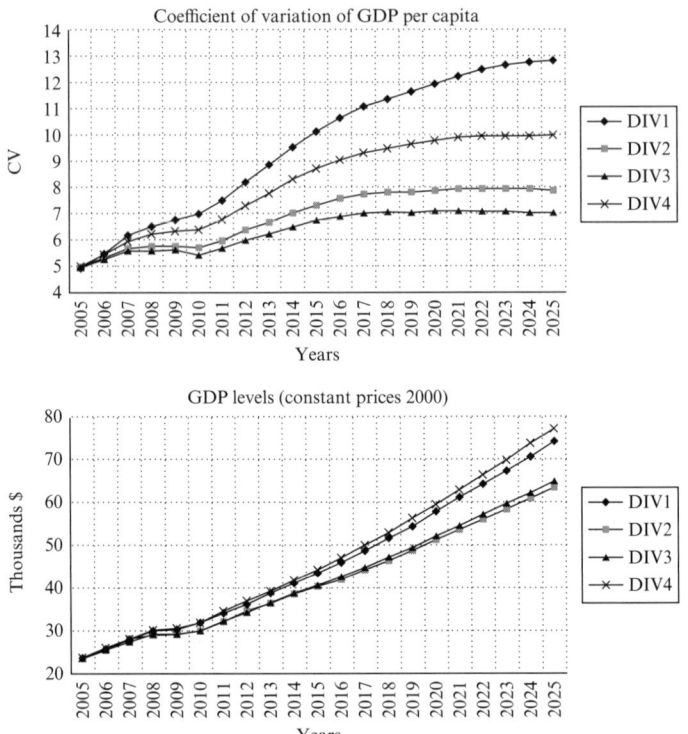

*Figure 7.10   Divergence and growth among EU27 countries in the four
            scenarios*

in slower countries. It is designed to test whether a differentiated policy
across EU27 countries will have an effect on growth and on the degree of
divergence among countries.

A first question to address is whether the scenarios imply different joint
patterns of growth and divergence among EU27 countries. Figure 7.10
shows in the upper panel the evolution of divergence among countries
in terms of GDP per capita, as measured by the coefficient of variation
of GDP per capita at country level. In the scenarios DIV2 and DIV3 we
observe a stabilization of differences among the countries starting from
year 2016. Meanwhile, in scenarios DIV1 and DIV4 the CV is always
increasing. Looking at this evidence, it seems that the first two scenarios
are preferable if we aim at reducing divergences. Note that the result is
obtained keeping at low impact level the e-inclusion policies for EU_
NorthWest and EU_North, enhancing the EU_South and EU_East effort

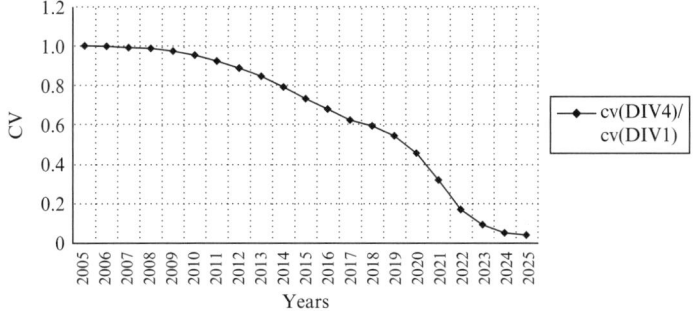

Figure 7.11 Ratio of the CVs in the scenarios DIV1 and DIV4 for the variable INFRANET – CV(DIV1)/CV(DIV4)

of e-inclusion (DIV2) and putting more effort on impact of e-inclusion on EU_East countries in DIV3 scenario. Unfortunately, there exists a trade-off between divergence and growth.

The lower panel of Figure 7.10 shows the level of GDP at constant prices (year 2000) in different scenarios. We note that the two lower divergence scenarios also ensure the lower level of GDP in EU27. At the same time DIV1 and DIV4 – high divergence scenarios – ensure the highest level of GDP along time. In particular, it is interesting to note that the DIV4 scenario ensures a pattern of growth of GDP that is close to the one of the high growth scenario (DIV1), and presents a level of divergence that becomes stable in the last years of the time window under scrutiny. In a sense, the DIV4 scenario shows that it is possible to find a compromise between growth and divergence once we design policies of e-inclusion that take into account the need for an additional effort in EU_East countries.

Moreover, a deeper investigation of the two scenarios DIV1 and DIV4 based on the Coefficient of Variation (CV) shows that the diversity among EU countries in terms of intensity of use of the Internet decreases over time following an s-shaped pattern (Figure 7.11).

ICT index and ICT broadband index patterns (respectively Figure 7.12 and Figure 7.13) in the two scenarios under analysis reveal that the EU_East countries are able to catch up with the other groups of countries some years earlier, allowing for the enhancement of their potential for growth. It is worth noting that, as a result of these changes in the patterns of EU_East, no modifications emerge in the other EU27 countries. In other words, the e-inclusion policies that give particular attention to EU_East countries do not have negative effects on the other countries.

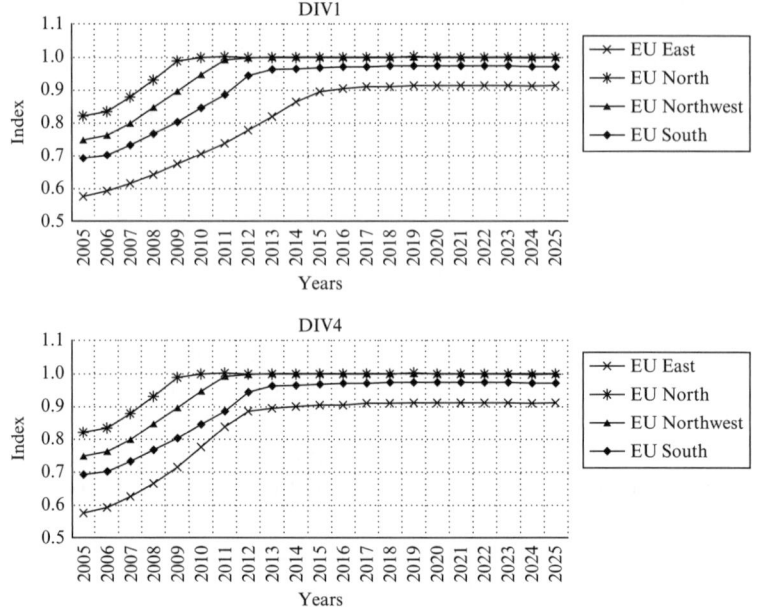

*Figure 7.12   Impact on ICT index (ICTINDEX) in the groups of
                European countries, scenarios DIV1 and DIV4*

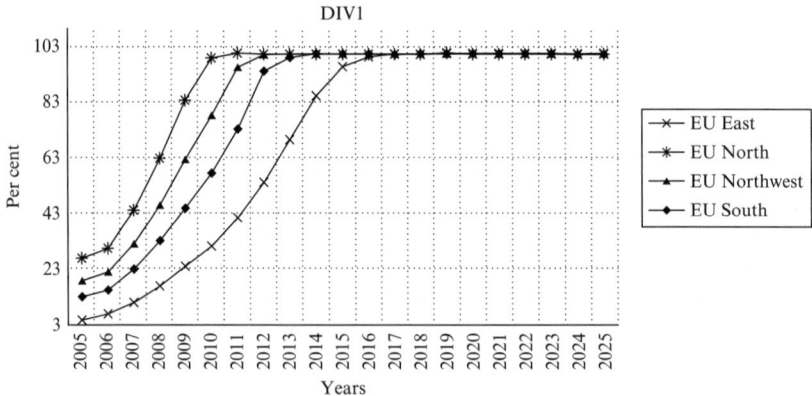

*Figure 7.13   Impact on ICT broadband percentage of connections
                (ICTBROAD) in the groups of European countries,
                scenarios DIV1 and DIV4*

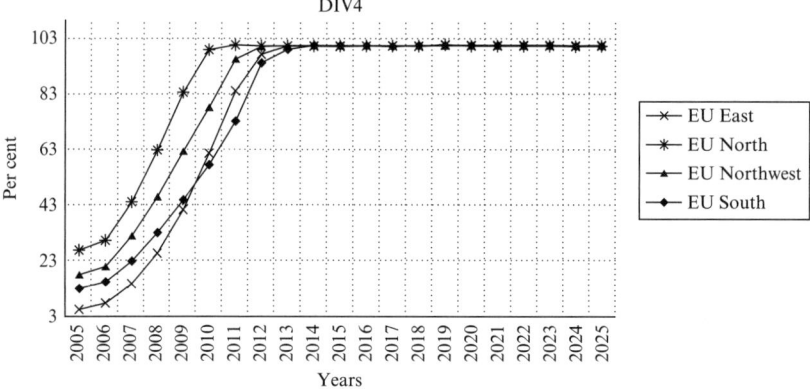

Figure 7.13 (continued)

NOTES

1. In this study we used IFs platform version 6.23. All the scenario files can be obtained upon request from the authors.
2. Henceforth, we use the adjective slower and faster referring to the slower or faster pace of advancement of e-inclusion in the countries.

8. Digital development: an overall EU policy framework

8.1 WHAT DOES E-INCLUSION REFER TO?

This final chapter attempts to bring together e-inclusion and ICT policies in an overall EU policy framework. Any EU policy framework should adhere to basic principles of EU policy making, such as subsidiarity, proportionality, non-intervention when market failures are absent and the integrity of the single market. The framework should be capable of employing effective means to pursue the set aims. Not least, it ought to achieve and maintain a tight complementarity between what is done at the Member State level – but for aims defined at EU level! – and what at EU level jointly.

Let's start by recalling the analytical decomposition of 'e-inclusion' as demonstrated in the European Development Digital Index (EDDI) shown in Figure 1.2 in Chapter 1. This is a useful tool for coming to grips with the notion of e-inclusion. In principle, the ingredients indicated could all serve as elements for policy, if given well-defined goals and if instruments can be identified. This decomposition shows immediately that any policy framework of e-inclusion will have to be broad-based and multivariate.

Infrastructure represents the supply side of electronic communication markets, whether the physical local presence of a network (rarely a problem in the EU given DSL technology, the simplest form of wired Internet connection, except perhaps in some rural areas of the new Member States), the quality range of the network connection offerings and their respective affordability given income distribution, local prosperity levels and the degree of price and non-price competition (for example entry and multiple suppliers). For infrastructure issues to be addressed in the framework of any e-inclusion policy framework, we have the EU's third telecoms package of regulation of December 2009,[1] EU and national competition policy (as a complement to the third package), and market forces. If the third telecoms package works well, helped by competition policies at the two levels of government, markets should work well too, because that is what these policies all aim at. Whether the EU internal market, rather than national e-comms markets, works well is a different matter. Indeed, the EU internal market for e-comms remains fragmented. In fact, what has been successfully achieved so far is the liberalization and modernization of national e-comms markets, with national regulators working under EU rules and assessing national competition issues under EU remedies guidelines and some scrutiny by the Commission. Infrastructure questions can thus be fine-tuned by detailing or differentiating the policies or regulation on network roll-out, in the infrastructure markets of networks, infrastructure conditions and interconnection. At every level of quality (for example properties such as stability in connectivity and of speed as well as different capacities of speed themselves, from say 0.5 MB to 100-plus MB) affordability can be influenced by demand and supply factors. As to the latter, the EU and national competition policies as well as the EU e-comms regime have been relatively successful in stimulating competition, helped considerably by market turbulence prompted by significant and continuous technological progress, which, so far, has facilitated market entry. As a consequence, prices of infrastructure and interconnection have come down drastically, thereby supporting affordability enormously. Moreover, networks have themselves become more sophisticated and the retail end can be both wired and wireless – the capacities of both have increased and are still increasing. On the demand side, it can hardly be surprising that higher income EU countries and a less skewed income distribution generally reduce the affordability barrier. The rapid catch-up of the new EU Member States (until the crisis) should, in and by itself, be regarded as a most powerful factor underpinning affordability, almost certainly more effective than any micro intervention could possibly be. Therefore, the general growth climate in the Union, and the return to high growth rates in Central Europe, are of the essence to the infrastructure dimension of e-inclusion, even though that appears not to be an 'inclusion-type' policy.

The availability aspect needs to be carefully defined. Figure 1.2 identifies both network and availability as determinants. On first sight, these two seem to be different terms for the same thing. However, this is not the case for e-inclusion. 'Network' refers to the act of buying a computer for the home or business premises with Internet connectivity, something that millions of households and even quite a few SMEs in the EU have not yet done. This elementary fact should make policy makers reflect on how deep the resistance to or hesitation about e-inclusion still is on the part of the very people that policy makers want to be included. Given the prices of PCs today, it is hard to believe that the sole reason for not buying a modern computer is poverty, even though that obviously does play a role. As a series of in-depth reports show clearly,[2] the main reason has to do with disinclination in certain age groups (say, the elderly), lack of even elementary schooling, the position of women, and so on. That fact has profound implications for the overall framework for addressing e-inclusion. Getting such groups of the population to overcome their inhibitions or weaknesses requires entirely different policies or activities and indeed mostly at national, better still at regional and local levels.

All in all, if a need is felt by EU policy makers to address the infrastructure dimension of e-inclusion as the foundation for any EU e-inclusion strategy, a myriad of very different policies at two, if not three (regional, too) or four (local as well) levels will be inevitable. Some of these distinct policies would have a relatively short to medium term character (for example, improving regulatory interventions about, say, the area coverage of mobile networks or about service versus network competition over time; or acting to promote competition in market segments) whilst other ones might well relate to long-run generational or structural characteristics such as poverty or near-illiteracy, or deeply-entrenched gender questions, or simply psychological resistance to newness amongst the elderly. Unsurprisingly but adding to the complexity, some of the deeper-seated reasons for not having infrastructure include of course the interrelation between 'infrastructure' and (the inability to enjoy) 'usage', and between 'infrastructure' and the insensitivity of segments of the population to either the temptation or societal pressures to respond to new forms of services (what is called 'impact' in Figure 1.2). Therefore, setting EU targets for e-inclusion appears to be an ambition requiring a very demanding framework, even for 'infrastructure' alone.

Internet usage   is what matters for societal and individual gains from e-inclusion. There is a lingering suspicion, supported by anecdotal evidence, that the mere possession of computers with an Internet connection still does not lead to actual usage of the Internet for certain segments of the population. These computers have often been given as a present by family and friends or obtained from schools (when replacing them) or public institutions at extreme discount prices. The problem for this category of potential but not actual users is the lack of even the slightest mastery of computer skills and/or ill-defined fears or resistance when having to tackle the usage problems of beginners alone. In Figure 1.2, the term 'autonomy' is used more broadly, but this zero-usage phenomenon (in the presence of infrastructure) could be regarded as the lack of any autonomy. For all those who actually use the Internet, e-inclusion can range from the absolute minimum participation (with slight autonomy) to the most sophisticated use. Autonomy would then be understood in degrees, from slight to full navigation including choice of content or even the creation of content in two-way configurations. Usage is also determined by the frequency of connecting and the number of hours per day online (together called 'intensity'), and by the level of 'skills', which is a moving indicator over time, especially when it comes to more advanced applications for business and a range of visual applications for consumers. One can ask the question here where the notion of e-inclusion ends and either ICT or economic growth policies begin, because the quantity and quality of IT specialists and the deepening the use of ICT inside companies, together with reorganization, are issues quite distinct from getting all and everybody included in the European information society. In any event, carefully characterizing usage in various ways, quantitatively and qualitatively, is an important step in understanding whether and to what extent the potential benefits of the information society, be it for personal preferences of entertainment or for business or education (and so on), can actually be attained in the EU.

The meaning of e-inclusion, beyond mere infrastructure, is found in stimulating EU citizens to acquire or improve the levels of skills needed for work, private use and student study, as well as focusing on the (changing) skills of workers required to support and execute new business and management tools based on ICT applications. Such tools are not only a matter of plain techniques or mastering new software, but, more often than not, imply different forms and styles of consumption or internal reorganization of business or new retail or logistical business models. In other words, usage can have ramifications which lead to adaptations of consumption and transformation of production and value chains. The EU level has few policies in place that can directly influence usage in this sense. The long-run approach is of course via public education and this is predominantly a matter for the Member States, or even their regions. In addition, there is a thriving market offering skill upgrade training, privately inside companies or institutions, but equally in the open market place as well as via publications and audio-visual means. At local level, elementary skills can be absorbed by citizens in various ways, as for example the (6000) UK online centres have shown with considerable success.[3] Inside European business, one would expect that competitive pressures and the prospect of gains in productivity or of lower costs and/ or higher quality or perhaps better traceability of products (for example in ISO9000 type systems) would render any particular concern of EU or national policy makers superfluous. Broadly, this presumption is undoubtedly correct, but a too limited extent of competitive pressure might be such that productivity gains from (ever more) sophisticated usage are reaped more slowly than by some competitors of the EU. If such patterns are systematic, they might reflect a European taste for gradualism in adapting to technological progress, but perhaps just as much a covert resistance to the organizational upheavals and changing the 'ways of doing things' which may accompany new, more advanced usage in business. A wide view of e-inclusion, incorporating this dynamic perception in particular in European business, would then turn into a strategy to prompt European business to accept the ICT dimension of competitiveness more wholeheartedly, and in so doing raise the EU growth rate for years to come. In the final analysis, however, the EU has few effective tools to stimulate more autonomous, more intense, and more sophisticated usage. The local level and market pressures, besides enlightened self-interest, seem to be the determinants an EU strategy would have to be content with. This is radically different from the elaborate policy regimes related to infrastructure. The indirect route of stimulating fiercer competition in certain segments of the services markets which, in the US, have demonstrated higher productivity growth linked to ICT use than the EU, could possibly augment the speed and scope of the uptake of advanced ICT solutions. This will be discussed later on.

Internet impact   in Figure 1.2 is divided into several classes of effects: three types of new (online) products and services (education, government and health); the impact on labour and employment (including delocalization); economic impact such as e-commerce and e-banking;[4] and the cluster of effects denoted as 'culture and communication'. The latter comprise emails and social networks, entertainment, media services, downloadable games and music, maps and routeplanners as well as other cultural services (from city advertising to cultural and historical background documentaries). The mere listing of these many new services or modes of communication makes one realize how much the interaction between people, and between people and business or government, has changed in a period of 10–15 years. And how easy it (often) has become to act in similar ways whether national or European or worldwide. If the vague notion of information society has any substance, it must be this new or drastically revised way of living and transacting, by means of entirely new services unimaginable two decades ago. E-inclusion has everything to do with the capacity to participate as fully as one would want – subject to preferences as well as normal budget and time constraints – in this rich, new way of life and the manifold benefits it gives rise to. These benefits are not given or static. On the contrary, these services deepen and widen in scope and new variants are tried out almost every day. Innovative other services are being invented, and the expectation that the results of a continuous wave of creativity will be experienced time and again is widely shared. Also, software and hardware developments have anything but petered out, and are in turn likely to magnify the benefits of the impact of e-inclusion and exclusion for a number of years to come.

It would be absurd to generalize about these many impacts and new services. Dependent on age, level of (recent) education, ICT skills, income, type of work (or study), location and other factors, many different profiles of persons can be distinguished as being more or less included or excluded in a highly differentiated fashion. It is also true that some services (for example government services such as tax forms, compulsory statistical information for firms, customs forms, and so on) may be supplied abundantly in one country and not yet in another one. To some degree, this might apply to educational services, tourist services such as reservations, and aspects of e-health (which is only beginning to be developed anyway) as well. Therefore, without trying to generalize, the question arises whether, and, if so, to what extent and how an EU policy framework could, or even should, attempt to stimulate the development and take-up of such numerous beneficial impacts, including the supply and sophistication of various services. The i2010 eGovernment Action plan and the Lisbon Agenda have already defined twelve basic online public services for citizens and eight for business. Their online availability has improved greatly from 21 per cent in 2001 to 71 per cent in 2009, albeit with better results for business (83 per cent in 2009) than for citizens (63 per cent), with the new Member States trying to catch up to the high average of the EU15.[5] The EU role might be perceived as one of general demonstration of the progress in and benefits of investing in such services, with awareness campaigns, best practices, conferences, websites and studies, targeted to specific stakeholders. Business and private Internet users of course exercise pressure too, and EU targets and comparative ranking of the Member States are a help for them. For the remainder, it would seem that it is up to the markets and national and regional governments to foster these developments. There are two clear exceptions to this general and modest policy vision of the EU: (1) where governments (or, rarely, EU bodies directly) require business or citizen information as a consequence of EU regulation, EU policies could be made more ICT-friendly, including refinement of regulation, which can promote beneficial impacts; (2) where cross-border hindrances inside the EU throttle or pre-empt the take-up or exploitation of these services, the Commission should either be active as the 'guardian of the treaty' based on overriding internal market (especially free movements or the right of establishment) principles, or, if that cannot be effective (say, for reasons of exceptions or national competences), initiate/ propose legislation facilitating cross-border services or overcoming the hindrances in this respect.

8.2   WHAT DOES ICT OR DIGITAL COMPETITIVENESS REFER TO?

After decades of almost permanent concern about the competitiveness of the EU ICT industry, the sector shows a mixed picture. Of course, ICT is a collective of rather distinct sectors in both goods and services.[6] These subsectors have very different factor intensity requirements, and hence display a spectrum of comparative advantages and disadvantages, first inside the EU, between low wage and high wage EU countries (or associated countries having open market infrastructure), and, beyond larger Europe, mainly between Asia and the Union. The value-added of the EU ICT industry is around € 600 bn,[7] some 5 per cent of GDP, with services accounting for 80 per cent. With ICT manufacturing assuming only 1 per cent of EU GDP, the EU shows a weak specialization compared to Japan (2.9 per cent) or China (far higher still). The 4 per cent of GDP assumed by ICT services compares more favourably with other countries (than manufacturing), although the US finds itself around 5 per cent of GDP. The EU ICT manufacturing sector has long had a trade deficit with the rest of the world whereas in ICT services the EU has a surplus. Its goods and services have seen rapid and sustained technological progress while prices of both ICT goods and services have fallen drastically over time. Moreover, many completely new goods and services have been introduced, and often successfully so, via own production, licensing or imports.

This is the traditional way to sketch 'the' competitiveness of the ICT industry. The picture can usefully be extended by adding the ICT R&D performance in the Union. The key aspects are worrying for the EU. Although the ICT sector is the largest R&D sector in the EU economy and its contribution consists almost entirely of business R&D (more than 90 per cent), the Japanese and US ICT R&D take a larger share in the overall business R&D in their economies (respectively 32.4 per cent and 39.2 per cent versus 24.9 per cent). However, one has to realize that overall business R&D in Japan and the US already has a higher share of GDP than in the EU. This double R&D gap may well be explained, to some extent, by the more modest size as well as the composition of the EU's ICT industry. In Europe, ICT R&D is mainly done by large companies whereas in the US there is a greater contribution from SMEs.

Recently, however, this traditional view of ICT competitiveness – though not necessarily irrelevant – has been overtaken by the far more encompassing idea of 'digital competitiveness'. So far this is a broad, encompassing approach, not yet a concept. The term 'competitiveness' should not be taken too literally here: it refers to a range of digital performance aspects on the supply and demand side of both goods and services, as well as to innovativeness and new goods or services. All these aspects hang together in complex ways. The traditional perspective on ICT competitiveness is now embedded in this far wider and more dynamic picture. The 2010 EU Digital Competitiveness Report combines the traditional basics of competitiveness with the impact of ICT investment on total factor productivity (TFP),[8] but also with an in-depth analysis of broadband, the use of Internet services (including e-commerce and Internet banking), an empirical analysis of e-inclusion, a survey of online public services and the take-up of ICT and e-commerce by business.

Such a holistic approach cannot be justified by merely regarding ICT as a sector. On the contrary, it is now routinely considered as a general purpose technology, a perspective pointing to profound and wide-ranging ramifications in the EU economy and society. This perspective entails many implications for reflection on, and design of, an effective EU policy framework. Indeed, in the extreme, one could expect EU digital competitiveness to remain a prominent EU policy concern, even if ICT manufacturing had largely vanished from Europe and even if many, for example, consumer Internet services were in fact worldwide (as is already the case for social networking sites[9]). Such a thought experiment would suggest that the traditional ICT competitiveness notion – although a possible and perhaps desirable element of digital competitiveness in the EU – might not be an indispensable element of a digital EU strategy. Such an extreme idea is solely suggested here to sharpen the contrast with the traditional reasoning and outlook. In fact, there are respectable reasons to support the view that wide-ranging ICT capabilities and R&D at the technology frontier are ingredients of an effective EU digital strategy which cannot be missed, if for example the EU is to remain innovative in advanced services (such as software for robotics) or for other manufacturing. Thus, it is striking that the car and pharmaceuticals sectors are amongst the top R&D ICT performers in Europe.

Is this new digital perspective nevertheless still predominantly supply-based, a typical characteristic of (sectoral) competitiveness policies? Even this cannot be confirmed since there is considerable attention to take-up and use in business and amongst citizens, indeed e-inclusion itself is seen as part and parcel of a digital strategy.[10]

Altogether, this renders it an extremely difficult proposition to develop any digital EU strategy, to obtain credible agreement between EU countries and in the EP (with sufficient backing of stakeholders) and to pursue it effectively. The scope of the various concerns and the respective ambitions hidden in the building blocks would seem to require a vast arsenal of instruments with highly distinct properties, some of which are legal, some merely persuasive, some with conditional funding, and some requiring active cooperative stakeholders (for example ICT standardization). It is possible that the EU level does not dispose of some such instruments, even when there is a case for assigning the policy task to that level. More often, the EU level might express certain desires or preferences for the EU public interest as elements of a digital EU strategy, but the instruments are unambiguously at the national (sometimes even local) level.

Upon reflection, these problems do not seem to be novel. Today's preoccupations with digital competitiveness and a new Digital Agenda were preceded by the eEurope Action Plan and later by i2010. But the widening of scope, the combination of supply and demand aspects, the emphasis on infrastructure (especially broadband), the incorporation of e-inclusion and the all-pervasive quest for growth enhancing transformations in business conduct, organization of companies and the public sector or citizens' digital literacy, makes for a much more radical, intrinsically different approach. Suggestions of 'virtuous circles' are tabled by the Commission.[11] The old ICT competitiveness approach may still matter to the sector, narrowly conceived, just as competitiveness matters to any other sector, but with a digital strategy or 'competitiveness' (in the sense of overall performance) the sectoral approach has been transcended, and broader aspects of EU growth and societal transformation have definitely taken over.

This actually raises the question whether e-inclusion policies are not undergoing the same fate. With a digital competitiveness perspective being all-encompassing, e-inclusion is becoming one element in a giga-puzzle to transform the EU and its society and exploit its full digital potential.

8.3 INSPIRED BY AN INDUSTRIAL POLICY PERSPECTIVE

It might be useful to consider e-inclusion as a part of a wide digital strategy for the EU as a whole. The new Digital Agenda shows how wide and encompassing such strategies can be. The question of e-inclusion is included in the Digital Agenda but is based on a fairly narrow notion of e-inclusion. In its section 2.6 on digital literacy, skills and inclusion, there is an open reference to possible adaptation of the Universal Service directive, a priority for digital literacy for the EU Social Fund, a proposal about EU-wide indicators of digital competences by 2013, and a commitment by Member States to implement digital literacy policies for disadvantaged groups (and in particular, those having disabilities) by 2011. This general language might end up being quite ambitious in the final analysis, but the Digital Agenda comprises 16 key actions and a host of other ones at two levels of government, and the e-inclusion provisions amount merely to one key action (no. 10) and just a few of the related actions specified in section 2.6. However, Annex 2 of the Agenda lists key performance targets taken from the Benchmark Framework 2011–2015 endorsed by the Member States in November 2009. Under Digital Inclusion, the targets for 2015 are as follows: regular Internet use up from 60 per cent to 75 per cent, and from 41 per cent (2009) to 60 per cent for disadvantaged people; and halving the number of people between 16–74 years old who have never used the Internet (30 per cent in 2009).

In order to appreciate the Digital Agenda for purposes of e-inclusion as analysed in the present project, we shall employ a framework adapted from the analysis of European industrial policy[12] and combine it with the decomposition of e-inclusion as in Figure 1.2.

At EU level the 1990 Bangemann Memorandum firmly put an end to interventionist EU industrial policy, accompanied by increasingly strict Commission surveillance of national state aids and preferential procurement by Member States' governments. The first 'victim' for which interventionist EU industrial policy was terminated was actually the ICT sector. What has remained of EU industrial policy today is a combination of (a) framework conditions at the EU level, (b) horizontal industrial policy, and (c) non-interventionist sectoral industrial policy. This does not mean that the EU and national government levels cannot and do not regulate, procure or fund policies or activities, but the crucial difference is that a market failure or overriding EU public interest has to be proven first. Intervening in markets when they do not fail is to be avoided, let alone on a national basis. The change in course was significant. Often, national or EU policy and national rescue operations were prompted by fears that a national industry or a national champion might be under threat or fail. Since 1990 (earlier for state aid), the EU level has been much more forthright and has mostly found that such threats were either an inevitable result of comparative disadvantage under globalization or the consequence of bad management or the price of prolonged protectionism. Shielding bad management or a sector with long-run comparative disadvantage is going against the long-run EU public interest in general and also against the proper working of the internal market as the paramount instrument to generate EU prosperity.

The framework aspects comprise the hard core of economic integration in the EU, including the establishment and proper functioning of the internal market and an effective competition policy for that internal market,[13] the general principles of regional and cohesion policy, 'better

EU regulation' and neutrality between private and state ownership of firms. Although the overall objective of the Digital Agenda is 'to maximize the social and economic potential of ICT. . . for doing business, working, playing, communicating and expressing ourselves freely', the actions proposed largely amount to a deepening and widening of a digital Single Market, complemented by numerous items to be pursued or delivered by the Member States. In attempting to understand the meaning and possible impact of the Digital Agenda for e-inclusion, it is therefore of the essence not to lose sight of the framework aspects, generating a better working of a single digital market, as this, in and by itself, will tend to enhance many activities and initiatives that may well matter for e-inclusion, from innovation or investment to increasing the variety of new services and their affordability. It is not impossible that a successful Digital Agenda will eventually lead to so many improvements of services that, in the margin, more 'excluded' citizens will decide to go digital and online. The framework conditions also discipline inclinations at EU or Member State level to employ interventionist measures, where no good case for such market interventions exists.

Besides the framework aspects, one may distinguish horizontal industrial policy and sectoral (non-interventionist) industrial policy. Under horizontal, one can classify research strategies, innovation policies, entrepreneurship and risk capital, skills and human capital, restructuring funds and (non-preferential and competitive) public procurement. Again, in e-inclusion, some such aspects may well be relevant. Under sectoral or specific industrial policy, actions may be specific to the sector, or may belong to trade policy, specific instruments of cohesion/ regional policies and technology policies (where some degree of choice is inevitable).

However, some adaptation of this approach is appropriate for the purpose of e-inclusion. After all, e-inclusion is mainly a problem of the demand side, but not in the usual meaning because the relevant ('excluded') citizens do not express preferences via market demand, or, if 'included', barriers to usage prevent them from fully participating in demand (subject to budget constraints). Unlike for industrial policies, where specific targeted measures can be classified as 'sectoral' and the orientation is mainly towards supply, there are good societal, social and economic reasons to induce citizens to begin to participate in the digital world in the first place, both in their personal interest and for the EU economy as a whole. Therefore, it is justifiable to first zoom in on measures or proposals directly affecting e-inclusion in its three components: infrastructure, usage and impact. When going beyond direct effects, the triple classification of industrial policy seems useful.

8.4 PROPOSALS DIRECTLY AFFECTING E-INCLUSION

Table 8.1 summarizes the items on the Digital Agenda that directly affect e-inclusion. They are divided into 'infrastructure', 'usage' and 'impact'.

Table 8.1 shows that the Digital Agenda incorporates proposals and policies in all three components of e-inclusion.

The four infrastructure proposals are about infrastructure coverage and (high) speed. All of these amount to prior conditions for improving e-inclusion, but the actual inclusion effect will be certain only where the lack of infrastructure is the obstacle to participation in the digital world. In the EU27 this has become exceedingly rare, the more so as various cheap and relatively simple DSL technologies can be (and are) applied almost everywhere, complemented by wireless in a range of applications. Therefore, the mere absence of infrastructure itself can usually be disregarded as a possible reason for remaining excluded. Indeed, the four proposals all concern broadband. But in broadband, infrastructure issues take on more conventional forms of differentiated services on offer over a wide range of prices. Other things being equal, this tends to raise the barrier to participation for the (say) 150 million non-included EU citizens. On the other hand, other things may not stay equal since all over the EU service

Table 8.1   EU Digital Agenda: items directly affecting e-inclusion

Infrastructure	Improving broadband coverage (EU + MS)
	Facilitating investment in broadband infra (various EU + MS)
	European Spectrum Policy programme, removing obstacles for high-speed (30mbps) (EU + MS)
	Possibly widening Universal Service Obligation (USO) rights in USO directive (EU)
Usage	Priority for digital literacy in Social Fund (EU)
	Long-term digital literacy policies and e-skills policies for disadvantaged groups and SMEs (MS)
Impact	e-Health and dignified living (MS)
	Ambient assisted living (AAL) technologies within reach of all (MS)
	Common minimum set of patient data
	Mutual recognition of e-identification and e-authentication
	Seamless cross-border e-government services
	Common list of key cross-border public services

providers are shifting to new modes of competition such as 'triple play' or 'quadruple play' in which services such as telephony, Internet and TV/radio are bundled. Almost all EU citizens already have telephone and TV/radio, so that triple play may have the effect of bringing in formerly non-included citizens if the bundled offers are competitive. In turn, whether offers are competitive depends first of all on infrastructure competition (for example between cable and telecoms networks or different telecoms networks), which is extremely unevenly spread in the EU. In EU countries which are not, or are hardly, cabled, triple play might therefore not induce many non-included for reasons of price. Taking the first proposal ('improving broadband coverage'), the EU has been promoting broadband for a decade in the expectation that virtuous circles with rapidly rising demand for products requiring high speeds as well as the emergence of new services and innovative developments in commerce and non-commercial activities would boost economic growth, create new and interesting jobs, and enhance worldwide competitiveness of many sectors. In the perspective of e-inclusion, one would expect such policies to have effects via usage. In other words, citizens and workers who are already included but at very low speed levels of infrastructure, are likely to understand the new possibilities sufficiently well to generate additional demand for higher infrastructure. This potential demand will be activated if price/quality combinations can be afforded. A harder question to answer is whether it would induce a migration from being excluded to being included in the digital world, especially where triple play is offered without competitive alternatives.

The other three proposals all help the first aim of improving broadband coverage in the EU. For this reason, there is no need to elaborate on them given our focus on e-inclusion. However, it is important to emphasize that all three proposals are far from easy to accomplish as stated. Investment in broadband is subject to strong density effects which renders extension to rural areas uninteresting or at least risky. One might suppose that Universal Service Obligation (USO) rights would be widened to include relatively low speeds of broadband infrastructure in remote and scarcely populated regions, but somebody will have to pay the bill. In the present post-crisis era of budgetary constraints, this bill will often be found too high, or such promises will have to be postponed. Moreover, the relatively poor Member States in Central Europe and a few poor regions in the EU15 are unlikely to be able to heed expanded USO commitments, other than by means of programmes from the Structural or Cohesion Funds (and even then, national co-funding might have to compete with other use of the national funds). The facilitation of investment in broadband infrastructure might of course help in the margin.[14]

On usage, the proposals would appear to be more directly addressing non-inclusion. Key Action 10 proposes to make 'digital literacy and competences' a priority for the EU Social Fund. Once effectively reaching citizens and workers in the EU, this may not only positively affect usage, but – perhaps with a lag – induce migration to buying computers and actually going online ('infrastructure') It should be noted, however, that this new priority for the Social Fund would only begin to be effectuated in 2014 which means that citizens will not notice any effect before 2015. The other proposal is directed to the Member States. By 2011 Member States should implement long-term e-skills and digital literacy policies and promote relevant incentives for SMEs and disadvantaged groups. Of course, several Member States already actively pursue such policies in different degrees. Although this item cannot, by definition, tackle the problem of affordability of infrastructure, it would seem by far the most immediate tool to reduce non-inclusion. As the example of the 6000 UK online centres shows, it will require a highly decentralized and practical approach which is neither desirable nor feasible at the EU level. The target of halving the 30 per cent excluded by 2015 will be a tall order since the relevant groups (the elderly, the poor, the unemployed and the less educated – with some overlap between these four categories) are not easily convinced and are likely to regard affordability as a central problem too. For the elderly, technically defined as the 65–74 age group, there is likely to be some automatism involved in reducing the excluded: by 2015 this cohort will itself be halved (deceased or older than 74) and, assuming that minimal e-literacy is higher for age groups just below 65 (in 2009), the rate of non-e-inclusion amongst the elderly is bound to fall anyway. A special issue, subsumed in the proposals on usage in Table 8.1, is the infrastructureibility and usability of Internet services for people with disabilities. Here, international treaty obligations (for example a UN Convention) apply, which have been incorporated in the third telecoms Framework of December 2009 as well as in the Audiovisual Media Services directive 2007/65/EC. Clearly, this should have a direct positive effect on usage for disabled persons insofar as Member States had not yet applied international web infrastructureibility standards to their public websites and other online services crucial for public life. Finally, it is good to notice that the Commission goes much further in digital literacy and skills than basic aspects of e-inclusion; this will be discussed when dealing with Table 8.2.

When it comes to 'impact', a range of proposals are found. Under e-Health there is a strong emphasis on facilitating independent dignified living and AAL (Ambient Assisted Living) technologies. This adds great value to the wellbeing of the elderly, and their generally powerful preference to continue to live independently in a dignified fashion might be a critical incentive to migrate to e-included citizens (link between

Table 8.2   EU Digital Agenda: items indirectly affecting e-inclusion

Improving framework conditions	
Usage	Pan-EU licensing for online right management (DSM) (EU)
	Review EU data protection (cf. citizens) (EU)
	Propose rules on jurisdiction (Eur/int.) (EU)
Impact	Update of e-commerce Directive (EU)
	Single Euro Payments Area (SEPA) / deadline introduction/ migration (EU)
	Review e-signature Directive (EU)
	Common contract law for consumers proposed (EU)
Horizontal Digital Agenda	
Impact	EU-wide online dispute resolution system for e-commerce (EU)
	More flexible rules for ICT standardization in Europe (EU)
Sectoral Digital Agenda	
Usage	Mainstream e-learning in national education (MS)
	New e-skills programme, as part of EU2020 'new jobs' flagship (EU)
Impact	Modernize ENISA (EU Agency for network security) (EU)
	Legal measures to combat 'cyber attacks' (EU + MS)

impact, infrastructure and usage). However, often the elderly concerned will be above the 74 years threshold and risk falling outside the indicators measured! A more general proposal is a common minimum set of patient data for purposes of intra-EU patient mobility, a sensitive issue in certain Member States. Under e-economy the mutual recognition of e-identification and e-authentication is proposed, a highly desirable consequence of a proposed revision of the e-signature directive which has had so far only limited effect for e-commerce. For consumers (and e-inclusion is mostly about consumers) this matters less as long as credit cards can be used for cross-border business-to-consumer (B2C) commerce, but for SMEs hesitant to initiate cross-border e-commerce (business-to-business, as B2B) it seems crucial. Under e-government, the proposals include seamless cross-border e-government services (which appears elementary but is not) and a common list of key cross-border public services between the Member States.

Altogether, the EU Digital Agenda exhibits a rich menu of highly diverse proposals which nonetheless can all be considered to address e-inclusion problems directly.

8.5 PROPOSALS AFFECTING E-INCLUSION INDIRECTLY

Table 8.2 applies the industrial policy framework, as adapted, in trying to understand the EU Digital Agenda proposals which affect e-inclusion problems indirectly. Of course, it is somewhat arbitrary to draw the line since one might take the view that all proposals in one way or another indirectly affect e-inclusion questions. Table 8.2 gives a selection by the author of the measures which could have a recognizable effect on questions of e-inclusion. There are no measures in Table 8.2 affecting infrastructure. Thus, all these indirect effects are concerned with citizens or workers already enjoying some kind of infrastructure, but where usage and/or impact can be appreciably improved and enriched. Presumably, one can extend this argument and suggest that the proposals in this respect might help to make the online services so attractive (or less problematic) that excluded citizens finally do decide to migrate and get included by taking infrastructure.

In wide EU strategies like the Digital Agenda, the broader EU framework aspects tend to assume considerable significance, even though the proposals might not seem to be focused on the key issue at stake, here, e-inclusion. Under 'usage', three proposals in fact deal with complex issues that have frustrated European digital users for quite a while: (1) data protection (what can and cannot be asked, what can be stored by whom or for how long and how privacy protection is guaranteed in various countries, and so on); (2) digital rights management which is organized on a country by country basis, thus fragmenting the internal market for users interested in legal downloading of, say music and films, whereas illegal piracy has no borders in Europe!, and (3) the problem of too easy escape for Internet spammers or even those damage services, by exploiting anomalies of jurisdiction. All three are framework questions, essentially internal market issues, broadly conceived. Their legal technicality is one thing; for users their resolution would surely make going online and making cross-border payments for goods and services a lot more attractive. Under 'impact' the four proposals all belong to e-economy. The revision of the e-signature Directive (beyond the mutual recognition aspects already mentioned in Table 8.1) and the update of the 2001 e-commerce Directive are straightforward cases. It is also important to terminate the endless delay in migrating from existing (national) payment systems to SEPA (Single Euro Payments Area), the EU payment system for all card and electronic transactions, which can serve the completion of digital services transactions in obvious ways. Its convenience would soon be known as a benefit of using online EU-wide services.

Insofar as EU online consumers are reluctant to buy across intra-EU borders other than from well-known international brand names (a widely documented fact recalled in the 2010 Monti report on the Single Market), a common contract law for consumers (perhaps as a 28th regime for consumer protection) would overcome such reticence to a large extent.

Table 8.2 also presents two horizontal proposals, both on 'impact'. One supplements the revision of the e-commerce Directive by setting up an EU-wide online dispute resolution system for e-commerce. It also supplements the common contract law for consumers mentioned above. Consumer redress online is (rightly) perceived as difficult and costly at the moment, and the more so when it is across an intra-EU border. For most consumers this is the litmus test of whether or not systematic buying in the entire internal market is worth it, unlike for B2B where the fear is less. The other proposal seems far removed from e-inclusion concerns, namely, more informal and faster ICT standardization via simple IP (Internet Protocol) workshops, fora and consortia.[15] However, it is expected to affect positively various items classified under impact. The following observation is telling:

> It is indeed imperative to modernize the EU ICT standardization policy and to fully exploit the potential of standard setting. Otherwise, the EU will fail to master the information society, will not realize a number of important European policy goals which require operability such as e-Health, infrastructureibility, security, e-Business, e-Government, transport, etc. and will face obstacles to. . . [promoting] international standards for personal protection.[16]

Finally, Table 8.2 comprises four sectoral proposals. On usage, it proposes mainstream e-learning in national education. On first sight, this: seems non-controversial. However, it is likely to require extra funding for computers in schools which renders the need less obvious for poorer EU countries. A more specific proposal relates to the ICT labour force in the EU, that is, high up the skills ladder when it comes to usage. It stretches the notion of e-inclusion to regard this as an element of it (rather than of modern industrial policy, education policy and growth strategy); however, once ICT skill shortages become problematic and chronic, as extrapolation suggests might happen in the EU, it is likely to harm e-inclusion sooner or later as well. The proposal would be a part of the EU2020 'new jobs' flagship.

On 'impact', the modernization of the EU Internet security agency ENISA is proposed in the framework of a 'reinforced and high level network and information security policy'. It should be remembered that ENISA was not allowed by Council to become part of the strengthened e-comms agency, finally entitled BEREC, in the third e-comms framework adopted in late 2009. However, the Digital Agenda strongly emphasizes the fight against cybercrime and large-scale attacks on, for example, EU and national government systems. The issue is whether the EU is capable of decisively pushing back the negative externalities of Internet use that are eroding the benefits of 'impact'.

8.6 POLICY RATIONALES OF E-INCLUSION POLICIES

Since e-inclusion amounts to a wide-ranging strategy, it is important to appreciate the (EU) policy rationales behind it. It is equally crucial to grasp the myriad of options the EU can choose in pursuing e-inclusion. In the narrow legal sense, 'the' EU is the EU level of law and decision making under the Community method (Commission proposes; usually, European Parliament and Council dispose). But the EU can, formally or more loosely, pursue strategies via coordination, or, at EU level, 'supplement or support' actions by Member States. More strongly, and formally outside the treaties, the EU can act as a voluntary club of countries which happen to be EU Member States, more or less like a European-style OECD, and pursue aims or precise targets for the countries, jointly, on a consensual basis. The potential strength of the club, as compared to the OECD, is that the very same countries and their decision makers are already bound in many other, often powerful, ways in common frameworks and policies, and are used to cooperating in consensual patterns. The Lisbon process since 2000 has shown, despite all its problems and weaknesses, that common wide-ranging strategies blending strict EU competences, coordinating policies and actions as well as voluntary endeavours, based on joint analysis, reporting and peer review, can achieve results when leaders and national decision makers are convinced of a national interest nested, as it were, in an EU common pursuit. The EU e-inclusion policies have to be positioned in this broad contextual setting in any attempt to grasp their rationale(s) and potential effectiveness.

In this light, the following first reminds the reader of the basic treaty provisions to which e-inclusion can be credibly linked. Subsequently, such possible links have to be tested for a sound rationale, and one has to verify at what level (EU, Member States, regions) and with what degree of binding the policies can be pursued. Secondly, the economic rationales for e-inclusion are briefly discussed. Non-economic rationales (for example, the societal desire to combat a digital divide, or not to exclude) have a political, social or ethical rationale which is simply taken for granted for the purpose of the present chapter. As Section 4.1 shows, the EU expressly

Table 8.3 EU treaty objectives and links with e-inclusion

Art. 3/1, EU	Well-being of its peoples
Art. 3/3, EU	Sustainable development
	Balanced growth
	Highly competitive social market economy
	(Full) employment and social progress
	Promote scientific and technological advance
	Combat social exclusion
	Economic, social and territorial cohesion

favours such a political choice in general language in the Lisbon treaty. Of course, there is the question of how far the EU level can or should go in ensuring the realization of such objectives.

The arrival of the information society amounts to a transformation of how EU citizens live, transact, communicate, work and entertain themselves. The costs and drawbacks of this momental change notwithstanding, there is a conviction all over the world that this new way of living and working entails such massive benefits that non-participation is generally a serious drawback, if not a handicap socially and economically. The concept of e-inclusion expresses this general idea, culminating in an extremely wide-ranging strategy, as noted above. Tables 8.3 and 8.4 show in a concise fashion that the two Lisbon treaties incorporate a series of broad objectives as well as a range of instruments of a highly differentiated nature and scope which can underpin such a wide strategy in a general sense. This does not mean that all elements of the strategy would be EU law or even EU policy in the formal sense; much of this could be policies of persuasion, funding and consent on joint objectives, sometimes called the 'open method of coordination', sometimes simply different degrees of cooperation. Much might actually have to be done by the Member States or authorities at the regional or local level.

The objectives specified by the (Lisbon) EU treaty, insofar as they are relevant for e-inclusion, are listed in Table 8.3. They do not fully overlap with those in the EU and EC treaties of Maastricht, Amsterdam and Nice. Apart from some reshuffling and the new term 'social market economy' (which seems quite open-ended), an explicit and new EU objective is to 'combat social exclusion'. This would seem to go further and is less fuzzy than 'social cohesion'. The adoption of this EU objective is remarkable because one would presume such an objective typically to be assigned to a local, regional or at most national level of government, given the fact that all EU countries cherish some form of welfare state. In any event,

Table 8.4   Treaty on the functioning of the EU provisions and e-inclusion

Exclusive powers	Art. 3/1 (b) Competition rules for the internal market
Shared powers	Art. 4/2 (a) Internal market 4/2 (b) Social policy 4/2 (c) Cohesion (economic, social, territorial) 4/2 (f) Consumer protection 4/2 (h) Trans-European networks Art. 4/3 Research and technology
Coordination	Art. 5 Coordination of economic and employment policies of the Member States
Supporting, coordinating and supplementing 'actions' of the Member States	Art. 6 (b) Industrial policy Art. 6 (e) Education
Other	Art. 9 Fight against social exclusion Art. 16 Protection of personal data

e-inclusion will obviously accord well with this overall EU objective. But all eight EU objectives mentioned here can in one way or another serve as a treaty-based rationale for an e-inclusion strategy. The 'well-being of its peoples' might be a little vague and 'scientific and technological advance' is likely to constitute more of a prerequisite in some sense, but the remaining four are undoubtedly relevant as a policy rationale: sustainable development, balanced growth (a term traditionally overlapping with what is now called economic cohesion, but which can be interpreted in terms of avoiding deep divides in the EU (information) society), a 'highly competitive social market economy' and '(full) employment and social progress'. In empirical economic work, such as a large part of this report, these four EU objectives cannot be incorporated in ways doing full justice to all the refinements and subtleties, but the thrust of this work accords well with text and spirit of the treaty.

The Lisbon Treaty on the Functioning of the EU (TFEU) (basically, the former EC treaty, as revised) specifies the EU instruments to pursue the EU objectives. The relevant ones for strategies of e-inclusion are summarized in Table 8.4. These instruments are characterized by different degrees of (de) centralization and of legal binding; these distinctions have been captured in the left column. The organization of this (former EC) treaty has been radically changed, especially by enumerating the powers of the EU and labelling them as 'shared' and 'exclusive', besides the clear grouping together of other, weaker powers. However, the substance is similar if not identical to the former EC treaty, except for Art. 9 – the fight against social exclusion, already a new EU objective in Table 8.3 – and Art. 16 – the protection of personal data.[17] Both are highly relevant for e-inclusion. The economic logic of the treaty has also remained the same, although the enumeration of the 'shared powers' has created a veil which seems unhelpful for a proper understanding. The logic has its foundation in the internal market.[18] It is and has always been the 'workhorse' of the EU, intended to generate more prosperity from deep commitments to work together.[19] Indeed, in Art. 3, EU, all the EU objectives specified (see Table 8.3) are preceded by the phrase that the Union 'shall establish an internal market. It shall work for. . .'. Thus, EU social policy, consumer protection, trans-European networks and the competition rules in Table 8.4 are part and parcel of the internal market, not separate stand-alone policies. For other EU policies specified in the table, the internal market acts as a consistency constraint on what can and cannot be done (for example industrial policy; social cohesion; coordination of economic and employment policies; research and technology). The links are weaker for education, a national competence but encouraged as a supplementary policy, and for the fight against social exclusion.

Considering Tables 8.3 and 8.4 together, it seems justified that economic growth (conditioned by sustainability and 'balanced'), driven by a competitive market economy (a proper functioning of the internal market and of (domestic, national) markets more generally), and a strong employment performance in the Union constitute the dominant rationales for EU strategies. However, they are not the only rationales – indeed, the EU market economy incorporates social elements, social exclusion is to be fought, social cohesion is to be pursued, personal data protection must be ensured and two national competences (infrastructure via TENs and education) play a complementary role where relevant. The conclusion is that, from a treaty perspective, the rationales for an e-inclusion strategy are powerful and justified.

One can be more specific in attempting to attribute treaty objectives and instruments to the (Digital Agenda) measures directly affecting e-inclusion (Table 8.1) and those indirectly affecting e-inclusion (Table 8.2). However, a word of caution is needed when engaging in such an exercise, because the chain of causation between instruments and final (treaty) goals can be extremely complicated (and indeed blurred by other factors influencing such goals). Attribution is perhaps easier for the instruments listed in Table 8.4. Thus, the infrastructure measures *directly* influencing e-inclusion are all internal market tools; also, two of the impact measures (common patient data and mutual recognition of e-identification) are typical of the internal market. As to usage measures from Table 8.1, digital literacy via the Social Fund is (socially) a form of impact, economically a bolstering of employability[20] and in EU policy terms a measure of economic and social cohesion and of employment. It is harder to classify long-term digital literacy for disadvantaged groups (and SMEs) under EU instruments; indeed, Member States have voluntarily agreed to this objective. Combining the fight against social exclusion with social cohesion and a supplementary EU role in education, an EU promotion of this idea is probably justifiable, clearly in close cooperation with the Member States.[21] The other four usage measures proposed are a mixed bag. It is difficult to attach the two on e-health and AAL to specific EU instruments, though the latter might be given a place under R&D.[22] But they can of course fall under voluntary cooperative ventures by the Member States collectively. The two under e-government services are plainly Member States activities where Commission studies or other actors can do little more than suggest.

For measures *indirectly* affecting e-inclusion, the bulk can be characterized as internal market items. This is true for all the framework conditions ('usage' and 'impact') in Table 8.2, for the two horizontal (impact) items and for the sectoral impact measures. This leaves two sectoral usage measures. The mainstreaming of e-learning in national education is clearly a Member State activity encouraged by the EU countries as a group, not by the EU as such. The new e-skills programme as part of the EU2020 strategy relates to advanced ICT skills, basically for ICT specialists, and can be seen as industrial policy (critical for the future competitiveness of EU business given the expected shortages) as well as education and vocational training.

8.7 ECONOMIC RATIONALES FOR E-INCLUSION POLICIES

As discussed in Section 8.1, the already broad notion of e-inclusion (based on infrastructure, usage and impact, including actions to improve online services both private and governmental) is more and more embedded in an even wider idea of digital competitiveness. Although conceptually ill-defined, the recent Commission reports on Digital Competitiveness and the 2010 EU Digital Agenda clarify that e-inclusion is regarded as a significant and complex component on the demand side whilst not losing sight of social exclusion risks, the existing digital divide in Europe between segments of the population, and the social impact aspects (for example on social capital and as a social communication tool). The domain is so wide, with such diversity of policy issues, that a single analytical framework cannot encompass it. In the following, the focus is on the economic rationales.[23]

There would seem to be four clusters of economic rationales for e-inclusion strategies in the Union. Three of the four clusters are not easily recognized as e-inclusion policies because they have wider purposes or other effects beyond e-inclusion. However, it would be a sad mistake to focus solely on measures directly targeting 'usage' and 'impact', beside the now well-known emphasis on broadband availability. These direct measures do matter economically in their own right, but there are sound economic rationales to complimentary approaches as well. In fact, all four clusters interact to some degree, hence e-inclusion is well served by paying attention to all of them. In turn, such a boost to EU e-inclusion can be shown to have considerable beneficial effects on the EU objectives listed in Table 8.3. The following clusters of EU policies, all affecting e-inclusion directly or indirectly, will be discussed:

- the pursuit of a digital Single Market;
- policies promoting EU ICT competitiveness and technology;
- specific measures augmenting e-inclusion;
- structural reforms at the Member State level affecting in-firm ICT-related reorganization under heightened competitive pressures.

Digital Single Market

The digital Single Market (DSM) has finally become a major EU priority, so it seems, as manifested by the Digital Agenda, the Monti report [24] and incorporation in the EU2020 strategy, not to speak of strong voices in the European Parliament. Section 8.3 clarifies that the Digital Agenda, insofar as the EU-level elements are concerned, is overwhelmingly about the DSM. In turn, Tables 8.1 and 8.2 demonstrate that this Digital Agenda comprises a large number of proposals which can reasonably be expected to influence positively, both directly and indirectly, e-inclusion in the EU. Therefore, the treaty rationale and economic rationales go together. The internal market is to serve the EU objectives, as specified in Table 8.3: in particular, economic growth (referred to in several EU objectives), a more competitive social market economy, higher employment (*ceteris paribus*) and – here, given the focus on e-inclusion – the fight against social exclusion.

The study by Copenhagen Economics (2010) on the economic impact of the DSM simulates that such a programme, if effective, could add 4 per cent to EU GDP by 2020 (or more than € 1000 for every EU citizen). This is the same order of magnitude as the EC-1992 programme was expected to generate at the time! The study also argues – probably correctly in qualitative terms – that this GDP increment is by no means the only benefit.

The authors conclude that (a) ICT usage would increase due to a genuine DSM, in turn fostering productivity growth – a result that squares with the empirical results of Chapter 5 of the present study, which shows that the usage dimension is critical for raising labour productivity; (b) a DSM tends to induce additional innovation, not least because in the EU successful digital firms tend to be knowledge-intensive, incur high R&D costs (which have much lower unit costs when infrastructure to a large DSM is ensured) and (currently still) suffer from high regulatory costs due to a fragmented digital regulatory environment which a DSM would improve considerably; (c) EU (online) consumers would benefit in terms of choice and fiercer price competition, which, in turn, might actually stimulate usage and impact, leading in the longer run to even higher growth; (d) a DSM should help to stimulate e-government, and hence online public services, leading to a betterment of impact also on this account. The Copenhagen study does not offer a simulation of employment gains, other than quoting studies on the job-creating effects of a decisive improvement of digital infrastructure. The present study, though not focusing directly on the DSM, finds that the impact (or empowerment) dimension captures the potential to transform modes of production in firms and value-chains, in turn leading to more jobs and a higher rate of growth via a higher TFP.

The economic rationale for the DSM is therefore powerful and accords well with an e-inclusion perspective. Moreover, the simulated increment to EU GDP as well as the potential to raise the EU's growth rate over time (via additional innovation and entrepreneurship) also help in and by themselves to reduce a possible divide between e-inclusion in rich and relatively poor EU countries. As noted before, e-inclusion scores not only differ between segments of the population, but show a clear correlation with the level of prosperity, too. Sustained economic growth in the Union as a whole is therefore good for overcoming a divide between Cohesion countries and the EU15, for example.

Policies Promoting EU ICT Competitiveness and Technology

As already noted, EU policies have moved away from the former, almost exclusive and at first interventionist, emphasis on research, technology and development in ICT and ICT sectoral competitiveness, whether hardware or software, to the very wide spectrum of digital competitiveness. Indeed, EU R&D in ICT is overwhelmingly (more than 90 per cent) private nowadays. Sectoral ICT competitiveness is worrying, with a comparative disadvantage in hardware production and a relatively modest position in software. Looking at companies (which may locate their output over the entire globe, of course, but might nonetheless be regarded as reflecting EU advantages, and are likely to exert positive influences on knowledge jobs and economic growth – given the dynamics of the sector – in the EU itself), the picture is little better.[25] The traditionally strong position in telecoms equipment (three companies in the top five worldwide in 2009) and telecoms services (two in the top five and several close behind) is mirrored neither in the computer industry (none in the top ten), nor in the software industry (one in the top five and four in the top twenty). Due to convergence, even the telecoms equipment positions have come under severe challenge now that IP (Internet Protocol) and Internet functions on handsets and tablets begin to dominate.

However, the EU is not withdrawing but reorientating. The EU2020 strategy and the Digital Agenda announce a reform of funding and increase in ICT support so as to reinforce the EU's technological strength in key strategic areas, stimulate ICT innovation, and create better conditions for SMEs in these domains to grow. In two Commission communications, the new approach is foreshadowed.[26] Is there a link with e-inclusion? Direct links with e-inclusion are somewhat speculative and not strong.[27] The more remote but nonetheless relevant connection is found in the competitiveness of other industries heavily using (if not developing) advanced ICT applications such as the car industry, medical devices and pharmaceuticals. These sectors contribute to EU economic growth and will also stimulate demand for new e-skills.

Specific Measures Augmenting e-Inclusion

The specific e-inclusion programmes at EU level and by the Member States pursuant to reaching the Riga targets as well as the direct and indirect measures affecting e-inclusion in the Digital Agenda (of course, the two overlap to some degree) can be justified by both a societal rationale and an economic rationale. The EU objectives of combating social exclusion and/or of social cohesion can easily be reconciled with notions such as the 'digital divide' having motivated e-inclusion strategies. However, measures fostering e-inclusion, if effective, also have positive economic effects. The present study provides a novel empirical analysis showing exactly that. In short,

- it is crucial to distinguish between the much heralded infrastructure dimension and the other two. As long as relatively low-speed broadband is targeted, infrastructure policies in and by themselves will have very limited effects on growth, labour productivity and employment (see Section 5.4). The present study does not go into the potential economic effects of high-speed broadband, but the literature now emerging[28] suggests that, if affordability barriers and the costs of density effects in remote areas can be overcome, such effects can be large and positive. However, unlike the present study, these studies are not capable of distinguishing empirically between the (pure) 'infrastructure' dimension of e-inclusion and other aspects – typically, these are amalgamated into overall effects;

- 'usage' is shown to influence positively the rate of growth of labour productivity via greater autonomy, intensity and more workers with e-skills. For disadvantaged groups, in particular people in the age group of 55–64 years old, what matters for their employability is the ability to use ICT in a company environment;
- the 'impact' (or empowerment) dimension is shown to matter for creating new jobs and for enhancing the rate of growth of the economy.

These findings would seem to suggest that Member States, and not merely the EU level, have a powerful incentive, an enlightened self-interest, to pursue e-inclusion actively for all three dimensions. Unlike many other reforms to improve market functioning or (say) remove disincentives in welfare states, e-inclusion policies typically do not produce temporary losers. Indeed, one might argue that the absence of e-inclusion policies is likely to turn non-participants of the information society into losers. Of course, they entail financial costs for enterprises, governments and individuals besides the invisible adjustment costs of learning new skills at a higher age or in a difficult social environment. Such financial and intangible costs act as a brake. The present study can act as a strong encouragement for goverments of EU countries to remain active promoters of e-inclusion, if only because it is bound to support much-wanted economic growth and higher employment, including for certain disadvantaged groups.

Structural Reforms at the Member State Level

There is a risk that legitimate concerns about the digital divide prompt e-inclusion policies with too narrow a focus. The narrowest approach consists of pursuing solely the specific measures augmenting e-inclusion. As this section shows, it is crucial to broaden approaches by incorporating far broader EU strategies (the DSM and ICT competitiveness) as they too tend to influence e-inclusion positively, in various ways. As noted, the new Digital Agenda and the intentions for a new EU industrial policy (also) related to ICT form a testimony that this is now well understood at the EU level.

Nevertheless, the approach to e-inclusion has to be drawn wider still, and for good reasons. So far, it has been hard to find convincing evidence for a further broadening of the e-inclusion spectrum by policy makers. But that reticence seems unjustified. There is increasingly strong empirical economic evidence that enterprises in the EU, compared to those in the US, have been insufficiently compelled by competitive pressures to reorganize themselves internally, boost the e-skills of staff, and to adapt their business models based on advanced and intrinsic applications of ICT and ICT use. At a slightly higher level of aggregation (goods or services markets), intrinsic ICT adoption requires flexible markets not merely for competitive pressures to emerge but also to allow the reallocation of resources from old to new activities and to new modes of production. The infamous productivity gap between the EU and the US since about 1995 is mainly attributed to ICT use in certain services sectors (see Chapter 1, note 9 for details), hence to more effective and intrinsic ICT adoption by firms going all the way to new organizational forms and other ways of doing business internally and externally.

The question is then: why do EU companies perform much more weakly in this respect and hesitate to go far in internal reforms, especially since these transformations lead, after a delay, to strong productivity effects? Early indications in the literature suggested that a systemically less fierce competitive climate in European markets might be attributable to restrictive regulation of goods, services and labour markets.[29] Barrios and Burgelman (2008) have analysed in a single framework the link between market rigidities, ICT diffusion and economic growth. The authors find a negative influence of market regulation on GDP growth through ICT investment deterrence. One striking illustration is the contrast they find between high regulation and low regulation countries in three aspects: labour regulation, business regulation, and credit market regulation. The ICT growth contribution is significantly lower for high regulation countries than for low regulation countries in all three cases. The study by Van Reenen et al. (2010) for the Commission, which employs firm-level data and should be more reliable and robust in this respect, finds that the relative strictness of national labour market regulation and product market regulation may be a significant determinant of cross-country differences in the impact of ICT. This effect seems to be most severe with respect to labour market regulation.[30] EU and national policy makers have often stated in general terms that they favour deep reforms for reasons of growth and productivity (if not to facilitate adjustment in the eurozone) but, in contrast to specific e-inclusion measures, these will inevitably create temporary 'losers', in particular in services and labour markets. Policy makers might also wonder whether and to what extent such intra-firm upskilling and reorganization should be considered as the extreme end of the e-inclusion spectrum, or as going beyond it, being a policy to engender more economic growth.

8.8 CONCLUSIONS

This chapter has developed an encompassing EU policy framework for pursuing e-inclusion. It attempts to come to grips with what e-inclusion can be understood to comprise (following the EDDI approach) in an EU perspective and how it relates to traditional and new ICT policies at EU and national levels. The infrastructure dimension has been dealt with quite effectively by the respective EU telecoms regimes, the current one being governed by the third e-comms package of December 2009. For the infrastructure dimension of e-inclusion, there is a clear correlation with the level of prosperity, which implies that general economic growth in the EU and catch-up growth for the new Member States act, de facto, also as e-inclusion policies insofar as the divide between richer and poorer EU countries is concerned. However, the broadband question is likely to hit affordability barriers once higher quality requirements are insisted on, particularly in rural and Cohesion areas. Since usage and impact are crucial in generating economic gains from e-inclusion, one is struck by the incredible ambition and enormous diversity of e-inclusion policy intentions at two or more levels of government in the Union. Such a demanding framework raises serious questions of complexity and effectiveness. Thus, the EU has few effective tools to stimulate more 'autonomous', more 'intense' and more sophisticated usage. The local level, market pressures and enlightened self-interest in national capitals seem to be more important. This is radically different from the e-comms regimes related to infrastructure. In slightly different ways, the same ambition and similar issues of complexity and effectiveness can be found for the impact (or, empowerment) dimension. Again, market pressures and insistence by citizens and business will be critical for such policies to yield results. Fortunately, the kind of reforms at stake do eventually lead to a transformation of consumption and business models, if not the provision of public services, but do not create temporary losers ; the resistance has more to do with up-front financial costs and the intangible efforts of adjustment by the 'excluded'.

The traditional EU way of approaching ICT competitiveness, though still playing a role, has been overtaken by the far more encompassing idea of digital competitiveness. It combines both supply and demand in a very wide range of aspects, based on the notion that ICT is a general purpose technology with wide ramifications in European society and the EU economy. This raises questions about the design of an effective policy framework. Indeed, the idea of digital competitiveness is so broad that e-inclusion is now regarded as part of it. In order to better understand how these two hang together, a detailed scrutiny of the direct and indirect (proposed) measures of the Digital Agenda influencing e-inclusion is provided. It turns out that, amongst the direct measures, all three aspects of e-inclusion are affected, a rich menu of highly diverse proposals. Most actions amount to a deepening and widening of the internal market, complemented by numerous items to be delivered by Member States. As to the indirect measures, only 'usage' and 'impact' are touched upon. What is striking is that many aspects which can reasonably be expected to help e-inclusion are in fact broader framework aspects related to the hard core of EU economic integration (for example the internal market).

Since e-inclusion amounts to a wide-ranging strategy, it is important to appreciate the EU policy rationales behind it. First, the treaty rationales (both EU objectives and TFEU instruments) are inspected. Besides the explicit treaty objective of combating social exclusion, it is found that the empiricial economic analysis conducted in the report accords well with the text and spirit of the treaty, given economic growth objectives ('sustainable' and 'balanced'), a 'highly competitive social market economy' and (full) 'employment and social progress'. As to the instruments, the economic logic of the TFEU treaty based on the workhorse function of the internal market is clearly recognizable in the EU Digital Agenda. Most of the other proposals are to be pursued by the Member States, except for an occasional reference to EU industrial (but non-interventionist) policy and the Social Fund.

Second, the economic rationales behind an e-inclusion strategy are discussed. It is of vital importance to understand that the broadest possible e-inclusion approach will magnify the economic effect on key objectives such as economic growth and employment. In this respect, embedding e-inclusion in the wide idea of digital competitiveness can be supported. There is still a risk that legitimate social or societal concerns driving e-inclusion policies might prompt a (too) narrow approach of attempting specific measures addressing access, usage and impact. A broader approach, with a strong economic rationale, would also include the pursuit of a digital Single Market (even though it does not 'look like' an e-inclusion policy on first sight) and, to a more limited extent, the promotion of ICT competitiveness. It is argued that the empirical economic literature not least the present report's econometric results (in Chapter 5), demonstrates the beneficial links between usage (labour productivity) and impact (economic growth and job creation), on the one hand, and these broader approaches. However, the economic rationale of going still further in this respect is also found in the literature. Member States can go beyond mere measures about e-learning, or the better provision of online services and so on, and credibly pursue deep reforms in domestic labour markets (and to some extent services markets, too), since these appear to be critical in obtaining much greater economic gains from e-inclusion improvements, especially inside companies in the EU. The conspicuous productivity growth gap between the US and the EU since 1995 can largely be attributed to insufficient competitive pressures in markets, in turn due to too restrictive regulation, making going-slow possible and rendering innovative approaches and deeper ICT investments less interesting or compelling for companies. This recommendation is harder to swallow for Member States than the conventional e-inclusion measures, precisely because such market reforms do risk creating temporary losers.

NOTES

1. Operating at two levels of government, that is, it also entails a regime of national regulators under a series of EU obligations at national level. See framework directive 2009/140 (also on licensing and interconnection) and the universal service and user rights directive 2009/136, both on in OJEU L 337, plus Regulation 1211/2009 on BEREC, in OJEU, idem.
2. UNCTAD, 2009; SEC (2009) 1103 of 4 August 2009, Europe's Digital Competitiveness Report, Vol. 1; and others.
3. See www.ukonlinecentres.com and the 2008 study 'Economic benefits of digital inclusion: building the evidence'.
4. This calls for a remark on what the distinction is between economic and social. Delocalization but also employment effects and relative wage shifts are clearly economic effects which entail social consequences. In Figure 1.2 they are classified as 'Labour'. Moreover, under economic impact, one can go beyond e-commerce and e-banking, for example, in C2C 'open market' sales, and – to give another example – co-makership between different companies in the global value-chain based on e-design, standardized quality control and permanent data exchange (EDI) between upstream and downstream. Yet another ICT-driven revolution is found in logistics, combining ICT and satellite GPS services for tracking.
5. All data from the 2010 Digital Competitiveness Report, 17 May 2010, Vol. 1, SEC (2010) 627, pp. 77/78.
6. The usual definition of 'the' ICT sector is actually an addition of six manufacturing sectors and two services sectors. ICT manufacturing consists of office machinery (computers, etc.), insulated wire (transmission cables, optical fibre), electronic valves, telecoms equipment, radio and TV receivers (including CD players, DVDs) and selected scientific instruments. ICT services include telecoms services (including Internet and audio-visual services) and computer-related services (including software, data processing, etc.). Source: European Commission, 2006 Competitiveness Report, chapter 7, p. 173 (Table 7.1).
7. European Digital Competitiveness Report 2010, 17 May 2010, Vol. 1, SEC (2010) 627.
8. TFP is a residual in growth accounting, beyond the contributions of labour and direct capital accumulation. The considerable difference in EU and (higher) US growth since the mid-1990s is due to a TFP gap. This gap is attributed, to a considerable extent, to an ICT performance gap. The US has outperformed the EU in both ICT manufacturing and ICT use in certain specific (for example retail and wholesale) services to such an extent that it largely explains a painful growth differential for over a decade or more. See Van Ark, O'Mahoney and Timmer, 2008; Jorgensen, Ho and Stiroh, 2008; and in even greater detail Bloom et al., 2010.
9. Google, Facebook, YouTube, Wikipedia, eBay and Amazon are examples.
10. Also in the 2009 Digital Competitiveness report there are extensive analyses on, respectively, e-inclusion, the impact of ICT on social capital, and 'impact' issues such as the

Internet as a communication tool and for entertainment. COM (2009) 390 of 4 August 2009 and SEC(2009) 1103 of the same date.

11. CEC (2010b), 'A Digital Agenda for Europe', p. 4.
12. See Jacques Pelkmans (2006a).
13. This EU competition policy includes, besides anti-trust, a strict effect-based state aids surveillance as well as a combination of competition policy and EU regulation to enable network industries to operate efficiently and competitively in the internal market.
14. It is extremely difficult to estimate how effective this item will be. The Digital Action plan mentions a range of funding options at EU level (ERDF, ERDP, EAFRD, TEN and CIP) as well as 'credit enhancement' backed by the EIB, without any explanation in the text. However, a Broadband Communication is announced for 2010 in which these options will be worked out.
15. Internet and world wide web standards are set in informal consortia, which cannot be legally refered to in EU legislation due to the strict (and exclusive) link between the CEN/CENELEC/ETSI system recognized in EU law and the EU. This strict link is justified by reasons of solidity (given safety and health issues involved), open inquiry requirements, open access for consumers and labour unions and the WTO Code on good standardization practices. In Internet questions, where a fast pace is critical, inter-operability is key and safety/health issues are minimal, the formal EU strictness in ICT standardization has become an Achilles heel.
16. From COM(2009) 324 of 3 July 2009, 'Modernising ICT standardisation in the EU – the way forward', p. 3. Support is also found in the EXPRESS report of February 2010 (expert panel on EU standardisation) in recommendations 9.1, 9.2 and 12.3.
17. The latter incorporates Art. 8 of the 2000 EU Charter of Fundamental Rights, together with a decision-making procedure at EU level. Art. 16 TFEU is far broader than the former Art. 286, EC (for example includes the Member States when carrying out EU-related activities). See also Art. 39, EU.
18. Nowadays also in EMU, which is left out because the link with e-inclusion is expected to be too weak or absent.
19. It would go much too far to elaborate. See Pelkmans (2006b), chapters 2–10 as well as chapters 12, 14, 15 and 16, explaining systematically the fundamental economic role of the EU internal market and how most of the other instruments in Table 8.4 are linked to or deeply influenced by it.
20. The term 'employability' is not mentioned in the Employment Title (IX) of the TFEU but is routinely used in the EU policy debate. However, Art. 145, TFEU speaks about 'promoting a skilled, trained. . . workforce'. Art. 146, TFEU also speaks about 'employment as a common concern'. Art. 162, TFEU on the European Social Fund states 'aim to render the employment of workers easier . . . and to facilitate their adaptation to industrial changes and to changes in production systems'.
21. Note that Art. 165, TFEU says that the Union 'shall contribute to the development of quality education. . . if necessary by supporting and supplementing' the actions of Member States. Art. 166, TFEU established a 'vocational training policy' (again, supporting Member States) and includes 'faciliate adaptation to industrial changes' via vocational training.
22. Art. 180, TFEU says that the Union, in complementing activities carried out by Member States, can carry out 'dissemination. . . of the results in Union research, technological development and demonstration'.
23. Chapter 3 of this study touches upon some of these questions. See also a recent report to the European Commission by University of Siegen and partners, Study on the Social Impact of ICT, 30 April 2010, dedicated to a range of social impacts in considerable detail.
24. Monti, 2010, pp. 44–47.
25. The following data are taken from the Copenhagen Economics study (2010).
26. See COM (2009) 116, 'A strategy for ICT R & D and innovation in Europe, Raising the Game', dealing mainly with software and communication technology (including

for example future internet); and COM (2009) 512 of 30 Sept. 2009, 'Preparing for our future: developing a common strategy for key enabling technologies in the EU', which deals with five such technologies, three of which deeply affect ICT in a modern, wider sense: micro-electronics, nano-electronics and photonics.

27. Four possible links can be suggested. One runs via broadband (Table 8.1) which might become cheaper, hence more affordable in the future due to further technical progress. Another one runs via ICT standardization (Table 8.2) which is continuously updated due to R&D. A third one might be the new e-skills programme (Table 8.2), by definition an area subject to permanent progress. The fourth one runs via the applications of these technologies in, for example, e-health (see Table 8.1) or in other domains which would enhance the 'impact' dimension of e-inclusion.

28. For example, MICUS, 2008; WIK, 2008.

29. See, for example, Gust & Marquez, 2004; Conway et al., 2006.

30. The labour market regulation effect offsets the main effect of ICT by no less than −45% while the product market regulation effect does this only for some −16%. This is in itself an important clue for the reforms to be undertaken. But the reader is warned that the product market regulation indicators (taken from the OECD) tend to suffer from a considerable EU-neglect bias (Pelkmans, 2010). Product market regulation at the Member State level is effectively disciplined by EU internal market rules in many ways, whilst anti-competitive outcomes are often caught (or prevented) by EU competition policy. These disciplines are ignored in the OECD indicators as they are solely country based.

Appendix: EDDI European Digital Development Index: definition of methodology

A.1 INTRODUCTION

The construction of an index has several problematic issues which can be solved only in connection with the cognitive objectives of the subject producing the index, and within the limitations set by the availability of information in the spatial-temporal context in which the index is constructed. Over the last decades, many international bodies, intergovernmental organizations, private institutions, and national and international foundations have developed various indexes on economic, social and governance issues which often get significant attention from the press and contribute to creating the national and international perception of the conditions of each country. The inclusion of the various countries in the lists produced on the basis of the values taken from the different indexes affects public opinion, opinion leaders, politicians, and economic, national and international decision makers, influencing the choices of investment localization and other primary economic, political and social activities. This, therefore, is a significant impact that is often determined by subjects who completely ignore the procedures according to which the various classifications are prepared. Some of these indexes adopt a complex methodology as they include a large number of indicators of a varying nature: *hard*, originating from national and international statistical organizations, or *soft*, originating from estimates produced by surveys conducted on population samples or from interviews with opinion leaders, entrepreneurs, financial operators, and so on. It is necessary to evaluate each single indicator and the technical criteria adopted in order to merge them into the index producing the final classification of the various countries. The more the index is the result of data processing, the more difficult it is to reconstruct the procedure leading to the final result, and the more difficult it is to provide an interpretation of the latter.

As a rule, indexes are intended to provide an empirical representation of very general and often multidimensional concepts. These concepts

Table A.1   Pros and cons of indexes

Pros	Cons
Can summarize complex, multidimensional realities with a view to supporting decision makers	May send misleading policy messages if poorly constructed or misinterpreted
Are easier to interpret than a battery of many separate indicators	May invite simplistic policy conclusions
Can assess progress of countries over time	May be misused, e.g. to support a desired policy, if the construction process is not transparent and/or lacks sound statistical or conceptual principles
Reduce the visible size of a set of indicators without dropping the underlying information base	The selection of indicators and weights could be the subject of political dispute
Thus make it possible to include more information within the existing size limit	May disguise serious failings in some dimensions and increase the difficulty of identifying proper remedial action, if the construction process is not transparent
Place issues of country performance and progress at the centre of the policy arena	May lead to inappropriate policies if dimensions of performance that are difficult to measure are ignored
Facilitate communication with general public (i.e. citizens, media, etc.) and promote accountability	
Help to construct/underpin narratives for lay and literate audiences	
Enable users to compare complex dimensions effectively	

cannot, by their nature, be detected directly and can rarely be defined in an unequivocal manner, especially at transnational level.

In a recent manual published by the OECD (2008, pp. 13–14) dedicated to the construction of indexes, a summary table indicating the related pros and cons was created (Table A.1).

The OECD manual aims to provide a set of methodological guidelines on how to design, develop and construct an index. It identifies an ideal sequence, subdivided into ten steps as shown below, for constructing an index (ibid., pp. 16–17):

1. *Theoretical framework*   A theoretical framework should be developed to provide the basis for the selection and combination of single indicators into a meaningful composite indicator under a fitness-for-purpose principle.
2. *Data selection*   Indicators should be selected on the basis of their analytical soundness, measurability, country coverage, relevance to the phenomenon being measured and relationship to each other. The use of proxy variables should be considered when data are scarce.
3. *Imputation of missing data*   Consideration should be given to different approaches for imputing missing values. Extreme values should be examined as they can become unintended benchmarks.
4. *Multivariate analysis*   An exploratory analysis should investigate the overall structure of the indicators, assess the suitability of the dataset and explain the methodological choices, for example weighting, aggregation.
5. *Normalization*   Indicators should be normalized to render them comparable. Attention needs to be paid to extreme values as they may influence subsequent steps in the process of building a composite indicator. Skewed data should also be identified and accounted for.
6. *Weighting and aggregation*   Indicators should be aggregated and weighted according to the underlying theoretical framework. Correlation and compensability issues among indicators need to be considered and either corrected for or treated as features of the phenomenon that need to be retained in the analysis.
7. *Robustness and sensitivity*   Analysis should be undertaken to assess the robustness of the composite indicator in terms of, for example, the mechanism for including or excluding single indicators, the normalization scheme, the imputation of missing data, the choice of weights, and the aggregation method.
8. *Back to the real data*   Composite indicators should be transparent and fit to be decomposed into their underlying indicators or values.
9. *Links to other variables*   Attempts should be made to correlate the composite indicator with other published indicators, as well as to identify linkages through regressions.
10. *Presentation and visualization*   Composite indicators can be visualized or presented in a number of different ways, which can influence their interpretation.

Each one of the ten steps illustrated above is extremely important. Each choice made at a given level has significant consequences for the subsequent levels. With respect to the various choices to be made during each phase, these need to be functional not only at the local level, but also and especially at the overall level (that is, aimed at obtaining the best possible results for the index). Furthermore, in order to reduce scepticism toward the index produced, it is recommended that ample documentation be provided, giving a detailed account of all the choices made during each phase. The entire procedure must be consistent and clear for any potential index users.

In summary, the recommendations provided by the OECD manual prescribe that the first phase should provide a clear understanding and definition of the multidimensional phenomenon to be measured; a specification of any dimensions underlying the phenomenon to be empirically investigated; a list of selection criteria for the underlying variables (indicators, by way of example, input, output and process indicators); and a clear and full documentation illustrating in detail the entire set of choices made.

At the end of the data selection phase the following should be available: a control of the quality (reliability and validity) of the available indicators; a discussion on the strengths and weaknesses of each selected indicator; a table containing the basic information on each indicator (source, type – hard, soft, or input, output, process – and availability in time and in space – that is, among the various countries considered in the study).

The phase involving the imputation of missing data is intended to produce a data matrix without missing values.

The statistical-methodological literature makes reference to various techniques, among which the following implicit models can be mentioned: hot deck imputation, which is based on the replacement of the missing value with the value of the case which is most similar to that showing the missing value; and cold deck imputation, replacement of missing values with values provided by other sources. Whatever the technique selected for the imputation of missing values, it will be useful to calculate a measure of the reliability of each single imputed value so as to evaluate the impact of the substitution of missing values on the final index. The presence of any outliers in the data matrix will also need to be verified, and their reliability determined. Finally, the imputation procedures adopted and the related results must be documented and explained.

In the fourth, multivariate analysis phase, the structure of the linkages between the selected indicators is analysed. The aim is to identify the structure underlying the data and how this develops both among the different variables and among the various countries under analysis.

Several techniques can be used for this: principal component analysis (pca), factorial analysis, cluster analysis, multidimensional scaling and so on. Each technique offers a number of very interesting possibilities for the analysis.

In the fifth phase, the appropriate normalization procedures are selected by taking account of both the theoretical framework and the nature of the available variables. The purpose of normalization is to make the values measured on different scales comparable. Several techniques can be used for this: ranking, standardization, Min-Max, distance to a reference value, categorical scales, indicators above or below the mean, cyclical indicators, balance of opinions, percentage of annual differences over consecutive years. Each technique has its advantages and drawbacks. The technique selected and the results obtained must be illustrated in detail.

In the sixth phase, the appropriate variable weighting and aggregation procedures are selected on the basis of the theory of reference. Several techniques can be used for this, obviously producing different results. Consequently, the possibility of using alternative techniques must be evaluated. Furthermore, during the weighting of each single variable, account must be taken of any correlations existing between them. In that case, the weights must be selected in such a way as to mitigate the high correlations between two or more variables. Finally, ample documentation must be provided on the executed weighting and aggregation procedures.

In the seventh phase, the robustness of the index produced must be assessed. To this end, an uncertainty and sensitivity analysis must be conducted, which enables the user to identify the sources of uncertainty and instability affecting the index and producing different results in it. The analysis must assess the following: what effects are produced by the inclusion or exclusion of an indicator in the construction of the index; an estimate of the errors present in the data based on the information available on variance estimation; the effects produced by the various techniques for imputing missing values; the effects produced by the various data normalization techniques; and the effects produced by the various weighting and aggregation techniques. All of the aforementioned phases and their respective results must be documented.

In the eighth phase, we need to return to the input data. The index must be broken down into its individual components, each of which must then be analysed in terms of their correlation and, if necessary, causality. Each country's performance must be plotted on each single indicator, and the indicators showing the greatest impact on index variability must be identified.

In the ninth phase, the correlations between the index and other measurements connected with the phenomenon under examination are analysed, taking account of the results of the sensitivity analysis. Following these analyses, an analytical interpretation of the results produced by the index is developed. As always, ample documentation must be provided on the analyses conducted in this phase.

The tenth and last phase is dedicated to the presentation of the index results, which must be addressed to the user. The most effective instruments in graphic and tabular format must then be selected in order to permit an immediate and effective communication of the results.

A.2 BACKGROUND TO THE CREATION OF A SINGLE INDEX OF DIGITAL DEVELOPMENT

A digital development index construction proposal is illustrated in the following pages. The index has been named EDDI (European Digital Development Index). The main objectives of EDDI are to track progress in the development of ICT in EU countries, and to monitor digital progress. The overall process of constructing the index was undertaken following the guidelines recommended by the OECD (2008).

The index has taken into account the 27 EU Member States. For a diachronic assessment of the development of EDDI, the historical series from 2004 to 2009 has been taken into account.

It is necessary to define the main objectives and purposes of EDDI, in other words, what exactly should be measured. This is critical as it determines the broader framework of the index, the main indicators to be included, and the methodology used to construct it.

EDDI should measure:

- The development of ICT in EU countries (that is, track ICT progress over time);
- The level of advancement of ICT in all EU countries;
- The differences among EU countries with different levels of ICT development;
- *The development potential* of ICT, or the extent to which countries can make use of ICT to enhance growth and development, based on available capabilities and skills.

The multidimensional nature of the digital development concept has been reduced to three dimensions and to twelve subdimensions.

From 2004 to 2009, the three main dimensions for each year are the following: (1) Infrastructure; (2) Usage; (3) Impact. Each dimension has been broken down into a given number of subdimensions.

Three subdimensions of Internet Infrastructure have been identified, namely: (1.1) Network; (1.2) Affordability, (1.3) Availability and Quality.

The Network subdimension consists of three indicators: (1) broadband penetration rate; (2) international Internet bandwidth per inhabitant (bit/s); (3) secure Internet servers (per 1 million people). All indicators are available from 2004 to 2009 with the exception of the second one, which is available from 2004 to 2007. The data related to 2008 and 2009 have been assessed starting from the average annual growth rate data of 2007 for each country calculated in the period 2004–07.

The Affordability subdimension is represented by a single indicator (information and communication technology expenditure per capita in US$) available from 2004 to 2007. The data related to 2008 and 2009 have been assessed starting from the average annual growth rate data for 2007 for each country calculated in the period 2004–07.

Finally, four indicators were selected to represent the Availability and Quality subdimension: (1) Internet subscribers (total fixed broadband) per 100 inhabitants (from 2004 to 2009); (2) Internet subscribers (total fixed) per 100 inhabitants (from 2004 to 2009); (3) level of Internet access of households (per cent) (from 2004 to 2009); (4) percentage of households using a broadband connection (from 2004 to 2009). The index of the sub-dimension consists of four indicators from 2004 to 2009.

The Internet Usage dimension has three subdimensions: (2.1) Autonomy; (2.2) Intensity; (2.3) Skills.

The Autonomy subdimension is represented by only one indicator (per-centage of individuals who accessed the Internet at home in the last three months). This indicator is available for the entire period considered.

The Intensity subdimension is represented by only one indicator (per-centage of individuals who accessed the Internet, on average, every day or almost every day in the last three months). This indicator is available for the entire period considered.

The Skills subdimension is subdivided into three indicators: (1) percent-age of individuals who have copied or moved a file or folder (data avail-able from 2004 to 2009); (2) percentage of individuals who have used basic arithmetic formulae (data available from 2004 to 2009); (3) percentage of individuals who have connected and installed new devices (data available from 2006 to 2009).

The index of the subdimension consists of two indicators from 2004 to 2005 and three indicators from 2006 to 2009.

The Internet Impact dimension has six subdimensions: (3.1) Educational area, label Education; (3.2) Employment and labour area, label Labour; (3.3) Health and wellness area, label Health; (3.4) Government interac-tion, label Government; (3.5) Economic area (e-commerce, e-banking), label Economy; (3.6) Cultural, communicative and recreational area, label Culture.

The Education subdimension is represented by four indicators: (1) percentage of individuals who used the Internet, in the last three months, for formalized educational activities (school, university) (from 2004 to 2006); (2) percentage of individuals who used the Internet, in the last three months, for other educational courses related specifically to employment opportunity (from 2004 to 2006); (3) percentage of individuals who used the Internet, in the last 3 months, for other educational courses related specifically to employment opportunity (from 2004 to 2006); (4) percentage of individuals who used the Internet, in the last three months, for training and education (from 2007 to 2009). From 2004 to 2006 the subdimension consists of three indicators; from 2007 to 2009 the dimension consists of one indicator.

The Labour subdimension consists of three indicators (the years for which data for each indicator are available are indicated in brackets): (1) percentage of persons employed using computers connected to the Internet in their normal routine at least once a week (from 2004 to 2009); (2) percentage of individuals who used the Internet to look for a job or send a job application (from 2004 to 2009); (3) percentage of persons employed working part of their time away from enterprise premises and accessing the enterprise's IT system from there (from 2004 to 2006). The sub-index of this subdimension for 2004, 2005 and 2006 consisted of three indicators; for 2007, 2008 and 2009 it consisted of two.

The Health subdimension consists of only one indicator: percentage of individuals who used the Internet to seek health information on injury, disease or nutrition (from 2004 to 2009).

The Government interaction subdimension consists of only one indicator: (1) Percentage of individuals who used the Internet, in the last three months, for interaction with public authorities (from 2004 to 2009).

The Economy (e-commerce, e-banking) subdimension consists of three indicators: (1) percentage of individuals who used the Internet, in the last three months, for Internet banking (from 2004 to 2009); (2) percentage of individuals who used the Internet, in the last three months, for selling goods and services (for example via auctions) (from 2004 to 2009); (3) percentage of individuals who used the Internet, in the last three months, for using services related to travel and accommodation (from 2004 to 2009). Hence, the index of this subdimension consists of three indicators from 2004 to 2009.

The e-culture, communication and recreation subdimension consists of six indicators: (1) percentage of individuals who used the Internet, in the last three months, for sending/receiving emails (from 2004 to 2009); (2) percentage of individuals who used the Internet, in the last three months, for playing/downloading games and music (from 2004 to 2007); (3) percentage of individuals who used the Internet, in the last three months, for reading/downloading online newspapers/news magazines (from 2004 to 2009); (4) percentage of individuals who used the Internet, in the last three months, for listening to web radios/for watching web television (from 2004 to 2009); (5) percentage of individuals who used the Internet, in the last three months, for downloading software (from 2005 to 2008); (6) percentage of individuals who used the Internet, in the last three months, for other communication uses (chat sites, and so on) (from 2004 to 2009). The subindex of this subdimension for 2004 consists of five indicators; six in 2005, 2006 and 2007; four in 2008; five in 2009.

A.3   SELECTION OF INDICATORS

The analytical framework underlying the construction of EDDI is therefore structured into three components (dimensions of the general concept) and into twelve sub-indexes. Obviously, the sub-indexes, the dimensions and the final index are strongly interdependent. Without Internet infrastructure and access there is no Internet use. Having access to Internet infrastructure is thus always a prerequisite for subsequent use. Internet use indicates the level of absorption of the technologies. During the Internet use stage, countries increase their use in terms of numbers and in terms of level of intensity and sophistication of use (for example, online banking or purchasing). Computer skills are needed to make best use of the Internet. They are critical to the potential impact that ICT can have on development, in particular the achievement of value added from Internet use. If countries are not capable of exploiting the new technologies and realizing their potential benefits, development and progress will be hampered. Internet impact therefore largely depends on the availability of skills and knowledge and the capability to use the Internet efficiently and effectively. Internet capability or skills are therefore an indispensable input measurement required to achieve maximum Internet impact on everyday life.

It should be noted that composite indexes by nature are subject to questioning and have to be interpreted with caution (OECD, 2008). They do serve one important purpose, though: they raise awareness among policy makers of areas that deserve particular attention in future policy decisions. This is also the case for information-society related policies.

As already said, in order to construct the twelve sub-indexes, various indicators were selected to properly represent the different concepts under analysis. Based on the above described framework, the selected indicators should correspond to the following three dimensions of the index (or sub-indexes): (1) Internet infrastructure and access; (2) Internet usage; (3) Internet impact.

For each type of dimension, a list of potential variables (or indicators) was established. Starting from this list of variables and following the analyses subsequently conducted, a final selection is made of the indicators considered most representative of each dimension and subdimension. The final selection of the indicators takes into account the following criteria:

- The availability of the data (and their quality) for a large number of EU countries;
- The results of multivariate analyses carried out. Principal components analysis (pca) is carried out to analyse the underlying nature of the data, to explore whether the different dimensions are statistically well balanced and to reveal how different indicators are associated and change in relation to each other;
- The relevance of a particular indicator for contributing to the main objectives and conceptual framework of the index.

The main objective of running multivariate analysis, such as pca, was to analyse carefully the underlying nature of the data used in the index. The application of the pca makes it possible to estimate the validity of each variable as an indicator of the assumed concept, producing component loadings which can be interpreted as quantitative estimates of the semantic similarity between indicator and concept. It is understood that such estimates must not be assigned an absolute and final value, as they obviously depend on the nature of the basket of variables examined and on the spatial-temporal context to which the matrix data refer. Another objective constituting the practical side of the conceptual development consists in the building of indexes through the calculation of the component scores. By taking account of the variables weight on the principal components, it is possible to calculate the score for each case of the matrix data on the identified component or components. Such scores are calculated in a way that the values are standardized (average equal to zero and standard deviation equal to one) and distributed in an approximately normal manner.

By using the pca, therefore, it is possible to reduce the number of variables and thus attain the maximum sparingness of the index, minimizing the loss of information. The results/outputs derived from pca include three main elements: eigenvalues, the percentage (%) of variance explained in each component, and the component loadings. Eigenvalues represent the relative importance of the components – components with high eigenvalues and which explain the maximum variance are retained.

Here follows an example concerning the construction of the 'Government interaction' (label eGovernment) sub-index of the Impact dimension relative to the 27 EU countries in the years 2004 to 2009. Four indicators were selected to represent this subdimension, all of which originate from the Eurostat database (the respective abbreviations are indicated in parenthesis): (1) percentage of individuals who used the Internet, in the last

Table A.2   *Communalities after the extraction of the first principal*
         component by year

	2004	2005	2006	2007	2008	2009
ngvif	.844	.963	.955	.975	.968	.955
ngvfm	.908	.958	.904	.957	.974	.946
ngvrt	.868	.920	.851	.897	.855	.852
nugov	.930	.979	.955	.979	.969	.967

Note: Extraction method: principal component analysis.

three months, for obtaining information from public authorities websites
(ngvif); (2) percentage of individuals who used the Internet, in the last
three months, for downloading official forms (ngvfm); (3) percentage of
individuals who used the Internet, in the last three months, for sending
filled forms (ngvrt); (4) percentage of individuals who used the Internet,
in the last three months, for interaction with public authorities (nugov).

From 2004 to 2009, all 27 European countries show valid data for all
the four variables taken into consideration. In this instance, therefore,
the problem of imputing the missing values does not arise. The linear correlations among the four pairs of variables are then analysed, to check
whether their structure of mutual associations makes them compatible
with the principal components analysis. All the coefficients calculated for
each pair of variables show values ranging between .76 and .99. Hence, the
conditions for performing a pca are met.

Table A.2 shows the values relative to the communalities of the four
variables subjected to the pca following the extraction of the first principal component. As you can see from the values shown in the table, the
variance percentages reproduced of each variable from the first principal
component range from 84% to 98%.

In the 2004 analysis, the first principal component reproduces 89% of
the overall variance, and it is the only one among all the extractable components showing an eigenvalue greater than one (Kaiser's principal component selection criteria). The first principal component reproduces 95%
of the overall variance in the 2005 analysis; 92% in the 2006 analysis; 95%
in the 2007 analysis; 94% in the 2008 analysis and 93% in the 2009 analysis.
Table A.3 show the pca statistics.

In each year all the variables have a high component saturation capacity, which shows the one-dimensionality existing among them in detecting
the dimension for which they were identified as indicators (see Table A.4).

In consideration of the high redundancy of the four variables, it
was deemed appropriate to represent the eGovernment interaction

Table A.3   Total variance explained for first principal component by year

Year	Eigenvalues first pc	
	Total	% of variance
2004	3.550	88.751
2005	3.820	95.497
2006	3.666	91.642
2007	3.808	95.199
2008	3.767	94.167
2009	3.720	93.002

Note: Extraction method: principal component analysis.

Table A.4   Component loadings matrix by year

	2004 Comp. 1	2005 Comp. 1	2006 Comp. 1	2007 Comp. 1	2008 Comp. 1	2009 Comp. 1
ngvif	.919	.981	.977	.987	.984	.977
ngvfm	.953	.979	.951	.978	.987	.972
ngvrt	.932	.959	.923	.947	.925	.923
nugov	.965	.989	.977	.989	.985	.983

Note: Extraction method: principal component analysis. a 1 components extracted.

subdimension from 2004 to 2009 with only one variable (nugov) that presents the high value of component loadings coefficient. The procedure shown in this example was applied to all twelve subdimensions of the three main dimensions.

A.4   IMPUTATION OF MISSING DATA

Following the selection of the indicators, the dataset has been completed for the years 2004 to 2009, whereby missing values have been estimated. In this respect, it is appropriate to quantify the entity of the missing data in the various matrices constructed from 2004 to 2009. Tables A.5, A.6 and A.7 show in detail, for each indicator, the number of missing data for each year considered.

The situation of missing data is as follows: in 2004, out of 23 indicators selected the complete data were 621 (27*23 = 621); missing data in the 27 European countries amount to 112. The impact of missing data on the

Table A.5   *Number of missing data for the indicators of the three*
                subdimensions of the Infrastructure dimension, by year

Label	Subdimension indicators	Source	04	05	06	07	08	09
	Subdimension: Network							
ni132	Broadband penetration rate (%)	Eurostat	2	2	0	0	0	0
nwpc	International Internet bandwidth per inhabitant (bit/s)	WDI	2	2	3	1	–	–
np6	Secure Internet servers (per 1 million people)	WDI	0	0	0	0	0	0
	Subdimension: Affordability							
npcd	Information and communication technology expenditure per capita (US$)	WDI	6	6	6	6	6*	6*
	Subdimension: Availability and Quality							
ni992	Internet subscribers (total fixed broadband) per 100 inhabitants	ITU	1	0	0	0	0	0
ni993	Internet subscribers (total fixed) per 100 inhabitants	ITU	0	1	3	4	4	0
niacc	Level of Internet access of households (%)	Eurostat	4	3	0	0	3	0
nhbro	Percentage of households using a broadband connection	Eurostat	7	3	1	0	3	0

Note: * = for 2008 and 2009 the values of this indicator have been estimated by taking into account the average variation rate weighted values of 2007 calculated in the period 2004–07.

total data is equal to 18%. In 2005, out of 23 indicators selected the complete data were 621; the missing data were 83, with an impact on the total data equal to 13%. In 2006, out of 24 indicators the complete data were 648; the missing data were 32, with an impact on the total data of 5%.

The situation improved greatly starting from 2007, where out of 21 indicators selected the complete data were 567; the missing data were 16, with an impact on the total data equal to 2.8%. In 2008, out of 20 indicators the complete data were 540; the impact of the 19 missing data on the total data was 3.5%. Finally, in 2009, out of 20 indicators the complete data

*Table A.6   Number of missing data for the indicators of the four
             subdimensions of the Usage dimension by year*

Label	Subdimension indicators	Source	04	05	06	07	08	09
	Subdimension: Autonomy							
nihm	Percentage of individuals who accessed Internet at home in the last 3 months	Eurostat	8	4	0	0	0	0
	Subdimension: Intensity							
niday	Percentage of individuals who accessed Internet, on average, every day or almost every day in the last 3 months	Eurostat	4	3	0	0	0	0
	Subdimension: Skills							
nccpy	Percentage of individuals who have copied or moved a file or folder	Eurostat	6	1	0	0	0	0
ncsum	Percentage of individuals who have used basic arithmetic formulae	Eurostat	5	1	0	0	0	0
ncins	Percentage of individuals who have connected and installed new devices	Eurostat	–	–	0	0	0	0

were 540; the missing data were only 7; the impact of the missing data on the total data was 1%.

The technique selected to calculate the missing data is based on the application of the pca. An analysis was conducted for each year which took into account all the variables showing complete data in all European countries. This analysis produced the first principal component, and the component scores for each of the 27 European countries were saved. These component scores are expressed in the form of standard values of a linear mix of all the variables entered in the analysis, and represent the best possible synthesis of the data. This choice is based on the following methodological considerations:

(a)   the analysis conducted takes into consideration cardinal values only, collected from a limited number of cases (only 27 European countries);

(b)   all the variables taken into consideration show positive correlations, many of which are very close;

*Table A.7   Number of missing data for the indicators of the six
                      subdimensions of the Impact dimension by year*

Label	Subdimension indicators	Source	04	05	06	07	08	09
	Subdimension: Education							
niedu	Percentage of individuals who used Internet, in the last 3 months, for formalized educational activities (school, university)	Eurostat	5	4	1	–	–	–
nduot	Percentage of individuals who used Internet, in the last 3 months, for other educational courses related specifically to employment opportunity	Eurostat	7	4	1	–	–	–
ndupt	Percentage of individuals who used Internet, in the last 3 months, for post educational courses	Eurostat	8	5	1	–	–	–
nedut	Percentage of individuals who used Internet, in the last 3 months, for training and education	Eurostat	–	–	–	0	0	0
	Subdimension: Labour							
npuse	Percentage of persons employed using computers connected to the Internet in their normal routine at least once a week	Eurostat	3	6	5	2	3	1
nujob	Percentage of individuals who used Internet for looking for a job or sending a job application	Eurostat	6	5	1	0	0	0
ntele	Percentage of persons employed working part of their time away from enterprise premises and accessing enterprise's IT system from there	Eurostat	5	7	6	–	–	–
	Subdimension: Health							
nihif	Percentage of individuals who used Internet for seeking health information on injury, disease or nutrition	Eurostat	11	4	0	0	0	0
	Subdimension: Government							
nugov	Percentage of individuals who used Internet, in the last 3 months, for interaction with public authorities	Eurostat	5	6	3	0	0	0

Table A.7 (continued)

Label	Subdimension indicators	Source	04	05	06	07	08	09
	Subdimension: Economy (e-commerce, e-banking)							
niubk	Percentage of individuals who used Internet, in the last 3 months, for Internet banking	Eurostat	5	4	0	0	0	0
nusel	Percentage of individuals who used Internet, in the last 3 months, for selling goods and services (e.g. via auctions)	Eurostat	6	7	1	3	0	0
nhols	Percentage of individuals who used Internet, in the last 3 months, for using services related to travel and accommodation	Eurostat	6	5	0	0	0	0
	Subdimension: Culture, Communication and Recreation							
niuem	Percentage of individuals who used Internet, in the last 3 months, for sending/receiving emails	Eurostat	5	4	0	0	0	0
niugm	Percentage of individuals who used Internet, in the last 3 months, for playing/downloading games and music	Eurostat	5	4	0	0	0	0
niunw	Percentage of individuals who used Internet, in the last 3 months, for reading/downloading online newspapers/news magazines	Eurostat	5	5	1	0	0	0
nuweb	Percentage of individuals who used Internet, in the last 3 months, for listening to web radios/for watching web television	Eurostat	6	5	1	0	0	0
nusof	Percentage of individuals who used Internet, in the last 3 months, for downloading software	Eurostat	–	6	1	0	0	0
nuoth	Percentage of individuals who used Internet, in the last 3 months, for other communication uses (chat sites, etc.)	Eurostat	6	5	0	0	0	–

(c)   in order to reduce any distorting effects, which are inevitable in any substitution technique, it was deemed appropriate to substitute the missing values strictly when the latter did not constitute the absolute majority of data of the variable (in the case at issue, they could amount to a maximum of 11 missing values out of 27 data);

(d)   the technique used for calculating the missing data must not, where possible, constrict the variance of the variables affected by missing data;

(e)   prior to actually substituting the missing data, the robustness of the technique adopted was verified (see below).

After conducting a pca for each year considered, we obtained a set of component scores which reflect the situation of any given country with respect to the other 26. This new variable was defined as 'Country score on missing scale index'. If a country is highly advanced in the digital development process, it will show a positive component score, which is expressed in units of standard deviation from the mean equal to zero. A country which shows a backward situation with respect to digital develpoment will have a low score in terms of units of standard deviation below average.

The variables used in the principal component analysis for each year considered are the following: ten in 2004; eight in 2005 and 2006; 46 in 2007; 67 in 2008; and 32 in 2008 and 2009.

The first principal components taken from the analysis of each year generated the following total variance values: 56.51% in 2004; 64.59% in 2005; 62.02% in 2006; 56% in 2007; 61.41% in 2008; and 61.73% in 2009. It is interesting to note that, in the years which show the greatest number of variables (2007, 2008 and 2009), the percentages of variance generated by the first components are very high. This confirms what has been asserted above concerning the presence of close positive correlations between all variables in each data matrix.

At this stage, we have a set of scalar values for each country and for each year (see Table A.8). In order to substitute the missing data of a given country in a given year over a variable date, the following formula was applied:

$$Xmcy = \bar{x} + \sigma x * mcy$$

where:
$Xmcy$ = missing data on variable X of country c in the year y;
$\bar{X}$ = average of variable X calculated on valid data;
σx = standard deviation of X calculated on valid data;
mcy = component score on the missing scale of country c in the year y.

Table A.8 Value on missing scale index for countries and by year

Country	2004	2005	2006	2007	2008	2009
Austria	0.56	0.56	0.47	0.41	0.28	0.60
Belgium	0.50	0.32	0.26	0.29	0.15	0.21
Bulgaria	−1.23	−1.34	−1.22	−1.50	−1.51	−1.55
Cyprus	−0.45	−0.45	−0.48	−0.85	−0.88	−0.99
Czech Republic	−0.47	−0.45	−0.52	−0.56	−0.68	−0.69
Denmark	2.04	1.66	1.59	1.90	1.75	1.72
Estonia	−0.11	−0.03	−0.03	0.43	0.35	0.45
Finland	0.93	0.95	0.67	1.62	1.42	1.24
France	0.28	0.37	0.45	−0.18	0.42	0.57
Germany	0.89	0.99	1.14	1.00	0.88	0.84
Greece	−0.84	−0.91	−1.00	−1.21	−1.34	−1.25
Hungary	−0.89	−0.91	−0.94	−0.35	−0.26	−0.22
Ireland	0.42	0.27	0.24	−0.22	−0.33	−0.40
Italy	0.20	0.41	0.36	−0.74	−0.77	−0.66
Latvia	−1.19	−1.18	−1.11	−0.53	−0.54	−0.54
Lithuania	−1.19	−1.08	−0.93	−0.65	−0.55	−0.57
Luxembourg	1.04	1.11	1.07	1.27	1.69	1.75
Malta	0.06	0.17	0.14	−0.40	−0.38	−0.45
Netherlands	1.15	1.41	1.53	1.64	1.74	1.62
Poland	−1.19	−1.24	−1.24	−0.71	−0.78	−0.88
Portugal	−0.52	−0.49	−0.59	−0.78	−0.68	−0.74
Romania	−1.67	−1.79	−1.75	−1.77	−1.76	−1.88
Slovakia	−0.91	−0.97	−1.00	−0.42	−0.46	−0.35
Slovenia	−0.32	−0.22	−0.22	0.03	0.05	0.06
Spain	−0.20	−0.23	−0.20	−0.11	−0.02	0.03
Sweden	1.98	1.76	1.83	1.60	1.42	1.31
United Kingdom	1.13	1.31	1.49	0.79	0.80	0.78

For example, assume that we need to estimate the data for Bulgaria on the variable ni132 (broadband penetration rate %) in the year 2008. The average of variable ni132 is equal to 21%, and the standard deviation is 8. The value of Bulgaria on the missing scale index of 2008 is equal to −1.55. Hence, the value of the missing data for Bulgaria can be estimated in the following manner:

$$21 + (8* − 1.55) = 21 − 12 = 9$$

The estimated value is very close to the actual value, which is equal to 10.

Table A.9   Correlations between real data and replaced data by 18 variables

Real data	Replaced data	r	Real data	Replaced data	r
	2004			2007	
ni99	m99	.917	ni99	m99	.975
ni992	m992	.818	ni992	m992	.896
ni993	m993	.909	nhdsl	Mhdsl	.855
	2005			2008	
ni99	m99	.919	ni99	m99	.950
ni992	m992	.857	ni992	m992	.912
ni993	m993	.943	niacc	Miacc	.946
	2006			2009	
ni99	m99	.884	ni99	m99	.952
ni992	m992	.904	ni992	m992	.899
ni993	m993	.934	niacc	miacc	.961

In order to verify the robustness and reliability of the technique used for substituting the missing data, it is possible to generalize this first example. This consists in taking the complete part of the dataset, eliminating some of the data (for the same countries and in the same proportion of the complete dataset in each year from 2004 to 2009), using our imputation methods and evaluating performance. The goodness of imputation can be checked using the correlation coefficient (r).

From each matrix available, three variables were selected which did not show any missing data and, for all countries, the values were estimated using our missing data substitution technique. By comparing real values with estimated values, it is possible to evaluate the effectiveness of the technique adopted. The three variables selected for examining the missing data substitution technique are the following: ni99 (Internet users per 100 inhabitants), ni992 (Internet subscribers total fixed broadband per 100 inhabitants), ni993 (Internet subscribers total fixed per 100 inhabitants) from 2004 to 2006; ni99 (Internet users per 100 inhabitants), ni992 (Internet subscribers total fixed broadband per 100 inhabitants), nhdsl (percentage of households using a DSL connection) for 2007; ni99 (Internet users per 100 inhabitants), ni992 (Internet subscribers total fixed broadband per 100 inhabitants), niacc (level of Internet access of households %) for 2008 and 2009. Table A.9 shows the coefficients of linear correlation between the actual data of the eighteen variables and the data estimated using our missing data calculation technique.

The average correlation is equal to .913. The maximum value of r is .975 (ni99 2007); 4 values of r are equal to or greater than .95 (ni99 2007, niacc 2009, ni99 2009, ni99 2008); 8 values are included between .90 and .946 (niacc 2008, ni993 2005, ni993 2006, ni99 2005, ni99 2004, ni992 2008, ni993 2004, ni992 2006); 6 values are included between .899 and .818 (ni992 2009, ni992 2007, ni99 2006, ni992 2005, nhdsl 2007, ni992 2004). These results positively validate our procedure for substituting missing data.

A.5 NORMALIZATION OF DATA

The data are normalized using different techniques. An important criterion for the selection of the normalization method is to choose one that could be replicated by countries. There has been strong interest among some countries in applying the index methodology at the national or regional level.

Normalization of the data is necessary before any aggregation can be made to ensure that the dataset uses the same unit of measurement. For the indicators selected for the construction of the index, it is important to transform the values to the same unit of measurement since some of them were expressed as a percentage (of the population or households where maximum value is 100), while other indicators (although expressed as a percentage) can have values exceeding 100, such as mobile cellular subscriptions or international Internet bandwidth.

There are certain particularities that need to be taken into consideration when selecting the normalization method for the index. For example, it is important to measure the relative performance of countries. Second, the normalization procedure should produce index results that allow countries to track the progress of their evolution towards an information society over time. As stated, a further important criterion for the selection of the normalization method was to choose one that can be replicated by countries.

The appropriate data normalization technique of both the theoretical framework and the nature of the available variables is that called distance to a reference value. The reference measure is the ideal value that could be reached for each variable (similar to a goalpost). In all of the indicators chosen, this will be 100, except for three indicators which are not expressed as percentages: (1) nwpc (international Internet bandwidth per inhabitant bit/s); (2) np6 (secure Internet servers per 1 million people); (3) npcd (information and communication technology expenditure per capita US$).

To diminish the effect of the large number of outliers at the high end of the value scale, the data were first transformed to a logarithmic scale on base ten. The ideal value was then computed by adding two standard deviations to the mean of the rescaled values. After the data had been normalized, the minimum of the respective distributions was subtracted and divided by the mean plus two standard deviations.

This technique has three advantages, namely: (1) it simplifies the diachronic comparison of data, given that the results of each country on the indexes calculated over the years are comparable and, hence, show the evolution over time of the digital development situation; (2) it allows for an immediate reading of the data which are expressed in an interval varying from zero to one; this proportion can be easily transformed, by multiplying by 100, into percentage points; (3) unlike other normalization techniques, such as the Min-Max transformation, which makes all normalized variables homogeneous with respect to their contribution to the final index, the technique based on the distance to a reference value does not in any way affect the contribution given by each variable to the final index. In other words, it is possible to define the normalization technique adopted as capable of self-weighting the weight of each variable on the final index.

A.6   STATISTICAL PROCESS FOR CONSTRUCTING EDDI

Once the data has been normalized, it is possible to construct EDDI and the related sub-indexes. The methodology described below has been used both for whole population and for disadvantaged groups for each country. We take as an example of calculation Sweden in 2009. Tables A.10, A.11 and A.12 show all the steps required to calculate the final index and the sub-indexes of the three principal dimensions and twelve subdimensions.

The index of each subdimension is calculated as the arithmetic mean of the number of indicators included in it. For example, the Network subdimension of the infrastructure dimension consists of three indicators; the calculation of the related index consists in adding the normalized values of the three indicators and dividing the result by the number of indicators used (in this case three).

The calculation of indexes using the arithmetic mean is made necessary for the purpose of normalizing the various indexes and sub-indexes with respect to the different number of indicators used each time.

Once all the indexes of a given subdimension have been calculated, the index of the dimension may be calculated. The procedure consists in

Table A.10 Example of how to calculate the sub-index of the Infrastructure dimension: Sweden 2009

Label	Subdimensions indicators	Ideal value	Value 2009	Normalization (value 2009/ ideal value)
Subdimension: Network (ni132 + nwpc + np6)/3 = (.33 + .30 + .58)/3 = .40				
ni132	Broadband penetration rate (%)	100	33	.33
nwpc	International Internet bandwidth per inhabitant (bit/s)*	5	1.5	.30
np6	Secure Internet servers (per 1 million people)*	3	1.7	.58
Subdimension: Affordability (npcd) = .21				
npcd	Information and communication technology expenditure per capita (US$)*	4	0.8	.21
Subdimension: Availability (ni992 + ni993 + niacc + nhbro)/4 = (.45 + .46 + .86 + .80)/4 = .64				
ni992	Internet subscribers (Total fixed broadband) per 100 inhabitants	100	45	.45
ni993	Internet subscribers (Total fixed) per 100 inhabitants	100	46	.46
niacc	Level of Internet infrastructure of households (%)	100	86	.86
nhbro	Percentage of households using a broadband connection	100	80	.80
Sub-index of the Infrastructure dimension = (network+affordability+availability)/3 = (.40+.21+.64)/3 = .42				

Note: * = normalization was performed for these variables by subtracting the minimum distribution and dividing by the mean plus two standard deviations.

calculating the arithmetic mean by adding the values of the indexes of the subdimensions and dividing by their number. For example, the formula for the index of the infrastructure dimension is as follows = (network + affordability + availability)/3.

In this case too, the calculation of the arithmetic mean makes the varying number of subdimensions of each of the three indexes of the infrastructure, usage and impact dimensions irrelevant. Finally, the calculation

Table A.11   Example of how to calculate the sub-index of the Usage dimension: Sweden 2009

Label	Subdimensions indicators	Ideal value	Value 2009	Normalization (value 2009/ ideal value)
	Subdimension: Autonomy = nihm = .85			
nihm	Percentage of individuals who accessed Internet at home in the last 3 months	100	85	.85
	Subdimension: Intensity = niday = .73			
niday	Percentage of individuals who accessed Internet, on average, every day or almost every day in the last 3 months	100	73	.73
	Subdimension: Skills = (nccpy + ncsum + ncins)/3 = (.63 + .43 + .44)/3 = .50			
nccpy	Percentage of individuals who have copied or moved a file or folder	100	63	.63
ncsum	Percentage of individuals who have used basic arithmetic formulae	100	43	.43
ncins	Percentage of individuals who have connected and installed new devices	100	44	.44
	Sub-index of the Usage dimension = (autonomy + intensity + skills)/3 = (.85 + .73 + .50)/3 = .69			

of EDDI consists in the arithmetic mean between the indexes of the three dimensions: (infrastructure + usage + impact)/3. Figure A.1 shows the values of EDDI for Sweden in 2009, the indexes of the three dimensions and those of the twelve subdimensions.

As already said, the normalization technique selected makes it easier to read the results obtained from the various indexes. For example, the value of .52 obtained from Sweden in 2009 represents an estimate of the population of that country which is included in the ITC society (obviously in accordance with the way we defined this concept in our study). By multiplying that value by 100 we can say that 52% of Sweden's population in 2009 is included. If a country registered the maximum value, that is 1, for all the indicators, then the final result of EDDI would also be equal to

Table A.12 Example of how to calculate the sub-index of the Impact
dimension: Sweden 2009

Label	Subdimensions indicators	Ideal value	Value 2009	Normalization (value 2009/ ideal value)
	Subdimension: Educational area = nedut = .45			
nedut	Percentage of individuals who used Internet, in the last 3 months, for training and education	100	45	.45
	Subdimension: Employment and labour area = (npuse + nujob)/2 = (.62 + .22)/2 = .42			
npuse	Percentage of persons employed using computers connected to the Internet in their normal routine at least once a week	100	62	.62
nujob	Percentage of individuals who used Internet for looking for a job or sending a job application	100	22	.22
	Subdimension: Health and wellness area = nihif = .36			
nihif	Percentage of individuals who used Internet for seeking health information on injury, disease or nutrition	100	36	.36
	Subdimension: Government interaction = nugov = .57			
nugov	Percentage of individuals who used Internet, in the last 3 months, for interaction with public authorities	100	57	.57
	Subdimension: Economic area = (niubk + nusel + nhols)/3 = (.71 + .48 + .31)/3 = .50			
niubk	Percentage of individuals who used Internet, in the last 3 months, for Internet banking	100	71	.71
nusel	Percentage of individuals who used Internet, in the last 3 months, for selling goods and services (e.g. via auctions)	100	48	.48
nhols	Percentage of individuals who used Internet, in the last 3 months, for using services related to travel and accommodation	100	31	.31

Table A.12   (continued)

Label	Subdimensions indicators	Ideal value	Value 2009	Normali-zation (value 2009/ ideal value)
	Subdimension: Cultural = (niuem + niunw + nuweb + nusof + nuoth)/5 = (.83 + .50 + .50 + .30 + .07)/5 = .44			
niuem	Percentage of individuals who used Internet, in the last 3 months, for sending/ receiving emails	100	83	.83
niunw	Percentage of individuals who used Internet, in the last 3 months, for reading/downloading online newspapers/ news magazines	100	50	.50
nuweb	Percentage of individuals who used Internet, in the last 3 months, for listening to web radios/for watching web television	100	50	.50
nusof	Percentage of individuals who used Internet, in the last 3 months, for downloading software	100	30	.30
nuoth	Percentage of individuals who used Internet, in the last 3 months, for other communication uses (chat sites, etc.)	100	7	.07
	Sub-index of the Impact dimension = (edu + lab + healt + gov + econ + cult)/6 = (.45 + .42 + .36 + .57 + .50 + .44)/6 = .46			

one. This would represent the maximum level of inclusion possible, equal to 100% of the population. According to the above, the various values of each single country on EDDI considered over the years may also determine the adjustment path towards maximum inclusion at diachronic level.

A.7   SENSITIVITY ANALYSIS AND RETURN TO THE INPUT DATA

A sensitivity analysis follows to assess the robustness of the index produced. The analysis assesses the following: what effects are produced

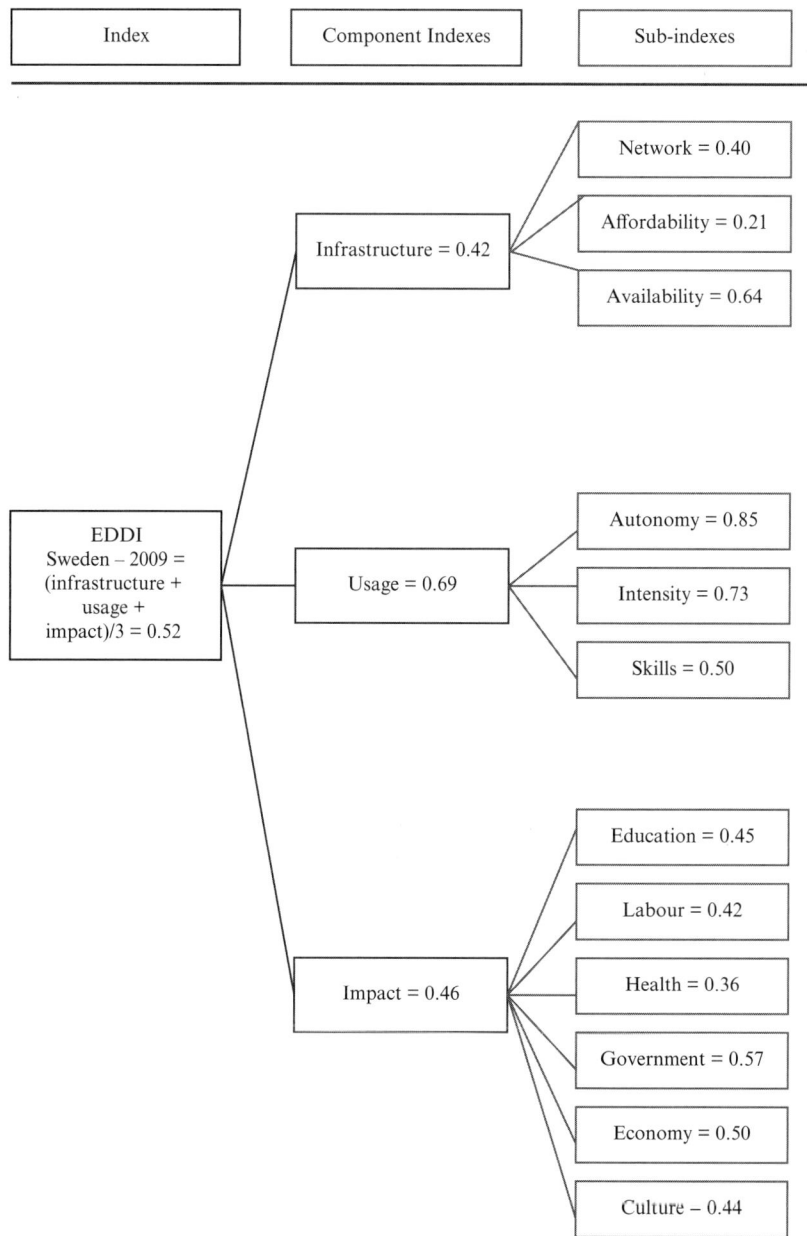

Figure A.1   Example of how to calculate EDDI: Sweden 2009

by the inclusion or the exclusion of an indicator in the construction of the index; an estimate of the errors contained in the data on the basis of the available information on data estimation; the effects produced by the different missing value imputation techniques; the effects produced by different data normalization techniques; the effects produced by different weighting and aggregation techniques. The index is then broken down into its single components and these are analysed in terms of their correlation and, if necessary, regression. The indicators with the greatest impact on index variability must be identified. After these analyses, an analytical interpretation of the results produced by the index is developed.

The first attempt to verify the robustness of the index produced was made using different combinations of methods and techniques to compute the index. More specifically, three indexes were constructed: the first through the principal component analysis (abbrev. pca_EDDI), the second using the arithmetic mean by weighting the three dimensions with alternative weights compared to those used in the principal component analysis (in particular, by assigning the weight of .3 to the Infrastructure dimension; .3 to the Usage dimension and .4 to the Impact dimension; abbrev. EDDI_p), and the third using the arithmetic mean without weighting the three dimensions (abbrev. EDDI). When possible, this verification was also carried out for the indexes of the dimensions and subdimensions with the same results as those obtained for the global index. For this additional verification, the indexes produced by the pca were compared with those produced using the arithmetic mean.

For all the years considered, the coefficients of linear correlation calculated between the three versions of EDDI indexes are systematically equal to the maximum value of one. Hence, the three versions of the index are perfectly superposable. Having acknowledged that, preference was given to the simplest index, that is, that constructed through the use of the arithmetic mean of the dimensions and subdimensions.

Proceeding with the verification of robustness, we now consider the linear correlations between the indexes of the subdimensions and the similar indexes constructed using the pca.

It is important to specify that these comparisons can be made only in the case that the variables available in a given subdimension are at least three, otherwise it would be impossible to perform a pca. The correlation coefficients are calculated between the indexes of the subdimensions constructed by calculating the arithmetic mean and through the principal component analysis. None of the correlation coefficients is less than .93. Many coefficients are near the maximum value. This verification also confirms that the results of the indexes constructed using the two techniques are absolutely superposable.

Tables A.13, A.14 and A.15 show the correlation matrices between the subdimensions of each dimension for every year considered. These tables make it possible to verify the internal consistency of each dimension.

For the Infrastructure dimension, the three subdimensions of network, affordability and availability show, throughout the years considered, correlations between .79 and .95. The only exception concerns the year 2008, in which case, due to the lack of the variable nwpc in the network subdimension and of the presence of estimating values in the variable npcd, two low values were registered in the correlations between network and affordability (.34) and in those between affordability and availability (.19). Even the three subdimensions of the Usage dimension are closely correlated. All the coefficients included in Table A.14 are between .84 and .97.

On average, the six subdimensions of the Impact dimension registered lower correlation values than those of the other two dimensions. By reading the values of correlation coefficients year by year, we see that these gradually grow over time. This confirms our expectations, given that the activities connected to this dimension are the result of the development of conditions which are determined by Internet access and usage. Furthermore, the recent diffusion of broadband must be taken into account, as it is a precondition for being able to access the vast majority of the services included in this dimension.

Table A.16 show the matrices of correlation between the three dimensions of EDDI from 2004 to 2009. In all the years considered, the two most closely correlated dimensions are those of Usage and Impact, with values starting from .94 in 2004 and reaching up to .97 in 2009. In general, all the correlations between the three dimensions are close, which confirms what has been asserted above concerning the high interdependence between the components of EDDI.

We now verify the relationship between EDDI and the indicators, the twelve subdimensions and the three dimensions. In order to verify this, we use the multiple regression technique, defining as dependent variable EDDI and, as independent variables, first all the indicators available, then the twelve indexes of the subdimensions and, finally, the three indexes of the dimensions.

The stepwise multiple regression technique was used for the first two types of verification, given that, especially in the case of the indicators, the number of independent variables is greater than the number of available cases (27). Hence, the procedure must be followed step by step. In the first stage, the independent variable showing the closest correlation with the dependent variable enters the model. In the second stage, the independent variable which passes the entry test enters. Each time a new independent variable enters the model, all the other variables are tested so as to be

Table A.13   Correlations matrix between the three subdimension indexes of the Infrastructure dimension by year

2004	Network	Affordability	Availability
Network	1		
Affordability	.926	1	
Availability	.910	.831	1

2005	Network	Affordability	Availability
Network	1		
Affordability	.918	1	
Availability	.928	.814	1

2006	Network	Affordability	Availability
Network	1		
Affordability	.850	1	
Availability	.952	.796	1

2007	Network	Affordability	Availability
Network	1		
Affordability	.904	1	
Availability	.955	.819	1

2008	Network	Affordability	Availability
Network	1		
Affordability	.336	1	
Availability	.924	.189	1

2009	Network	Affordability	Availability
Network	1		
Affordability	.890	1	
Availability	.950	.826	1

Table A.14   Correlations matrix between the three subdimension indexes of the Usage dimension by year

	2004		
	Autonomy	Intensity	Skills
Autonomy	1		
Intensity	.939	1	
Skills	.939	.936	1

	2005		
	Autonomy	Intensity	Skills
Autonomy	1		
Intensity	.952	1	
Skills	.912	.897	1

	2006		
	Autonomy	Intensity	Skills
Autonomy	1		
Intensity	.965	1	
Skills	.913	.893	1

	2007		
	Autonomy	Intensity	Skills
Autonomy	1		
Intensity	.974	1	
Skills	.892	.898	1

	2008		
	Autonomy	Intensity	Skills
Autonomy	1		
Intensity	.971	1	
Skills	.880	.894	1

	2009		
	Autonomy	Intensity	Skills
Autonomy	1		
Intensity	.969	1	
Skills	.841	.851	1

Table A.15   *Correlations matrix between the six subdimension indexes of the Impact dimension by year*

				2004		
	Education	Labour	Health	Government	Economy	Culture
Education	1					
Labour	.385	1				
Health	.786	.708	1			
Government	.623	.889	.899	1		
Economy	.701	.830	.914	.945	1	
Culture	.656	.835	.867	.935	.910	1

				2005		
	Education	Labour	Health	Government	Economy	Culture
Education	1					
Labour	.480	1				
Health	.674	.813	1			
Government	.480	.893	.888	1		
Economy	.564	.916	.908	.929	1	
Culture	.604	.863	.894	.931	.888	1

				2006		
	Education	Labour	Health	Government	Economy	Culture
Education	1					
Labour	.377	1				
Health	.466	.849	1			
Government	.362	.846	.854	1		
Economy	.450	.930	.847	.914	1	
Culture	.346	.841	.866	.884	.881	1

				2007		
	Education	Labour	Health	Government	Economy	Culture
Education	1					
Labour	.746	1				
Health	.763	.822	1			
Government	.846	.921	.875	1		
Economy	.785	.940	.858	.963	1	
Culture	.703	.833	.862	.894	.869	1

Table A.15 (continued)

	2008					
	Education	Labour	Health	Government	Economy	Culture
Education	1					
Labour	.711	1				
Health	.757	.848	1			
Government	.744	.897	.905	1		
Economy	.744	.939	.868	.904	1	
Culture	.732	.887	.848	.893	.914	1

	2009					
	Education	Labour	Health	Government	Economy	Culture
Education	1					
Labour	.759	1				
Health	.779	.835	1			
Government	.726	.943	.854	1		
Economy	.728	.945	.853	.933	1	
Culture	.617	.881	.846	.900	.888	1

removed from the model. This procedure is repeated until no other variable enters the model and no other is removed.

As in all the other cases, the analyses have been conducted for all the years considered. We begin by evaluating which are the first variables that, year by year, enter the model, considering first the single indicators, then the indexes of the twelve subdimensions and, finally, the three dimensions.

In the analyses of 2004, the first variable to enter the model is the percentage of individuals who used the Internet, in the last three months, for sending/receiving emails (niuem). This variable is the best predictor of EDDI as it explains 95% of the variance of the index. In the three subsequent years, from 2005 to 2007, the best predictor is the percentage of individuals who accessed the Internet at home in the last three months (nihm). The values of explained variance of the dependent variable were 98% in 2005 and in 2006; 96% in 2007, respectively. The best predictor for 2008 is level of Internet access of households (niacc), which explains 94% of the variance of the dependent variable. Finally, the best predictor for 2009 is again the percentage of individuals who accessed the Internet at home in the last three months (nihm), which explains 94% of the variance of the dependent variable.

Table A.16   Correlations matrix between the indexes of the three dimensions of EDDI by year

2004

	Infrastructure	Usage	Impact
Infrastructure	1		
Usage	.918	1	
Impact	.855	.945	1

2005

	Infrastructure	Usage	Impact
Infrastructure	1		
Usage	.918	1	
Impact	.893	.968	1

2006

	Infrastructure	Usage	Impact
Infrastructure	1		
Usage	.941	1	
Impact	.923	.972	1

2007

	Infrastructure	Usage	Impact
Infrastructure	1		
Usage	.943	1	
Impact	.927	.958	1

2008

	Infrastructure	Usage	Impact
Infrastructure	1		
Usage	.882	1	
Impact	.881	.965	1

2009

	Infrastructure	Usage	Impact
Infrastructure	1		
Usage	.915	1	
Impact	.918	.966	1

We now consider the results of the models which consider as independent variables the indexes of the twelve subdimensions. In 2004, the best predictor is the index of the Skills subdimension (95% of variance explained); in the subsequent two years, it is the index of the Autonomy subdimension (98% and 98% of variance explained, respectively); in 2007 and in 2008, the index of the Availability subdimension (96% and 96% of variance explained, respectively), in 2009, the index of the Economy subdimension (95% of variance explained). For the results of the models which consider as independent variables the indexes of the three dimensions, we used the regression 'enter' method, in consideration of the fact that these models contain only three independent variables. In this case, in order to evaluate the impact of the independent variables on the dependent variable, we have taken into consideration the standardized multiple regression coefficient (beta weight), which makes it possible to evaluate the impact of each independent variable on the dependent variable net of the other independent variables. As regards the models related to all years (2004 to 2009), the Usage dimension is that which shows the greatest impact on the EDDI.

In 2006 and 2007, the Infrastructure dimension is the most influential and, in 2008, the Impact dimension. We can explain these results by taking into consideration the advent of broadband as the engine of a different quality of access to the Internet. In fact, with the advent of broadband, which provides a higher speed of data transmission than the previous technologies, it was possible to implement many activities and services which have gradually spread among network users. We can therefore define a development in two phases: from 2004 to 2005, it was the Usage dimension that marked EDDI; in the two subsequent years, it was the dimension of Infrastructure, with the higher speed of broadband connections; and in 2009, and probably in the future, that which will increasingly mark EDDI is the quality of the activities carried out within the network.

The models analysed up to now have made it possible to identify which have been the first variables (whether these be indicators, indexes of subdimensions or of dimensions) for each year to be most closely correlated with the dependent variable (that is, EDDI). As already said above, we have to consider the fact that, in general, all the variables taken into consideration show close positive correlations. A coefficient of correlation takes account strictly of the common variance existing between the two variables used for its computation, and does not take into account all the other variables which are connected to them. It is therefore necessary to replace the bivaried coefficients with multivaried coefficients which express the value of the linkages between two variables without expressing the linkages with the other variables. For this purpose, it is useful to analyse the results of the multiple regression models.

The best multiple regression stepwise models by year using as independent variables all the indicators available for each year are:

- six independent variables entered the 2004 model. The goodness-of-fit statistics of the model are R^2 adjusted = .995; Standard error of the Estimate = .000.
- six independent variables entered the 2005 model. The goodness-of-fit statistics of the model are R^2 adjusted = .976; Standard error of the Estimate = .006.
- seven independent variables entered the 2006 model. The goodness-of-fit statistics of the model are R^2 adjusted = .998; Standard error of the Estimate = .000.
- eight independent variables entered the 2007 model. The goodness-of-fit statistics of the model are R^2 adjusted = .999; Standard error of the Estimate = .000.
- eight independent variables entered the 2008 model. The goodness-of-fit statistics of the model are R^2 adjusted = .998; Standard error of the Estimate = .000.
- eight independent variables entered the 2009 model. The goodness-of-fit statistics of the model are R^2 adjusted = .998; Standard error of the Estimate = .000.

Let us now take a close look at each model. In 2004 the best model shows the following six variables, in order of entry:

1. Percentage of individuals who accessed Internet, on average, every day or almost every day in the last 3 months (niday; beta weight = .420);
2. Information and communication technology expenditure per capita in US$ (npcd; beta weight = .158);
3. Percentage of individuals who used Internet, in the last 3 months, for selling goods and services (nusel; beta weight = .141);
4. Percentage of individuals who used Internet, in the last 3 months, for sending/receiving emails (niuem; beta weights = .133);
5. Secure Internet servers per 1 million people (np6; beta weight = .130);
6. Percentage of individuals who used Internet for seeking health information on injury, disease or nutrition (nihif; beta weight = .097).

As can be verified by reading the beta coefficients, in 2004 the variable which shows the greatest impact on EDDI is percentage of individuals who accessed the Internet, on average, every day or almost every day in the last three months (niday) with a beta value of .420.

We can interpret this value as follows: if, in 2004, in a given European country we register an increase of 1% on this variable, the EDDI index of that country increases by approximately four percentage points, holding constant all the other variables included in the model. Generalizing any standardized multiple regression coefficient indicates the rate of change in the dependent variable with each unitary change in the independent variable net of the other independent variables included in the model.

The best model for 2005 shows the following six variables:

1. Percentage of individuals who accessed Internet at home in the last 3 months (nihm; beta weight = .338);
2. Percentage of individuals who accessed Internet, on average, every day or almost every day in the last 3 months (niday; beta weight = .228);
3. Percentage of individuals who used Internet, in the last 3 months, for sending/receiving emails (niuem; beta weight = .227);
4. Percentage of persons employed using computers connected to the Internet in their normal routine at least once a week (npuse; beta weight = .126);
5. Information and communication technology expenditure per capita in US$ (npcd; beta weight = .109);
6. Percentage of individuals who used Internet, in the last 3 months, for other educational courses related specifically to employment opportunity (nduot; beta weight = .049).

The best model for 2006 includes the following seven variables:

1. Percentage of individuals who accessed Internet at home in the last 3 months (nihm; beta weight = .395);
2. Percentage of individuals who used Internet, in the last 3 months, for interaction with public authorities (nugov; beta weight = .149);
3. Level of Internet access of households (niacc; beta weight = .146);
4. Broadband penetration rate (ni132; beta weight = .122);
5. Percentage of individuals who have used basic arithmetic formulae (ncsum; beta weight = .106);
6. Percentage of individuals who used Internet for looking for a job or sending a job application (nujob; beta weight = .080);
7. Information and communication technology expenditure per capita in US$ (npcd; beta weight = .062).

The best model for 2007 consists of eight variables:

1. Percentage of individuals who accessed Internet at home in the last 3 months (nihm; beta weight = .300);
2. Percentage of individuals who used Internet, in the last 3 months, for interaction with public authorities (nugov; beta weight = .212);
3. Percentage of individuals who accessed Internet, on average, every day or almost every day in the last 3 months (niday; beta weight = .167);
4. Percentage of individuals who have connected and installed new devices (ncins; beta weight = .114);
5. Broadband penetration rate (ni132; beta weight = .081);
6. Secure Internet servers per 1 million people (np6; beta weight = .069);
7. Information and communication technology expenditure per capita in US$ (npcd; beta weight = .064);
8. Percentage of individuals who used Internet for seeking health information on injury, disease or nutrition (nihif; beta weight = .048).

The best model for 2008 consists of the following eight variables:

1. Percentage of individuals who accessed Internet at home in the last 3 months (nihm; beta weight = .220);
2. Percentage of individuals who accessed Internet, on average, every day or almost every day in the last 3 months (niday; beta weight = .181);
3. Percentage of individuals who used Internet for seeking health information on injury, disease or nutrition (nihif; beta weight = .141);
4. Secure Internet servers per 1 million people (np6; beta weight = .122);
5. Percentage of individuals who used Internet, in the last 3 months, for training and education (nedut; beta weight = .109);
6. Level of Internet access of households (niacc; beta weight = .106);
7. Percentage of persons employed using computers connected to the Internet in their normal routine at least once a week (npuse; beta weight = .103);
8. Percentage of households using a broadband connection (nhbro; beta weight = .101).

Finally, the best model for 2009 includes the following eight variables:

1. Percentage of individuals who accessed Internet at home in the last 3 months (nihm; beta weight = .315);

2. Percentage of individuals who accessed Internet, on average, every day or almost every day in the last 3 months (niday; beta weight = .136);
3. Percentage of individuals who have connected and installed new devices (ncins; beta weight = .131);
4. Percentage of individuals who used Internet, in the last 3 months, for interaction with public authorities (nugov; beta weight = .127);
5. Level of Internet access of households (niacc; beta weight = .126);
6. Percentage of individuals who used Internet, in the last 3 months, for training and education (nedut; beta weight = .087);
7. Broadband penetration rate (ni132; beta weight = .086);
8. Information and communication technology expenditure per capita in US$ (npcd; beta weight = .066).

Generally, bearing in mind the fact that the independent variables are not the same for each year considered, we may conclude that the results of these multiple regression models confirm that the three dimensions identified are still important in explaining the general EDDI. They also show how the advent of broadband between 2005 and 2006 is a determining factor in the development of all the activities contemplated in the Impact dimension: Education, Labour, Government, Health, Economy and Culture.

By comparing in each model the most important variables by year we can clearly see how the three dimensions which specify the general EDDI are always present and to a fairly balanced extent.

In the last two years considered, 2008 and 2009, the variable 'Percentage of individuals who accessed Internet at home in the last 3 months' (nihm) assumes a beta weight of .220 and .315 respectively, and the variable 'Percentage of individuals who accessed Internet, on average, every day or almost every day in the last 3 months' (niday) assumes a beta weight of .181 and .136 respectively. This confirms what has been asserted concerning the predominant role that the diffusion of broadband has played.

We now take into consideration the multiple regression stepwise models which adopt as independent variables the indexes of the twelve subdimensions. The best models for each year are:

- eight independent variables entered the model related to 2004. The goodness-of-fit statistics of the model are R^2 adjusted = .999; Standard error of the estimate = .000.
- seven independent variables entered the model related to 2005. The goodness-of-fit statistics of the model are R^2 adjusted = .999; Standard error of the estimate = .000.

- twelve independent variables entered the model related to 2006. The goodness-of-fit statistics of the model are R^2 adjusted = 1; Standard error of the estimate = .0000.
- twelve independent variables entered the model related to 2007. The goodness-of-fit statistics of the model are R^2 adjusted = 1; Standard error of the estimate = .0000.
- seven independent variables entered the model related to 2008. The goodness-of-fit statistics of the model are R^2 adjusted = .999; Standard error of the estimate = .000.
- eleven independent variables entered the model related to 2009. The goodness-of-fit statistics of the model are R^2 adjusted = 1; Standard error of the estimate = .0000.

Note that in all years considered the indexes of all the subdimensions are present.

The best model for 2004 includes eight subdimensions. Given that it is easier to make comparisons for these models, the independent variables are as follows, with beta weights shown in brackets: (1) Intensity (.239); (2) Autonomy (.195); (3) Skills (.173); (4) Network (.141); (5) Affordability (.110); (6) Health (.092); (7) Economy (.068); (8) Government (.045).

The best model for 2005 shows the following seven subdimensions: (1) Autonomy (.294); (2) Intensity (.221); (3) Skills (.150); (4) Network (.133); (5) Health (.114); (6) Affordability (.077); (7) Labour (.068).

Twelve subdimensions entered the best model for the year 2006: (1) Autonomy (.189); (2) Intensity (.147); (3) Skills (.126); (4) Availability (.124); (5) Network (.116); (6) Economy (.078); (7) Affordability (.070); (8) Government (.061); (9) Health (.051); (10) Culture (.042); (11) Labour (.041); (12) Education (.022).

The best model for the year 2007 includes twelve subdimensions: (1) Autonomy (.172); (2) Intensity (.136); (3) Availability (.124); (4) Skills (.118); (5) Network (.102); (6) Economy (.077); (7) Government (.071); (8) Affordability (.064); (9) Health (.058); (10) Education (.056); (11) Culture (.043); (12) Labour (.041).

The best model for 2008 includes seven subdimensions: (1) Economy (.294); (2) Availability (.270); (3) Skills (.196); (4) Intensity (.115); (5) Culture (.109); (6) Affordability (.077); (7) Education (.036).

Finally, the best model for 2009 includes eleven subdimensions: (1) Availability (.188); (2) Intensity (.144); (3) Economy (.120); (4) Skills (.117); (5) Autonomy (.099); (6) Culture (.089); (7) Affordability (.082); (8) Health (.067); (9) Government (.062); (10) Education (.061); (11) Network (.044).

Overall, the results of these multiple regression stepwise models also confirm the trends highlighted in the previous pages and show the

Table A.17   *Beta coefficients of three dimension indexes on the EDDI*
index by year (method enter, dependent variable: EDDI
index; independent variables: indexes of the three dimensions
by year)

	Beta_04	Beta_05	Beta_06	Beta_07	Beta_08	Beta_09
Infra-structure	.301	.290	.412	.280	.265	.268
Usage	.458	.452	.416	.416	.432	.436
Impact	.271	.281	.193	.323	.332	.317

fair balance of the various components constituting our global EDDI index.

At this point, we can examine the last three models of regression 'enter' method which use as independent variables the three indexes of the following dimensions: Infrastructure, Usage and Impact; and EDDI as dependent variable. Obviously, all the models explain for each year 100% of the variance of the dependent variable. What is most important here, however, is the impact that each dimension has year by year on EDDI. Table A.17 show the standardized multiple regression coefficients (beta weights) of the three independent variables for each year. In all years the Usage dimension show the greatest impact with beta weights values of .458 in 2004; .452 in 2005, .416 in 2006 and in 2007, .432 in 2008 and .436 in 2009.

In the years analysed the Usage dimension, even if always at the first place, loses importance.

The Infrastructure dimension follows a similar trend, moving from .301 in 2004 to .268 in 2009. The Impact dimension follows a growing trend: .271 in 2004; .281 in 2005; .193 in 2006; .323 in 2007; .332 in 2008 and .317 in 2009.

References

Agree, P. (1998), 'The Internet and public discourse', in *First Monday*, **3**, available at http://131.193.153.231/www/issues/issue3_3/agre/.

Alden, C. (2003), 'Let them Eat Cyberspace: Africa, the G8 and the digital divide', in *Millennium: Journal of International Studies*, **32** (3), 457–76.

Anderson, B. and K. Tracey (2002), 'The impact (or otherwise) of the Internet on everyday British life', in B. Wellman and C. Haythornthwaite (eds), *The Internet in Everyday Life*, Blackwell Publishing, Malden, MA.

Antonelli, C. (2003), 'The digital divide: understanding the economics of new information and communication technology in the global economy', in *Information Economics and Policy*, **15** (2), 173–99.

Arvanitis, S. (2004), *Information Technology, Workplace Organisation, Human Capital and Firm Productivity: Evidence for the Swiss Economy*, in OECD (2004).

Atkinson, R.D., D.K. Correa and J.A. Hedlund (2008), 'Explaining international broadband leadership', Washington, Information Technology & Innovation Foundation.

Atrostic, B.K. and S. Nguyen (2006), 'How businesses use information technology: insights for measuring technology and productivity', US Bureau of the Census, Center for Economic Studies, CES 06–15, June.

Atrostic, B.K., P. Boegh-Nielsen and S. Nguyen (2004), *IT, Productivity and Growth in Enterprises: New Results from International Micro-data*, in OECD (2004).

Azari, R. and J.B. Pick (2009), 'Understanding global digital inequality: the impact of government, investment in business and technology, and socioeconomic factors on technology utilization', paper presented at the International Conference on System Sciences, Hawaii.

Bakardjieva, M. (2005), *Internet Society. The Internet in Everyday Life*, Sage, London.

Baliamoune-Lutz, M. (2003), 'An analysis of the determinants and effects of ICT diffusion in developing countries', in *Information Technology for Development*, **10** (3), 151–69.

Barney, D. (2004), *The Network Society*, Polity Press, Cambridge.

Barrios, Salvador and Jean-Claude Burgelman (2008), 'Europe needs

CEC (2007a), i2010 – Annual Information Society report 2007', COM (2007) 146 final, available at ec.europa.eu/information_society/. . ./ i2010/. . ./annual_report/2007/i2010_ar_2007_en.pdf.

CEC (2007b), 'European i2010 initiative on e-Inclusion "To be part of the Information society"' Impact Assessment, SEC (2007) 1469, COM (2007) 694 final, SEC (2007) 1470, available at http://ec.europa.eu/ information_society/activities/einclusion/docs/i2010_initiative/comm_ native_com_2007_0694_f_en_acte.pdf.

CEC (2008a), 'Broadband access in the EU: situation at 1 July 2008', COM08-41 Final, http://ec.europa.eu/information_society/policy/ ecomm/.doc/implementation_enforcement/broadband_access/Broadba nd_data_july_08.pdf.

CEC (2008b), Broadband Internet Access Cost (BIAC) Final Report, http://ec.europa.eu/information_society/eeurope/i2010/docs/benchmark ing/broadband_access_costs_1st_half_2008.pdf.

CEC (2009), 'Europe's digital competitiveness report Volume 1, Volume 2: i2010 – Annual Information Society Report 2009. Benchmarking i2010: Trends and main achievements', COM (2009) 390, available at http://ec.europa.eu/information_society/eeurope/i2010/key_documents/ index_en.htm#EDCR.

CEC (2010a), 'Europe 2020. A strategy for smart, sustainable and inclusive growth', COM (2010) 2020, available at http://ec.europa.eu/eu2020/ index_en.htm.

CEC (2010b), A digital agenda for Europe', COM (2010) 245 final/2, available at http://ec.europa.eu/information_society/digital-agenda/ index_en.htm.

Chen, W., J. Boase and B. Wellman (2002), 'The global villagers: comparing internet users and uses around the world', in B. Wellman and C. Haythornthwaite (eds), *The Internet in Everyday Life*, Blackwell Publishing, Malden, MA.

Chen, W. and B. Wellman (2004), 'The global digital divide – within and between countries', in *IT & Society*, **1** (7), 39–45.

Chinn, M.D. and R.W. Fairlie (2004), 'The determinants of the global digital divide. A cross-country analysis of computer and internet penetration', Paper No. 881, Economic Growth Center, Yale University.

Chinn, M.D. and R.W. Fairlie (2007), 'The determinants of the global digital divide: a cross-country analysis of computer and internet penetration', in *Oxford Economic Papers*, **59**, 16–44.

Clayton, T. (2009), 'ICT usage behaviours and productivity of enterprises', paper presented to the Conference 'Bridging micro and macro in ICT: statistics, methodologies, research', IPTS, Seville, February 26–27.

Clayton, T., C. Criscuolo, P. Goodridge and K. Waldron (2004), 'Enterprise e-commerce: measurement and impact', in OECD (2004).

Clement, A. and L. Shade (2000), 'The access rainbow: conceptualising universal access to the information/communication infrastructure', in M. Guerstein (ed.), *Community Informatics*, Iotea Publishing, Hershey, PA, pp. 32–51.

Codagnone, C. (2009), *Vienna Study on Inclusive Innovation for Growth and Cohesion: Modelling and Demonstrating the Impact of eInclusion*, DG Information Society and Media, ICT for Inclusion Unit.

Compaine, B.M. (ed.) (2001), *The Digital Divide: Facing a Crisis or Creating a Myth?*, MIT Press, Cambridge, MA.

Connected Nation (2008), 'The economic impact of stimulating broadband nationally', www.connectednation.org.

Conway, P., Donato de Rosa, Giuseppe Nicoletti and Faye Steiner (2006), 'Regulation, competition and productivity convergence', OECD Economics Department Working Papers 509, OECD Publishing.

Cooper, M. (2000), 'Disconnected, disadvantaged, and disenfranchised: exploration in the digital divide', Consumer Federation of America/ Consumer's Union Report. Retrieved July 16 (http://www.consumer sunion.org/pdf/disconnect.pdf).

Copenhagen Economics (2010), 'The economic impact of a European digital single market', Final Report March, European Policy Centre.

Crandall, R.W. and C.L. Jackson (2001), *The $500 Billion Opportunity: The Potential Economic Benefit of Widespread Diffusion of Broadband Internet Access*, Criterion Economics, Washington DC.

Crandall, R.W., W. Lehr and R. Litan (2007), 'The effects of broadband deployment on output and employment: a cross-sectional analysis of US data', in *Issues in Economic Policy*, The Brookings Institution, 6.

Crenshaw, E.M. and K.K. Robison (2006), 'Globalization and the digital divide: the roles of structural conduciveness and global connection in internet diffusion', in *Social Science Quarterly*, **87** (1).

Crespi, G., C. Criscuolo, J. Haskel and M. Slaughter (2007), 'Productivity growth, knowledge flows and spillovers', CEP Discussion Paper No. 785.

Dasgupta, S., S. Lall and D. Wheeler (2001), 'Policy reform, economic growth, and the digital divide – an econometric analysis', Policy Research Working Paper 2567, The World Bank.

Davison, E. and S.R. Cotton (2003), 'Connection discrepancies: unmasking further layers of the digital divide', in *First Monday*, **8**, 9–19.

Digital Impact Group, Econsult Corporation (2010), 'The economic impact of digital exclusion', study commissioned by the US Federal Communications Commission (FCC) (http://www.digitalimpactgroup. org/costofexclusion.pdf).

Digital Inclusion Team (2007), 'The digital inclusion landscape in England. Delivering social impact through information and communications technology', available at digitalinclusion.pbworks.com/. . ./The+Digital+Inclusion+Landscape+In+England.pdf.

DiMaggio, P.J. and E. Hargittai (2001), 'From the "digital divide" to "digital inequality": studying internet use as penetration increases', Working Paper 19, Center for Arts and Cultural Policy Studies, Woodrow Wilson School, Princeton University, Princeton, NJ.

DiMaggio, P.J., E. Hargittai, C. Celeste and S. Shaker (2004), *From Unequal Access to Differentiated Use: A Literature Review and Agenda for Research on Digital Inequality*, in K. Neckerman (ed.), *Social Inequality*, Russell Sage Foundation, New York.

DiMaggio, P.J., E. Hargittai, W.R. Neuman and J.P. Robinson (2001), 'Social implication of the Internet', in *Annual Review of Sociology*, **27**, 307–36.

Di Nardo, J. and J. Pischke (1997), 'The returns to computers revisited: have pencils changed the wage structure too?', in *Quarterly Journal of Economics*, **112** (February), 291–303.

Dolton, P., and P. Pelkonen (2007), 'The impact of computer use, computer skills and computer use intensity: evidence from WERS 2004', CEE Discussion Papers 0081, Centre for the Economics of Education, LSE.

Dostie, B. and R. Jayaraman (2008), 'Organizational redesign, information technologies and workplace productivity', IZA Discussion Papers 3612.

Draca, M., R. Sadun and J. Van Reenen (2006), 'Productivity and ICT: a review of the evidence', CEP Discussion Paper No. 749, Centre for Economic Performance, LSE.

Dunnewijk, T., H. Meijers and A. van Zon (2007), 'Accounting for the impact of information and communication technologies on total factor productivity', JRC Scientific and Technical Reports, European Communities.

Dutton, William H. and Ellen J. Helsper (2007), *Oxford Internet Survey 2009 Report: The Internet in Britain*, available at http://www.oii.ox.ac.uk/research/oxis/OxIS2007_Report.pdf.

Dutton, W.H., S.E. Gillett, L.W. McKnight, and M. Peltu (2003), 'Broadband Internet: the power to reconfigure access', Forum Discussion Paper 1, Oxford Internet Institute, Oxford.

Entorf, H. and F. Kramarz (1997), 'Does unmeasured ability explain the higher wages of new technology workers?', in *European Economic Review*, **41** (15), 1489–1509.

European Commission (2009), 'eInclusion Public Policies in Europe. Final Report', available at ec.europa.eu/information. . ./einclusion/. . ./einclusion_policies_in_europe.pdf.

Fornefeld, M., G. Delaunay and D. Elixmann (2008), 'The impact of broadband on growth and productivity', MICUS management consulting GMBH.

Foster, S.P. (2000), 'The digital divide: some reflections', in *International Information and Library Review*, **32** (3/4), 437–51.

Fox, S. (2005), *Digital Divisions*, Pew Internet & American Life Project, Washington, DC.

FreshMinds (2008), 'Economic benefits of digital inclusion: building the evidence', http://www.ukonlinecentres.com/corporate/images/stories/downloads/economic%20benefits%20of%2digital%20inclusion%20-%20building%20the%20evidence.pdf.

Friedberg, L. (2003), 'The impact of technological change on older workers: evidence from data on computer use', in *Industrial and Labour Relational Review*, **56** (3), 511–29.

Fuchs, C. (2009), 'The role of income inequality in a multivariate cross-national analysis of the digital divide', in *Social Science Computer Review*, **27** (1), 41–59.

Giddens, A. (1987), *Social Theory and Modern Sociology*, Polity Press, Cambridge.

Giddens, A. (1990), *The Consequences of Modernity*, Polity Press, Cambridge.

Golding, P. (2000), 'Forthcoming features: information and communications technologies and the sociology of the future', in *Sociology*, **34** (1), 165–84.

Golding, P. and G. Murdock (2001), 'Digital divide communications policy and its contradictions', in *New Economy*, **8** (2), 110–15.

Guerrieri, P. and P.C. Padoan (2007), *Modelling ICT as a General Purpose Technology*, *Collegium*, 35, Spring, Special Edition, College of Europe, Bruges, Belgium.

Guillén, M.F. and S.L. Suàrez (2005), 'Explaining the global digital divide: economic, political and sociological drivers of cross-national internet use', in *Social Forces*, **84** (2).

Gunkel, D.J. (2003), 'Second thoughts: toward a critique of the digital divide', in *New Media Society*, **5** (4), 499–522.

Gust, C. and J. Marquez (2002), 'International comparison of productivity growth: the role of information technology and regulatory practices', *International Finance Discussion Papers*, Federal Reserve Board no. 727, Federal Reserve System, Washington, DC.

Gust, Christopher and Jaime Marquez (2004), 'International comparisons of productivity growth: the role of information technology and regulatory practices', in *Labour Economics*, **11** (February).

Hacker, L.K. and S. Mason (2003), 'Ethical gaps in studies of the digital divide', in *Ethics and Information Technology*, **5** (2), 99–115.

Haddon, L. (2004), *Information and Communication Technologies in Everyday Life*, Berg, Oxford.

Haller, S. and I. Traistaru-Siedschlag (2007), 'The adoption of ICT: firm-level evidence from Irish Manufacturing industries', WP204, Economic and Social Research Institute (ESRI).

Hanna, N.K. (2010), *ICT Services Industry for an Innovation Economy*, Springer, New York.

Hargittai, E. (1999a), 'Weaving the western web: explaining differences in Internet connectivity among OECD countries', in *Telecommunications Policy*, **23** (10/11), 701–18.

Hargittai, E. (1999b), 'Explaining differences in internet connectivity among OECD countries', in *Telecommunications Policy*, **23**, 701–18.

Hargittai, E. (2003), 'The digital divide and what to do about it', in D.C. Jones (ed.), *The New Economy Handbook*, Academic Press, San Diego, CA, pp. 821–41.

Hargittai, E. (2004), 'Internet access and use in context', in *New Media & Society*, **6**, 137–43.

Hargittai, E. (2007), 'A framework for studying differences in people's digital media uses', in N. Kutscher and Otto H. Uwe (eds), *Cyberworld Unlimited*, VS Verlag für Sozial wissenschaften/GWV Fachverlage GmbH.

Herrera, Amilcar O., et al. (1976), *Catastrophe or New Society? A Latin American World Model*, International Development Research Centre, Ottawa.

Hitt, L.M. and P. Tambe (2007), 'Broadband adoption and content consumption', in *Information Economics and Policy*, **19** (3–4), 362–78.

Hoffman, D.L. and T.P. Novak (1998), 'Bridging the racial divide on the Internet', in *Science*, **280** (17), 390–91.

Hollenstein, H. (2004), 'Determinants of the adoption of information and communication technologies (ICT): an empirical analysis based on firm-level data for the Swiss business sector', in *Structural Change and Economic Dynamics*, **15** (3), 315–42.

Horrigan, J. (2007), 'Home broadband adoption 2007', Pew Internet & American Life Project, Washington, DC. Retrieved 15 July (http://www.pewinternet.org).

Horrigan, J. and L. Rainie (2002), *The Broadband Difference: How Online Americans' Behaviour Changes with High-Speed Internet Connections at Home*, Pew Internet & American Life Project, Washington, DC.

Howard, P.N., K. Anderson, L. Busch and D. Nafus (2009), 'Sizing up information society: toward a better metric for the cultures of ICT adoption', in *Information Society*, **25**, 3.

Howard, P.N. and N. Mazaheri (2009), 'Telecommunications reform, internet use and mobile phone adoption in the developing world', in *World Development*, **37**, 7.

Hughes, A. and M.S. Scott Morton (2005), 'ICT and productivity growth: the paradox resolved', Centre for Business Research, Cambridge University, Working Paper No. 316.

Hughes, Barry B. (1980), *World Modeling*, Lexington Books, Lexington, MA.

Hughes, Barry B. and Evan E. Hillebrand (2006), *Exploring and Shaping International Futures*, Paradigm Publishers, Boulder, CO.

Husing, T. and H. Selhofer (2004), 'DiDix. A digital divide index for measuring inequality in IT Diffusion', in *IT&Society*, **1** (7), 21–38.

Infoxchange–A.T.Kearney (2009), 'Assessing the economic benefits of digital inclusion', Infoxchange Australia.

ITU (2003), 'Digital Access Index', report available at http://www.itu.int/ITU-D/ict/dai/.

ITU (2005), 'Digital Opportunity Index', report available at http://www.itu.int/ITU-D/ict/doi/index.html.

ITU (2006), 'World Telecommunication/ICT development Report: measuring ICT for social and economic development', available at http://www.itu.int/dms_pub/itu-d/opb/ind/D-IND-WTDR-2006-SUM-PDF-E.pdf.

ITU (2009), 'Measuring the Information Society: the ICT Development Index', report available at http://www.itu.int/ITU-D/ict/publications/idi/2009/material/IDI2009_w5.pdf.

ITU (2010), 'Measuring the Information Society 2010', report available at http://www.itu.int/ITU-D/ict/publications/idi/2010/index.html.

James, J. (2007), 'Evaluating latecomer growth in information technology: a historical perspective', in *Technological Forecasting and Social Change*, **75**, pp. 1339–47.

Jorgenson, D.W., M. Ho and K.J. Stiroh (2008), 'A retrospective look at the US productivity growth resurgence', in *Journal of Economic Perspectives*.

Katz, J.E. and R.E. Rice (2002), *Social Consequences of Internet Use. Access, Involvement, and Interaction*, MIT Press, Cambridge, MA.

Kennedy, T., B. Wellman and K. Klemnet (2003), 'Gendering the digital divide', in *IT&Society*, **1** (5), 72–96.

Kiiski, S. and M. Pohjola (2002), 'Cross country diffusion of the internet', in *Information Economics and Policy*, **14** (2).

Kim, M.C. and J.K. Kim (2001), 'Digital divide: conceptual discussion and prospect', in W. Kim (ed.), *Human Society & Internet*, Springer-Verlag, Berlin.

Koellinger, P. (2008), 'The relationship between technology, innovation, and firm performance: empirical evidence on e-business in Europe', ERIM Report Series Reference No. ERS-2008-031-ORG.

Kominski, R. and E. Newburger (1999), 'Access denied: changes in computer ownership and use: 1984–1997', paper presented at the Annual Meeting of the American Sociological Association Chicago, Illinois. Population Division US Census Bureau, Washington DC (http://www.census.gov/population/socdemo/computer/confpap99. pdf).

Koutroumpis, P. (2008), 'Broadband infrastructure and economic growth: a simultaneous approach', mimeo, Imperial College, London.

Krueger, A. (1993), 'How computers have changed the wage structure: evidence from microdata, 1984–1989', in *Quarterly Journal of Economics*, **108** (1), 33–60.

Lash, S. (1994), 'Reflexity and its doubles: structures, aesthetics, community', in U. Beck, A. Giddens and S. Lash (eds), *Reflexive Modernisation*, Polity Press, Cambridge, pp. 110–73.

Lash, S. (2002), *Critique of Information*, Sage, London.

LECG (2009), *Economic Impact of Broadband: An Empirical Study*, LECG Ltd, London (www.lecg.com).

Leigh, A. and R. Atkinson (2001), 'Clear thinking on the digital divide', Progressive Policy Institute, at www. pponline.org.

Leontief, Wassily, Anne Carter and Peter Petri (1977), *The Future of the World Economy*, Oxford University Press, New York.

Lucas, H.C. and R. Sylla (2003), 'The global impact of the internet: widening the economic gap between wealthy and poor nations', in *Prometheus*, 21.

Luciani, M. and P.C. Padoan (2007), 'Endogenizing ICT: quantitative results', in P. Guerrieri and P.C. Padoan (eds), *Modelling ICT as a General Purpose Technology*, *Collegium*, **35**, pp. 147–71.

Maliranta, M. and P. Rouvinen (2004), 'ICT and business productivity: Finnish micro-level evidence', in OECD (2004).

Manrique, C.G. and G.G. Manrique (2009), 'The global digital divide: what the indices reveal', paper presented at Annual Meeting of the American Political Science Association, Toronto, Canada.

Mesarovic, Mihajlo D. and Eduard Pestel (1974), *Mankind at the Turning Point*, E.P. Dutton & Co, New York.

MICUS Management Consulting Group (2008), 'The impact of broadband on growth and productivity', Brussels, available at http://

ec.europa.eu/information_society/eeurope/i2010/docs/benchmarking/broadband_impact_2008.pdf.

Milner, H. (2006), 'The digital divide: the role of political institutions in technology diffusion', in *Comparative Political Studies*, **39** (2).

Miniaci, R. and M.L. Parisi (2005), 'Which plans to reduce the digital divide? Policy evaluation and social interactive', Università di Blescia, Discussion Paper No. 509, October.

Miniaci, R. and M.L. Parisi (2006), 'Social interactions and the digital divide identification and policy implications', in *B.E. Journal of Economic Analysis and Policy*, Berkeley Electronic Press, 1.

Monti, M. (2010), 'A new strategy for the single market at the service of Europe's economy and society', Report to the President of the European Commission José Manuel Barroso, Brussels, 9 May.

Mossberger, K., C.J. Tolbert, and M. Stansbury (2003), *Virtual Inequality. Beyond the Digital Divide*, Georgetown University Press, Washington DC.

Mossberger, K., C.J. Tolbert and R.S. McNeal (2008), *Digital Citizenship. The Internet, Society, and Participation*, MIT Press, Cambridge, MA.

Mueller, M.L. (2001), 'Universal service policies as wealth redistribution', in B.M. Compaine (ed.), *The Digital Divide: Facing a Crisis or Creating a Myth?*, MIT Press, Cambridge, MA.

NTATREP (National Technical Assistance, Training, Research, and Evaluation Project) (2006), 'Measuring broadband's economic impact', Final Report prepared for the US Department of Commerce, Economic Development Administration Project #99-07-13829, February.

Neckerman, K. (ed.) (2004), *Social Inequality*, Russell Sage Foundation, New York.

Norris, P. (2001), *Digital Divide. Civic Engagement, Information Poverty, and the Internet Worldwide*, Cambridge University Press, Cambridge.

Norris, P. (2004), 'The bridging and bonding role of online communities', in P.N. Howard and S. Jones (eds), *Society Online. The Internet in Context*, Sage, Thousand Oaks, CA, pp. 31–56.

OECD (2004), *The Economic Impact of ICT: Measurement, Evidence and Implications*, OECD, Paris.

OECD (2007a), 'Working party on communication infrastructures and service policy', DSTI/ICCP/CISP (2007) 8/FINAL, available at https://www.tuanz.org.nz/library/a8657153-be09-495c-8acd-ac115d6a3e.cme.

OECD (2007b), 'Broadband and ICT access and use by households and individuals', DSTI/ICCP/IE(2007)4/FINAL.

OECD (2008), 'Handbook on constructing composite indicators: methodology and user guide', available at www.oecd.org/dataoecd/37/42/42495745.pdf.

OECD (2009), 'Network developments in support of innovation and user needs', DSTI/ICCP/CISP(2009)2/FINAL (http://www.olis.oecd.org/olis/2009doc.nsf/linkto/dsti-iccp-cisp(2009)2-final).

Ono, H. and M. Zavodny (2003), 'Gender and the Internet', in *Social Science Quarterly*, **84**, 111–21.

Ono, H. and M. Zavodny (2007), 'Digital inequality: a five country comparison using microdata', in *Social Science Research*, **36**, 1135–55.

Pelkmans, J. (2006a), 'European industrial policy', in P. Bianchi and S. Labory (eds), *International Handbook on Industrial Policy*, Edward Elgar, Cheltenham, UK and Northampton, MA, USA, pp. 45–78.

Pelkmans, J. (2006b), *European Integration: Methods and Economic Analysis*, FT Press, Harlow.

Pelkmans, J. (2010), 'Product market reforms in EU countries: are the methodology and evidence sufficiently robust?', CEPS Working Documents, Regulatory Policy, 16 July.

Pew Internet & American Life Project (2007), 'Internet activities', at www.pewinternet.org.

Pew Internet & American Life Project (2009), 'Technology user types, mobile, digital divide. The mobile difference', at www.pewinternet.org.

Pohjola, M. (2003), 'The adoption and diffusion of ICT across country: patterns and determinants', *The New Economy Handbook*, Academic Press, New York.

PricewaterhouseCoopers (2009), 'Champion for digital inclusion', PricewaterhouseCoopers.

Rice, R.E. and J.E. Katz (2003), 'Comparing internet and mobile phone usage: digital divides of usage, adoption, and dropouts', in *Telecommunications Policy*, **27**, 597–623.

Riga Ministerial Declaration on an Inclusive Information Society (2006), Riga, Latvia, 11 giugno, available at http://ec.europa.eu/information_society/events/ict_riga_2006/doc/ declaration_riga.pdf.

Rincon-Aznar, A., C. Robinson and M. Vecchi (2005), 'The productivity impact of e-commerce in the UK, 2001: evidence from microdata', NIESR (National Institute of Economic and Social Research) Discussion paper 257.

Robinson, J.P., P.J. DiMaggio and E. Hargittai (2003), 'New social survey perspectives on the digital divide', in *IT & Society*, **1** (Summer), 1–22.

Robison, K.K. and E.M. Crenshaw (2002), 'Post-industrial transformations and cyber-space: a cross-national analysis of internal development', in *Social Science Research*, **31**.

Rogers, E.M. (2001), 'The digital divide', in *Convergence: The International Journal of Research into New Media Technologies*, 7(4), 96–111.

Rogers, E.M. (2003), *Diffusion of Innovation. Fifth Edition* (first edition 1965), The Free Press, New York.

Ryan, B. and N. Gross (1943), 'The diffusion of hybrid seed corn in two Iowa communities', in *Rural Sociology*, **8**, 15–24.

SARU (Systems Analysis Research Unit) (1977), SARUM 76 Global Modeling Project, Departments of the Environment and Transport, 2 Marsham Street, London, 3WIP 3EB.

Sassi, S. (2005), 'Cultural differentiation or social segregation? Four approaches to the digital divide', in *New Media & Society*, **7**, 684–700.

Schleife, K. (2006), 'Computer use and employment status of older workers – an analysis based on individual data', in *Labour*, **20** (2), June, 325–48.

Sciadas, G. (ed.) (2005), *From the Digital Divide to Digital Opportunities*, Orbicom, Montreal.

Sehrt, A.M. (2004), 'Digital divide into digital opportunities', in *UN Chronicle*, **40** (4), 45–46.

Selwyn, N. (2004), 'Reconsidering political and popular understandings of the digital divide', in *New Media Society*, **6** (3), 341–62.

SIBIS (2003), 'Statistical indicators. Benchmarking the information society', report available at http://www.sibis-eu.org/.

Skirbekk, V. (2004), 'Age and individual productivity: a literature survey', in G. Feichtinger (ed.), *Vienna Yearbook of Population Research*, Australian Academy of Science Press, Vienna, pp. 133–153.

Thompson, H.G. and C. Garbacz (2007), 'Mobile, fixed line and Internet effects on global productive efficiency', *Information Economics and Policy*, **19**, 189–214.

Thompson, H.G. and C. Garbacz (2008), 'Broadband impacts on State GDP: direct and indirect impacts', mimeo (http://www.canavents.com/its2008/abstracts/62.pdf).

Tichenor, P.J., G. Donohue and C. Olien (1970), 'Mass media flow and differential growth in knowledge', in *Public Opinion Quarterly*, **34**, 150–70.

Trémembert, J. (2010), 'Indicators of the digital divide and its link with other exclusions', paper presented at the Conference Internet, Politics, Policy 2010: An Impact Assessment, 16 September, Oxford Internet Institute, Oxford.

US Department of Commerce (1999), 'Falling through the net: defining the digital divide', http://www.ntia.doc.gov/ntiahome/fttn99/contents.html.

US Department of Commerce (2004), 'A nation online: entering the broadband age', September (http://www.ntia.doc.gov/reports/anol/NationOnlineBroadband04.pdf).

Van Ark, B., M. O'Mahony and M.P. Timmer (2008), 'The productivity gap between Europe and the United States: trends and causes', in *Journal of Economic Perspectives*, **22** (1) Winter.

Van Dijk, J.A.G.M. (2005), *The Deepening Divide. Inequality in the Information Society*, Sage Publications, Thousands Oaks, CA.

Van Dijk, J.A.G.M. (2006), 'Digital divide research, achievements and shortcomings', in *Poetics*, **34**, 221–35.

Van Dijk, J.A.G.M. (2009), 'One Europe, digitally divided', in A. Chadwick and P.N. Howard (eds), *Internet Politics*, Routledge, London and New York.

Van Dijk Management Consultants (2008), Broadband Internet Access Cost (BIAC), available at ec.europa.eu/. . ./broadband_access_costs_1st_half_2008.pdf.

Van Reenen, J., N. Bloom, M. Draca, T. Kretschmer, R. Sadun, H. Overman and M. Schankerman (2010), 'The economic impact of ICT', Final report, Centre for Economic Performance, London School of Economics, London.

Varian, Hal, R.E. Litan, A. Elder and J. Shutter (2002), 'The net impact study: the projected economic benefits of the Internet in the United States, United Kingdom, France and Germany', (http://www.netimpactstudy.com/NetImpact_Study_Report.pdf).

Venturini, F. (2008), 'Information technology, research & development, or both? What really drives a nation's productivity', Working Papers 321, Universita' Politecnica delle Marche (I), Dipartimento di Economia.

Warschauer, M. (2001), 'What is the digital divide?', at www.gse.uci.edu/markw.

Warschauer, M. (2003), *Technology and Social Inclusion. Rethinking the Digital Divide*, MIT Press, Cambridge, MA.

Waverman, L. and K. Dasgupta (2010), 'Connectivity Scorecard 2010', LECG, Nokia Siemens Network.

Webster, F. (1995), *Theories of the Information Society*, Routledge, London.

Webster, F. (2002), *Theories of the Information Society*, Second Edition, Routledge, London.

Wellman, B. and C. Haythornthwaite (eds) (2002), *The Internet in Everyday Life*, Blackwell Publishing, Malden, MA.

WIK Consulting Group (2008), 'The economics of next generation access, study for the European Competitive Telecommunication Association

(ECTA)', Bad Honnef, September, available at: http://www.ectaportal.com/en/upload/ECTA NGA_masterfile_2008_09_15_V1.zip.

Wilson, E.J. (2000), *Closing the Digital Divide. An Initial Review*, Internet Policy Institute, Washington.

Witte, J.C. and S.E. Mannon (2010), *The Internet and Social Inequalities*, Routledge, London.

Wong, P.K. (2002), 'ICT production and diffusion in Asia: digital dividends or digital divide?', in *Information Economics and Policy*, **14** (2), 167–87.

Yu, L. (2006), 'Understanding information inequality: making sense of the literature of the information and digital divides', in *Journal of Librarian and Information Science*, **38** (4), 229–52.

Index

21